AF801018

The Political Dimension of Constitutional Law

Miguel Nogueira de Brito • Luís Pereira Coutinho
Editors

The Political Dimension of Constitutional Law

Springer

Editors
Miguel Nogueira de Brito
School of Law
University of Lisbon
Lisbon, Portugal

Luís Pereira Coutinho
School of Law
University of Lisbon
Lisbon, Portugal

ISBN 978-3-030-38458-6 ISBN 978-3-030-38459-3 (eBook)
https://doi.org/10.1007/978-3-030-38459-3

© Springer Nature Switzerland AG 2020
This work is subject to copyright. All rights are reserved by the Publisher, whether the whole or part of the material is concerned, specifically the rights of translation, reprinting, reuse of illustrations, recitation, broadcasting, reproduction on microfilms or in any other physical way, and transmission or information storage and retrieval, electronic adaptation, computer software, or by similar or dissimilar methodology now known or hereafter developed.
The use of general descriptive names, registered names, trademarks, service marks, etc. in this publication does not imply, even in the absence of a specific statement, that such names are exempt from the relevant protective laws and regulations and therefore free for general use.
The publisher, the authors, and the editors are safe to assume that the advice and information in this book are believed to be true and accurate at the date of publication. Neither the publisher nor the authors or the editors give a warranty, expressed or implied, with respect to the material contained herein or for any errors or omissions that may have been made. The publisher remains neutral with regard to jurisdictional claims in published maps and institutional affiliations.

This Springer imprint is published by the registered company Springer Nature Switzerland AG.
The registered company address is: Gewerbestrasse 11, 6330 Cham, Switzerland

Contents

Introduction

Miguel Nogueira de Brito and Luís Pereira Coutinho

Abstract This introductory chapter presents the book "The Political Dimension of Constitutional Law" which discusses in what sense constitutional law has a political dimension, raising the question whether constitutional law is fundamentally political - or theologico-political - as to its validity, terms of its origin, conceptual structure and/or corresponding practice.

In what sense does constitutional law have a political dimension? In other words, is constitutional law fundamentally political, as to its validity, origin, conceptual structure and/or corresponding practice? And is that dimension a political-theological dimension? These are the core questions of this book.

A positive answer to those questions means to challenge a prevailing vision in continental Europe, according to which constitutional law is to be conceived strictly as positive higher-order law, entrenched at a certain historical moment by a particular kind of power. Moreover, according to that vision, the corresponding body of rules and principles can be determined as a strict matter of *legal* interpretation, thus regardless of any political considerations.

The first part of this book, composed of essays by Martin Loughlin and Miguel Nogueira de Brito, approaches the said questions by examining the concept of fundamental law.

According to Loughlin, fundamental law is a politicized species of law, thus incompatible with a firm separation between law and politics and a strict differentiation between legal reason and political reason. There is a correspondence between fundamental law and what Loughlin names the world of the political: a world which, even though advanced through the language of law, shapes the conditions of human existence by establishing structures of authority and obedience and by framing what is just or unjust, good or evil, right or wrong. The conflicts that emerge in that world—which at its core concern contestable expressions of fundamental law—are

M. Nogueira de Brito · L. Pereira Coutinho (✉)
Lisbon's School of Law, Lisbon University, Lisbon, Portugal
e-mail: miguelbrito@fd.ulisboa.pt; lpcoutinho@fd.ulisboa.pt

© Springer Nature Switzerland AG 2020
M. Nogueira de Brito, L. Pereira Coutinho (eds.), *The Political Dimension of Constitutional Law*, https://doi.org/10.1007/978-3-030-38459-3_1

articulated through the medium of constitutional discourse. Those conflicts cannot be approached as matters of legal interpretation since their settlement necessarily involves political judgment.

Miguel Nogueira de Brito discusses Loughlin's account of the formation and decline of political right, a discipline that emerged at the dawn of modernity in order to frame the legal and political rationality of national and centralized states, but which would subsequently be dislodged by the gradual establishment of constitutional legality and administrative rationality. In his view, Loughlin—despite his "decline and fall" account of public law—provides us with a relevant proposal for understanding current constitutional theory and law, that is, the hypothesis of a dualist structure of the main concepts that make up public law and the constitutional state. This structure ultimately depends on a distinction between what is constitutive and what is constituted in a political community, and even more so on the hypothesis that this distinction is itself constitutive of the very possibility of a political community.

What is constitutive in the abovementioned sense is also the ultimate focus of Paul Kahn's essay, which opens the second part of the book and centers on the question whether there are legal interpretations on constitutional matters that are innocent of politics. For Kahn, the role of political decision in law—i.e. of what is constitutive—should be accounted for in a way that acknowledges the fact that it both precedes and is a condition of legal interpretation. A political decision in this context corresponds to the imaginative structure informing the political community's understanding of itself and shaping interpretative practices. That framework is theological-political since it regards the core beliefs standing behind constitutional law and practice. In this context, and addressing specifically the American constitutional law and practice, Kahn sustains that it has been dominated by two competing imaginative structures, that of *project*—which prevailed in a first moment—and that of *system*—which took form alongside nineteenth century economic thought.

A constitutive dimension of constitutional law is also addressed by Luís Pereira Coutinho, even though he approaches it in different terms. For Pereira Coutinho, that dimension is formed by constitutive concepts, such as *national sovereignty*, the *people*, and the concept of *Constitution* itself. Those concepts are constitutive in the sense that there wouldn't be a "law" that could be predicated as "constitutional", nor would there be a "constitutional state", without implicit or explicit reference to them, at least in the continental tradition developed after the French Revolution. Since the mode of significance of those concepts is negative and anticipatory—and thus analogous to that of theological concepts—the political dimension of constitutional law is considered a *negative* theological-political dimension. As *negative*, political theology is considered in very different terms from the ones originally proposed by Carl Schmitt.

The third part of the book explores the degree in which constitutional law is political—thus escaping the legalistic paradigm—as to its origin and change. In this context, Manon Altwegg-Boussac discusses the existence of informal constitutional changes in the very framework of written constitutionalist cultures, assessing the way in which the corresponding "political law" has been considered from different theoretical perspectives. Even though Altwegg-Boussac is skeptical regarding perspectives merely aimed at legitimizing unconstitutional practices—stressing the need to preserve a critical distance allowing for the distinction between valid law and mere violations of the Constitution—she insists in the need to take "political constitutional law" seriously.

Carlos Blanco de Morais also focuses constitutional change, addressing the crisis of a classic paradigm in which a rigid constitution established by a constituent power persists in time. According to Blanco de Morais that paradigm has now been challenged by a phenomenon of "liquefaction of the constitution", resulting from the contamination of constitutional adjudication by politics and implying the intrusion of highly politicized courts in the realm that was once typically reserved to the constituent power.

The last part of the book is composed of essays by Massimo La Torre, Agustin Jose Menendez and Pedro Lomba. All of them address European law, which is still only arguably constitutional law. Their arguments however address the core of the political dimension of constitutional law, since at issue is to know whether constitutionalism can be split from national sovereignty, political decision and democratic deliberation.

According to Massimo La Torre's diagnosis, that split has already occurred with the development of the European ordo-liberal project—which presides over the improperly named "European constitution", that according to dubious argumentative strategies tends to disconnect the idea of constitution from the idea of citizenship. That results in "a politics without politics, a State without State, a Constitution without Constitution". La Torre not only formulates such a diagnosis but also offers a fascinating reconstruction of its historical and intellectual origins, which he associates to the emergence of radically individualistic anthropological premises.

Agustin José Menendez similarly considers that European law has become a force of de-politicisation and de-democratisation. For Menendez, in an order devoted to the primacy of private property, entrepreneurial freedom and sound money, democratic decision-making has been limited both at the substantive and at procedural level. Public power is fragmented and pulverized and, as a result, non-representative institutions and private actors are empowered.

Pedro Lomba challenges the prevailing description of a depoliticized and undemocratic Europe. He holds that European politics presents itself in many faces. While acknowledging the challenges emerging from a more centralized, expert-based and politically sensitive European economic and monetary union, Lomba holds that these are not unaddressed, namely by courts which are concerned with maintaining the multilevel chain of legitimacy and with reinforcing the democratic safeguards of the new economic governance. He also notes that epistemic governance itself can been exercised to reinforce democratic politics and political commitments. Even if that may sound paradoxical, past decisions taken by epistemic authorities (e.g. European Central Bank) point to a significant politicization of the European system and cannot be taken as antagonistic to democratic politics.

Part I
Fundamental Law

Fundamental Law

Martin Loughlin

Contents

Abstract Fundamental law is a politicized species of law which is incompatible with a firm separation between law and politics and a strict differentiation between legal reason and political reason. There is a correspondence between fundamental law and the world of the political, a world which, even though advanced through the language of law, shapes the conditions of human existence by establishing structures of authority and obedience and framing what is just or unjust, good or evil, right or wrong. The conflicts that emerge in that world—which at its core concern contestable expressions of fundamental law—are articulated through the medium of constitutional discourse. Those conflicts should not be approached solely as matters of legal interpretation since their settlement necessarily involves political judgment.

This paper was presented at the seminar, The Return of Politics to Constitutional Law, held at the University of Lisbon on 22–23 May 2018. I should like to thank the organisers, Professors Miguel Nogueira de Brito and Luís Pereira Coutinho, and the seminar participants for comments.

M. Loughlin (✉)
London School of Economics & Political Science, London, UK
e-mail: m.loughlin@lse.ac.uk

© Springer Nature Switzerland AG 2020

M. Nogueira de Brito, L. Pereira Coutinho (eds.), *The Political Dimension of Constitutional Law*, https://doi.org/10.1007/978-3-030-38459-3_2

1 Introduction

The concept of fundamental law occupies an ambivalent status in the history of legal thought. In early modern constitutional debate it was the pivot around which contrasting views about juristic foundations of medieval and modern constitutionalism revolved. But with the transition to modernity the concept has been converted into a particular category of positive law. Fundamental law is now generally regarded simply as an expression of the higher status of entrenched constitutional law as distinct from the 'ordinary' law enacted by legislatures. This paper examines the continuing relevance of a broader sense of the concept that persists in modern constitutional thought. It argues that the concept of fundamental law still has significance as a juristic expression of the intrinsic political dynamics of modern constitutional practice.

As it was in the early modern context, fundamental law is a perennially contested concept. But it has the particular importance today of enabling us to identify a relatively new and highly politicized species of law. This new species of law is a consequence of the growing importance of modern constitutions in shaping political life and of the extending influence of constitutional jurisdiction. It is sometimes called 'constitutional legality' or 'superlegality' but by referring to it as fundamental law we retain its connection with those earlier incarnations. The modern concept of fundamental law I am concerned with now presents itself as the architectonic form of the political regime though, because it blends political reason with legal reason in ways that make it difficult to differentiate politics and law, this modern type of fundamental law is contentious.

I will examine the basic features of this modern type of fundamental law in what follows. Before doing so, I look at the origins of the term and the context for its emergence.

2 State Formation

The modern world is divided into a grid of territories called states. This grid has been created through continuous evolution as states have been formed either by the integration of adjacent land areas or by the disintegration of older imperial structures. Although this evolution has been continuous, it does not follow a precise developmental path. Rather, the process has been punctuated by particular circumstances, such as annexation (whether by conquest, treaty or marriage between ruling families) or partition (as a result of rebellion and insurgencies). One result is that modern states vary dramatically in size, resources, and spatial characteristics. And just as their basic features exhibit considerable variation, so too do their governing arrangements.

These conditions of state formation mean that it is difficult to generalize about their characteristics. Most commonly constructed from above by the consolidation of ruling power, it can be assumed that states are not spontaneously evolving organic communities. The bond of allegiance that subjects feel towards their state is more likely to have been forged through an imposed discipline and a manipulation of their desire for security than from some innate sense of common feeling. Even so, it would be less than accurate to characterize states simply as brute power formations. One reason is that the authority of their governing practices has over time been bolstered by various creeds which have instilled a strong sense that the state expresses the natural order of things.[1] In the early stages of state formation these creeds often inculcated the belief that the governing regime had been established in conformity to divine will, or replicated a natural 'chain of being', or had been ordained by ancient custom. But in the modern era it is most commonly claimed that their authority rests on the 'consent of the people'.[2]

Subjugation, regimentation and the inculcation of beliefs have all played major roles in explaining how states could impose their authority, but this is not the whole story. Subjects have often freely acquiesced in servitude to their rulers,[3] and many have come to believe that establishing the authority of the state is an essential condition of human flourishing.

3 The Political and the Legal

Whatever the complexities of state formation, one thing seems certain: the fact that the modern world has come to be organized into territorial entities forms a separate strand of human experience. Reflection on the processes of state formation opens up a distinctive way of looking at the world. This is the world of the political. The political in this sense should not be confused with conventional understanding of politics as a set of institutional practices operating as a particular sub-system within society. The political constitutes the distinctive way in which human experience has been formed by governing structures of authority and obedience which shape our sense of justice and injustice, right and wrong, freedom and servitude, good and evil.

For evidence of this, we need look no further than the classic works of modern political thought, which from Hobbes to Rawls seem like accounts of universal significance but are actually the products of the interests of a particular time and

[1] See only Anderson (1991) and Hobsbawm and Ranger (1983).

[2] For an insightful study of the appropriation of religious sensibility for political purposes see Beiner (2011).

[3] de La Boétie (1975), p. 48, who argues that the people, being captivated by the image of the prince, bring about their own ruin: "All this havoc, this misfortune, this ruin, descends upon you not from alien foes, but from the one enemy whom you yourselves render as powerful as he is, for whom you go bravely to war, for whose greatness you do not refuse to offer your own bodies unto death. He who thus domineers over you has only two eyes, only two hands, only one body, no more than is possessed by the least man among the infinite numbers dwelling in your cities; he has indeed nothing more than the power that you confer upon him to destroy you". See also Hume, "That politics may be reduced to a science" (1994), pp. 4–15.

place. That the political expresses an aspect of human experience both local and historical is of specific relevance to any inquiry into fundamental law. This is because once the political is identified as a specific mode of experience and the basis for any investigation into the character of the state, a second condition follows. The inquiry into the world of the political—that is, into the way that regimes have been established and have augmented their authority—can be advanced only through the language of law. The political worldview generates its power through the medium of law.

Jurists of the modern era have generally understood this, though recently it seems to have been lost from view. What is now commonly called 'the history of political thought' is not just an expression of political arguments of a particular time and place; it is also in large part a history of reflection on how the constitution of political authority can be explained in the language of rights and duties, powers and liabilities. This field of study might more precisely be labelled 'political jurisprudence'. In Latin it can be expressed as *jus politicum*, in French as *droit politique*, or in German as *allgemeine Staatslehre*, but because English uses only one word for law, specification of the field is not so easy. 'Political law' sounds oxymoronic and 'political right' too ambiguous. I have previously referred to it simply as public law, by which is meant public law as political jurisprudence.[4] But in a generic sense, it might simply be called 'fundamental law'.

4 The Origins of Fundamental Law

The term 'fundamental law' has an unusual genealogy. One might be forgiven for thinking that it is of ancient lineage, but in fact it seems to have first appeared in legal discourse in the late sixteenth century.[5] Once coined, the expression was liberally employed by various protagonists in the intense debates during the following century over the nature and source of governmental authority. These disputes generated great passion. Against a background of economic, social, technological and cultural change, inherited assumptions about ruling authority were being questioned. Throughout Europe, jurists were grappling with a set of political changes we now recognize as a transition from a medieval world order into a modern arrangement of constitutional states. But though it was widely invoked, the expression 'fundamental law' had by the end of the late-eighteenth-century almost disappeared from usage. Why did this happen?

[4]Loughlin (2010), p. 157 ss.; id. (2018), p. 11 ss.

[5]The term seems first to have appeared in Theodore Beza's work of 1574, *Du droit des magistrats* (1574), where it was deployed to bolster his argument that magistrates had the right to have the king deposed if he failed to keep within the lawfully-conferred powers under "les loix fondamentales d'un Royaume". See Kingdon (1970) and Franklin (1969).

One reason is that throughout these debates fundamental law remained what German scholars would call a *Kampfbegriff*, a concept whose very meaning was bound up with the ideological struggles of the period. That the term was so widely employed owes much to its plasticity. The idea conveyed a sense that the prince, restrained by 'fundamental laws', could not possess untrammelled power, but otherwise its meaning was ambiguous. The phrase acquired such powerful rhetorical traction precisely because of its protean character.

Some jurists argued that fundamental law referred to an existing body of law that determined the powers—and the limits to the powers—of the office of the ruler.[6] But others turned to the past in more imaginative ways. They claimed that fundamental law expressed an ancient, immemorial customary authority that existed before all positive law.[7] This exposed a tension between those who conceived law as authoritative enactment and those who were still appealing to the timeless values of classical natural law. But both claims were contested by radical jurists who, working from first principles, sought to locate the source of a ruler's authority in a respect for the natural rights of the individual.[8] Foremost among this group were the Huguenot jurists who argued that the commonwealth had been created by an original contract by which the people bestowed a (limited) ruling authority on the prince.[9] That original contract, they argued, was the *lex fundamentalis regnis*.

The expression 'fundamental law' therefore carried a wide variety of discordant meanings. These meanings were imbued with figurative language ranging from an assumed contractual relationship between ruler and people,[10] to a view of the kingdom as an architectural edifice erected on certain vital pillars.[11] Yet metaphor here obscured as much as it illuminated. Some accounts sought to enhance the status of fundamental law with reference to its supposed ancient lineage while others stressed its novelty. Some treated it as an empirical fact, others as a virtual phenomenon. Some conceptions were underpinned by an organic imagery of social order, while others asserted its individualistic basis. And throughout these debates it was

---

[6]Francis Bacon used the term in 1596 to refer to the laws of Edward I, which provided the basis of the English state on which it 'ever since hath principally rested' and made it clear he did not mean immemorial, customary law: Bacon, *Works*, 4:6. It has also been noted that in the proceedings of the French Estates Generals of 1588 and 1593, "an idea of fundamental law emerged as positive law, concerned with the framework of government, distinct from ancient customs": see Thompson (1986), p. 1109.

[7]The most influential English exponent of this argument was Sir Edward Coke: see Pocock (1987), pp. 30–69.

[8]Tuck (1987), pp. 99–122.

[9]See Althusius (1995), p. 93.

[10]Althusius (1995), p. 128: the state alone possessed sovereignty, and that sovereignty was located in the organized body of the commonwealth: "This fundamental law is nothing other than certain covenants by which cities and provinces come together and agree to establish and defend one commonwealth. If that consent is withdrawn, the commonwealth ceases to exist."

[11]Gentillet (1968), arguing that fundamental laws are the columns on which the edifice of king and kingdom was erected.

uncertain whether the authority of fundamental law was supposed to rest on history, or reason, or reason in history.

The impact of these different interpretations varied according to local political circumstances. That fundamental law provided the basic rules defining the office of the king resonated strongly in French thought, whereas Sir Edward Coke's use of the term to express customary law that exists 'time out of the mind of man' was distinctively English. And in Germany fundamental law was vigorously deployed in the early-eighteenth century for the purpose of asserting the superiority of the traditions of Teutonic public law over Romanist imperial law.[12] Overlaying these local cultural differences were philosophical questions that became more urgent with the transition from medieval to modern thought, questions expressing basic tensions between the concrete and the abstract, the visible and the invisible, the incarnate and the disembodied. Whether fundamental law continues to have relevance in modern constitutional regimes depends on the ways in which these philosophical tensions were handled.

5 Sovereignty

Many of the complications concerning the meaning of 'fundamental law' in modern thought coalesce around the question of sovereignty. Medieval jurists had a concrete notion of a sovereign, exhibited in the hierarchical relation between ruler and subject, but no real grasp of the abstract idea of sovereignty, which is why sovereignty can be said to be a purely modern concept. The emergence of the abstract concept is significant because once jurists come to explain the political as the domain of sovereignty fundamental law is seen to be bound up with contested understandings of sovereignty's true meaning. Consider the contrasting accounts of sovereignty given by two of its most influential exponents: Thomas Hobbes and Jean-Jacques Rousseau.

Hobbes brings us to the threshold of modern legal thought. Life in a state of nature—life without a regime of government—is characterised as 'solitary, poor, nasty, brutish and short'. He demonstrates how, if free to exercise our inherent natural rights, we would end up destroying ourselves. He also explains that certain laws of nature, such as mutual respect and fair treatment, might exist *in foro interno* but they carry no authority without the establishment of a governing regime to enforce them; they become true laws—that is, obligatory—only once enacted and enforced by the sovereign.

Hobbes directly engages with the claims of natural law and natural rights—the two main reference points for those promoting fundamental law in the early-modern period—only to show how they are ineffective or destructive. Instead he founds the state on a fictional social contract entered into by individuals, in which all their

[12] Thompson (1986), pp. 1121–1122.

natural rights are extinguished and unconditional authority is vested in the sovereign. His purpose is to demonstrate that in the modern world there can be only one fundamental law: subjects must obey the laws enacted by the sovereign.[13]

In Hobbes' seventeenth-century worldview, sovereignty expressed a concrete relationship between sovereign and subject. Only in the eighteenth century does an abstract idea of sovereignty evolve. Rousseau presents the definitive analysis. He argues, against Hobbes, that the basis of the political cannot be derived simply from the desire to have order. The ambition must be to show how law can be transformed from an instrument defining the hierarchical relationship of sovereign and subject into a medium through which freedom can be realized. Rousseau maintains, against Hobbes, that liberty is not the mere absence of constraint: liberty entails self-government. For Rousseau, liberty and law are reconciled in a state where people live under laws that they themselves have made. And for this to be feasible, the sovereign created by the social contract cannot be the office of the ruler: it must be 'the people' themselves. The sovereign is the artificial person formed by the union of all: that is, the state.

The challenge Rousseau faces is to show how this artificial person of the state might be said to possess a single will. He meets this by demonstrating that, unequal in nature, individuals become equals only in the world of the political. It is the principle of political equality that transforms them from a multitude into a people. This claim of political equality is the precondition for the formation of a single will. Each citizen acquires the same rights over others as are granted over themselves. This is what Rousseau calls the 'general will'. The general will is the will of the sovereign, that is, the will of 'the people' understood as free and equal beings.[14] For Rousseau, the concept of the general will, expressing the principle of equal liberty, becomes in effect the fundamental law of the modern state.

6 The Modern Idea of Fundamental Law

The idea of fundamental law persists into the modern era, though it is still as ambiguous and diverse as when early-modern jurists were grappling with shifts in the basis of ruling authority. The accounts of Hobbes and Rousseau give us the two poles of meaning. At one extreme, that of the concrete, the fundamental law of the state dictates that subjects must obey the laws enacted by the established office of the ruler. At the other, the abstract, fundamental law is conceived as a continuing struggle to realize the principle of equal liberty within the state. Between these two poles, a third influential modern conception of fundamental law now emerges with a focus on the principle of representation.

[13]Hobbes (1990), p. 44.

[14]Rousseau (1962), p. 32.

For Hobbes, the sovereign is a representative office that incorporates all the powers of the state. Rousseau, by contrast, argues that sovereignty cannot be represented. 'The moment a people gives itself representatives', he asserts, 'it is no longer free'.[15] The realities of governing in the modern world, then, require modification. Contra Rousseau, the sovereign people must elect representatives; the business of governing is too complex to be handled by the body of citizens in its entirety. Contra Hobbes, the representative office of the sovereign cannot be a singular entity. Instead, the business of governing requires that the office be put into commission and its various powers differentiated. These modifications—expressing principles of representation and differentiation—lead to the construction of a third conception of fundamental law, as a type of positive constitutional law.

In this third conception, the 'sovereign people' express their authority by adopting a document that delineates the main institutions, powers and responsibilities of government. The document allocates the sovereign powers of rule between legislative, executive and judicial authorities and includes a catalogue of the basic rights of citizens which governing authorities must respect. In setting out the terms of the governing relationship, this document takes effect as the state's constitution. This innovation, a product of the late-eighteenth century revolutions in North America and France, gives the constitution a sense of higher-order law. In this way modern constitutions acquire the status of fundamental law. The legislature established by the constitution may be able to make laws that regulate social conduct, but the constitution itself is to be regarded as the higher-order law which grants those powers to the legislature. The constitution is fundamental law.[16]

This new idea of the constitution as a text adopted in the name of the sovereign people means that, far from there being a body of laws enacted by the sovereign, a hierarchy of laws exists. The 'higher-order' law of the constitution becomes the modern expression of fundamental law.

This idea may have become received wisdom among constitutional lawyers, but it does not resolve all questions of authority. The problem was clearly recognized by the Abbé Sieyes, one of the most influential architects of this new conception. Writing in the throes of the French Revolution, Sieyes maintained that although it was essential that the state draft a constitution of fundamental laws, this was purely a consequence of the principle of delegation. Constitutional laws are fundamental only 'because bodies that can exist and can act by way of these laws cannot touch them'.[17] Fundamental law is fundamental only with respect to the office of government. It would be 'ridiculous', he explained, 'to suppose that the nation itself was bound by the formalities or the constitution to which it had subjected those it has mandated'.[18] Behind government, Sieyes argued, lies the nation and the nation is 'prior to

[15]Rousseau (1962), p. 98.

[16]Madison et al. (1987), p. 439.

[17]Sieyès (2003), pp. 92–162, at 136.

[18]Sieyès (2003), p. 136.

everything'. The nation is the source of law, 'its will is always legal'.[19] The powers of governmental bodies might have been conferred by the fundamental law of the constitution, but fundamental law itself is the product of the constituent power of the sovereign people. True fundamental law, Sieyes was indicating, is the common will of the people.

Sieye's argument suggests that the enacted constitution does not offer an adequate expression of the modern idea of fundamental law. It can do so only if the concept of law is limited to that of a body of rules posited by the authorized law-making institutions under the constitution. To so limit our understanding of law would effectively cut off any inquiry into the idea of fundamental law before it began. Such an inquiry in modern regimes could not avoid examining the ways in which political authority is constituted. The ambiguities of sovereign and sovereignty, the concrete and the abstract, remain.

In the perspective of the political, modern constitutions are institutional arrangements of the first importance. But although they operate both to empower and regulate they do not constitute the domain of the political. Constitutional rules might regulate political activity in the normal course of affairs but, especially at critical moments, their authority can be questioned. These are occasions when the unanticipated happens, circumstances and events that seem outside the boundaries of constitutional rules. In these moments of exception should the issue be referred to the sovereign people to determine? The problem is that 'the people' can only be assumed to act effectively through their representatives.[20] In exceptional circumstances, questions concerning the concrete and abstract expressions of sovereignty are left unresolved.

Who then is authorized to exercise sovereign power of action in an emergency? Even more fundamentally: who determines that a situation is exceptional? To the extent that there are still moments of exception, it might be claimed that a concrete sovereign in the Hobbesian sense, i.e. a power authorized to make law through decision (pure will), must remain as an element of the fundamental law of the modern state.[21] But consider by contrast the implications of Rousseau's concept of sovereignty. This is the argument that sovereignty cannot be possessed by any agent but is a quality permeating the entire order of the political. It can therefore never be fully absorbed in a constitutional text. The constitution of sovereignty—that is, the constitution of the state in contrast to the constitution of its office of government—promotes the struggle to establish equal liberty, an ambition never fully realized by mere words on paper with a meaning that cannot be handed over to governmental agents. In this abstract conception, the state and its constitution are analogous to a living organism that evolves as 'the conditions of the civil association' evolve.[22] The

[19]Sieyès (2003), p. 136.

[20]de Maistre (1965), p. 93.

[21]This is essentially Carl Schmitt's argument in *Political Theology: Four Chapters on the Concept of Sovereignty*. See Schmitt (2005), p. 1.

[22]Rousseau (1962), p. 50.

struggle to realize equal liberty in conditions of solidarity expresses the fundamental law of the political domain. But the problem remains: since 'the people' as such cannot speak as one voice, some constituted entity is obliged to speak in their name, and that will remain contestable.[23]

In his *Law of Nations* in 1758, Vattel stated:

> The fundamental regulation (*le règlement fondamentale*) that determines the manner in which the public authority is to be executed, is what forms the *constitution of the state*. In this is seen the form in which the nation acts in the quality of a body-politic, – how and by whom the people are to be governed, – and what are the rights and duties of the governors. This constitution is in fact nothing more than the establishment of the order in which a nation proposes to labour in common for obtaining those advantages with a view to which the political society was established.[24]

Vattel here states a problem that has yet to be resolved.

7 The Ideological Dimension of Modern Fundamental Law

I have suggested that the political—the way we have been shaped through our common historical experience of living in governmental units—is the product of a long history of group living but emerges only with the formation of modern regimes. Because modern states have come into existence at different historical moments, consciousness of the political varies according to particular circumstances, expressing the moment at which, in the face of change, people begin to reflect on the conditions of their collective existence. It is at such moments, when the authority of traditional order is placed in question, that the concept of fundamental law acquires importance.

Fundamental law therefore emerged as an influential idea when the ties that bound medieval societies together were unravelling and new ways of explaining and justifying order were required. In that early modern debate, the concept was invoked initially by those who, in the face of modernizing changes, sought to locate the ruler's authority in some mythical past.[25] Those claims were then challenged by radicals who based the authority of the ruler on a (virtual) contract entered into between individuals. But because these 'social contracts' were idealized constructions, their arguments could similarly be subjected to criticism as mythical creations. The concept of fundamental law comes into its own when the established regime is placed in question and this is when we enter the age of ideology.

[23]Elements of this problem can be seen in the debate between Schmitt and Kelsen over the agent that acts as guardian of the Weimar constitution. See Vinx (2015).

[24]de Vattel (2008), p. 92.

[25]A good example is Coke's use of the myth of the ancient constitution in seventeenth century England, though this had an earlier parallel claim in François Hotman's *Francogallia* (1972).

Ideological discourse is a product of modernization. It is generated when the political is conceived as an autonomous domain of thought and action and, unable to take its authority from transcendent sources, must generate authority immanently. The function of ideology is to conceal the contingency and partiality of particular group claims by presenting them as universals. This role is strengthened in modern constitutional order by the proliferation of claims about the meaning of fundamental law: does it find its basis in 'order and security' (Hobbes), 'equal liberty' (Rousseau), or 'common will' (Sieyes)? Fundamental law is presented as a series of contestable expressions of the basic law through which the institutionalized authority of the political is maintained.

In modern political regimes that institutionalized authority is expressed through a state's constitution. Constitutional discourse thus becomes the medium through which contestable expressions of fundamental law are articulated. Its ideological dimension acquires a greater prominence once constitutions assume a greater role in the regulation of political life. Political scientists have recently come to recognize that constitutions are 'crucial variables for explaining vital political and economic outcomes, such as the stability of democracy, economic policy and economic performance, and the rate of policy changes across political regimes'.[26] Following this, they have developed models of constitutional design to help constitution-makers improve governmental performance. Yet this type of exercise addresses only one aspect of constitutional ordering. There is undoubtedly a significant instrumental aspect to constitutions: they have an important technical role in co-ordinating decision-making and checking strategic or partisan political action. But there is also the symbolic dimension of constitutions which cannot be ignored without obscuring what is distinctive about political action.

The symbolic dimension is alluded to in Durkheim's observation that not everything in a contract is contractual: the contract depends for its acceptance on a set of prior beliefs.[27] The arrangement works because of certain background assumptions. It is similarly alluded to in Böckenförde's dictum that 'the liberal, secularized state is nourished by presuppositions that it cannot itself guarantee'.[28] The constitutional state establishes its authority only by acting contrary to its ostensible liberalism and imposing certain values on its citizens. In each instance, an indirect allusion is being made to the concept of fundamental law.

This work has taken on a greater degree of prominence as a result of the emergence of the constitutional jurisdiction of courts. Alongside political debate over public policy proposals within the executive and debate over legislative proposals in parliaments, there is intense debate about judicially-determined constitutional obligations. But the exercise of determining constitutional requirements is often mistakenly presented as a specialized and relatively technical assessment. With the extension of constitutional jurisdiction, constitutional deliberation has become

[26]Negretto (2013), p. 1.

[27]Durkheim (1984), p. 158.

[28]Böckenförde (1991), p. 45.

both more rarified and more intense. Many theories of constitutional interpretation are posited and, although expressed as forms of legal reason, they are intrinsically political. The ideological aspects of this practice are played out both through contested conceptions of law and constitution.

Constitutional interpretation has become an interminable interplay between the relative authority of text, precedent, and principle. No matter how much constitutional scholars seek to finesse this, the fact is that no authoritative method exists for weighing the different factors. Jurists have produced rigorous analyses of the canons of textual interpretation, of techniques for reasoning with precedents, and of methods of balancing general principles. But they have been unable to produce robust methods of comparing the relative importance of the different factors. This is not surprising because these factors express different interpretations of the meaning of fundamental law.

Schematically, the different conceptions we are addressing might be called law, legality and superlegality. By *law* is meant an artificial reason acquired through deep immersion in source-based legal materials. Law is local knowledge evolving incrementally in accordance with contemporary requirements. As skilled practitioners of this art, judges maintain their autonomy by recognizing a distinction between *jurisdictio* and *gubernaculum*, between matters legal and matters political. *Legality*, by contrast, is a modern form of law, the expression of will of the sovereign authority. The modern science of legality is promoted by jurists who see the state as a formal-rational regime using legislation as its normal working tool and who develop precise criteria for rule-governed action and consistent canons of rule interpretation. The third iteration, law as *superlegality*, is a recent innovation that has gathered momentum from the so-called rights revolution of the last fifty years. Superlegality is a conception of law as a set of fundamental norms that derive from general principles of liberty and equality, ideally of equal liberty. Superlegality is an elaboration of scholastic reason. It is neither a set of practices operating in a discrete sphere of government (law), nor an instrument of political power (legality). Superlegality is a set of abstract principles that limits the range of legitimate action of governing majorities.[29]

Many disputes in law are over facts while others involve ambiguities in the interpretation of texts and precedents. Operating in these ordinary ways, law evolves as an autonomous practice. But the closer one gets to the core matter of the constitution of political authority, the more disputes turn on the relative authority of conflicting conceptions of law, legality and superlegality. Constitutional disputes invariably entail claims about the relative authority of case law versus legislation, of legislative will versus constitutional principles, of constitutional principles versus judicial precedents. These conflicts cannot be resolved by legal method; they require the exercise of political judgment.

Conflicts like this make the very idea of a constitution the subject of intense dispute. Is it a text whose meaning is discoverable through normal canons of legal

---

[29] See further Loughlin (2018), pp. 5–7.

interpretation (Hobbes: *auctoritas, non veritas facit legem*), a product of the constituent power of the people that possesses a special status (Sieyes), or an expression of a society's fundamental political principles (Rousseau)? The relative importance of these interpretations varies according to time and place. But there can be no avoiding the fact that this judgment depends on prudential assessments of what is needed to maintain political authority. This exercise is masked in legal forms and methods, suggesting that fundamental law performs an ideological function of presenting partial, fluid and provisional interpretations as objective judgments.

8 Conclusion

At roughly the same time as the term fundamental law emerged in the early-modern period, a precise doctrine called 'reason of state' also was formulated. It maintained that the state is an autonomous institution operating according to its own laws, logic, standards and criteria. The doctrine played an influential, though persistently controversial, role in shaping policy in the early stages of state formation. With the establishment of the modern constitutional state, however, its power diminished, not least because this expression of political reason has become extensively institutionalized. It is not my intention here to explain the various ways in which reason of state has been transformed[30]; my point only is to assert that with the establishment of the modern constitutional state the type of political reason contained in that doctrine has been absorbed into a form of 'constitutional reason'. This type of constitutional reason is what I am calling modern fundamental law.

The modern constitutional state establishes a regime of governing according to law. But governing according to law no longer means governing in accordance with enacted rules or governing according to established precedents. Governing according to law—governing in accordance with constitutional legality—requires the exercise of political judgment about what is needed in order to maintain political authority. Determining the legality of governmental action requires an assessment of the relative importance of text, precedent and principles in contested political contexts. This method—the method of modern fundamental law—draws on political reason as much as legal reason; the institutionalization of political reason leads to the politicization of legal reason. Since there is no rational means of choosing between these different conceptions of law or between the different senses of the constitution of the state, modern fundamental law presents itself as a novel—and contestable—expression of political-legal reason.

[30]See Loughlin (2018), p. 141 ss.

References

Althusius, J. (1995). *Politica: Politics methodically set forth and illustrated with sacred and profane examples [1603]* (F. S. Carney, Ed. & Trans.). Indianapolis: Liberty Fund.
Anderson, B. (1991). *Imagined communities: Reflections on the origin and spread of nationalism.* London: Verso.
Beiner, R. (2011). *Civil religion: A dialogue in the history of political philosophy.* Cambridge: Cambridge University Press.
Böckenförde, E.-W. (1991). The rise of the state as a process of secularisation. In *State, society and liberty.* New York: Berg.
de Bèze, T. (1970). In R. M. Kingdon (Ed.), *Du droit des magistrats.* Geneva: Droz.
de La Boétie, É. (1975). *Discourse on Voluntary Servitude [1548]* (H. Kurz, Trans.). Auburn, Alabama: Mises Institute.
de Maistre, J. (1965). Study on sovereignty. In *The generative principle of political constitutions: studies on sovereignty, religion and enlightenment* (J. Lively, Ed. & Trans.). New York: Transaction Publishers.
de Vattel, E. (2008). *The Law of Nations, or Principles of the Law of Nature applied to the conduct of affairs of nations and sovereigns [1758].* Indianapolis: Liberty Fund.
Durkheim, E. (1984). The division of labour in society. In H. D. Halls (Trans.), *Introduction by Lewis Coser.* New York: Palgrave.
Franklin, J. H. (1969). *Constitutionalism and resistance in the sixteenth century: Three treatises by Hotman, Beza and Mornay.* New York: Pegasus.
Gentillet, I. (1968). In C. E. Rathé (Ed.), *Antimachiavel [1576].* Geneva: Droz.
Hobbes, T. (1990). In S. Holmes (Ed.), *Behemoth or the Long Parliament [c.1668].* Chicago: University of Chicago Press.
Hobsbawm, E., & Ranger, T. (Eds.). (1983). *The invention of tradition.* Cambridge: Cambridge University Press.
Hotman, F. (1972). In R. E. Giesey & J. H. M. Salmon (Eds.), *Francogallia [1573].* Cambridge: Cambridge University Press.
Hume, D. (1994). That politics may be reduced to a science. In K. Haakonssen (Ed.), *Political essays.* Cambridge: Cambridge University Press.
Loughlin, M. (2010). *Foundations of public law.* Oxford: Oxford University Press.
Loughlin, M. (2018). *Political jurisprudence.* Oxford: Oxford University Press.
Madison, J., Hamilton, A., & Jay, J. (1987). In I. Kramnick (Ed.), *The federalist papers.* London: Penguin.
Negretto, G. (2013). *Making constitutions: Presidents, parties, and institutional choice in Latin America.* Cambridge: Cambridge University Press.
Pocock, J. G. A. (1987). *The ancient constitution and the feudal law.* Cambridge: Cambridge University Press.
Rousseau, J.-J. (1962). Du Contrat Social. In *The political writings of Jean Jacques Rousseau, Edited from the original MSS. and authentic editions with introduction & notes by C. E. Vaughn* (Vol. II). Oxford: Basil Blackwell.
Schmitt, C. (2005). *Political theology: Four chapters on the concept of sovereignty* (G. Schwab, Trans.). Chicago: University of Chicago Press.
Sieyès, E. J. (2003). What is the third estate? In *Political writings* (M. Sonenscher, Trans.). Indianapolis: Hackett.
Thompson, M. P. (1986). The history of fundamental law in political thought from the French wars of religion to the American revolution. *American Historical Review, 91.*
Tuck, R. (1987). The "modern" school of natural law. In A. Pagden (Ed.), *The languages of political theory in early-modern Europe.* Cambridge: Cambridge University Press.
Vinx, L. (2015). *The guardian of the constitution: Hans Kelsen and Carl Schmitt on the limits of constitutional law.* Cambridge: Cambridge University Press.

Martin Loughlin is Professor of Public Law, London School of Economics & Political Science. Before that he taught at the Universities of Glasgow and Manchester. His books include *Sword and Scales: An Examination of the Relationship between Law and Politics* (Hart, 2000), *The Idea of Public Law* (Oxford University Press, 2003), *Foundations of Public Law* (Oxford University Press, 2017), *Political Jurisprudence* (Oxford University Press, 2017) and as co-editor *The Twilight of Constitutionalism* (Oxford University Press, 2010) and *The Paradox of Constitutionalism* (Oxford University Press, 2007).

Expanding Legality and Losing Fundamental Law: On Martin Loughlin's Dualist Conception of Public Law

Miguel Nogueira de Brito

Contents

Abstract What if political right, or fundamental law, were a distant star already dead, but whose brilliance we still capture in a world submitted, however, to a very distinct kind of domination, predominantly managerial and administrative in nature? This is the disturbing hypothesis that Martin Loughlin advances in his work on the formation and decline of political right, a discipline that emerged at the dawn of modernity in order to frame the legal and political rationality of national and centralized states, but which would subsequently be dislodged by the gradual establishment of constitutional legality and administrative rationality.

If in drawing this decline the work of Loughlin has a somewhat archaeological inclination, the truth is that at the same time it provides us with a relevant proposal for understanding current constitutional theory and law, that is, the hypothesis of a dualist structure of the main concepts that make up public law and the constitutional state. This structure ultimately depends on a distinction between what is constitutive and what is constituted in a political community, and even more so on the hypothesis that this distinction is itself constitutive of the very possibility of a political community.

M. N. de Brito (✉)
School of Law, University of Lisbon, Lisbon, Portugal
e-mail: miguelbrito@fd.ulisboa.pt

© Springer Nature Switzerland AG 2020

M. Nogueira de Brito, L. Pereira Coutinho (eds.), *The Political Dimension of Constitutional Law*, https://doi.org/10.1007/978-3-030-38459-3_3

1 Introduction

The political is an elusive concept. And the same can be said of fundamental law, the juridical refraction of the political. The political is different from politics, and fundamental law cannot be simply equated with constitutional law.

Whereas the political refers to the embedding of the state "in structures of authority and obedience whose power is such that they shape their members' sense of justice and injustice, right and wrong, freedom and servitude, good and evil", politics points to the managing of conflicts that arise between individuals or groups.[1]

Fundamental law, on the other hand, is not to be simply equated with constitutional law as the set of rules and principles that regulate the organization and functioning of political power and its relations with the individual. The difference between fundamental law and constitutional law correspond to the distinction made by Carl Schmitt in his *Verfassungslehre* between the material constitution as a political unity and the formal constitution as an institutional frame.[2] Differently put, fundamental law is the blending of political reason and legal reason that made possible the appearance of the modern constitutional state.[3]

The specificity of both the political and fundamental law has been the subject of Martin Loughlin work for several years and perhaps it would not be an overstatement to claim that in his view the state is at the very centre of both concepts. This naturally invites the questions: is the political even possible or viable beyond the state? Is fundamental law necessarily a law of the state?

At one, basic, level the answer to the last question seems obviously positive, and the answer to first one evidently negative. The historical point of view from which Martin Loughlin approaches the concepts of the political and of fundamental law naturally relates to the state. But at a more profound level it appears that the very possibility of the political as a meaningful dimension of human experience, as he envisages it, points to the concept of the state. And this inevitably drives us to Carl Schmitt's famous dictum: "the concept of the state presupposes the concept of the political".[4] Schmitt's dictum inverted the traditional view of German state theory and meant that the political "was not only independent of the state but could even end up opposed to it". In Schmitt's view this was confirmed in Weimar's time by the agonistic competition between political movements, all trying to conquer and use the

[1]Cf. Loughlin (2018a), p. 1; idem, "Fundamental Law", in this volume.

[2]Cf. Loughlin (2009), p. 10.

[3]Fundamental law is the core of public law, the subject of Martin Loughlin investigation, and a specific modern concept, not to be confused with the fundamental law of medieval times, which was understood as "natural law, a type of law regarded as 'higher' than and prior to ordinary (or positive) law": cf. Loughlin (2018a), p. 12.

[4]Cf. Schmitt (1979), p. 11; idem (2007), p. 19. Martin Loughlin repeats this claim *verbatim*: see Loughlin (2003), p. 32.

state's legal apparatus for their own purposes.[5] The political, in the sense of the opposition between friend and foe, defines what it is to be human which means in turn the centrality for human existence of those who are with you and those against whom you fight. Fighting and the possibility of violent death are necessary for there to be something like the political. These features of the political have certain legal consequences for Schmitt: the acknowledgement that politics requires authority and decisions that are singular, absolute and final rather than deliberation and general law.

In Schmitt's thought all these aspects had to be brought from the outside into the structure of the state, which in the meantime had, according to him, fallen prey to an excessively legalistic and liberal vision. Martin Loughlin takes a similar view but from a different perspective: the existential dimension of the political is constitutive of the modern state and its inner rationality. Whereas Schmitt looks at the state and sees the final product of German's *Staatsrechtslehre*, Loughlin sees the state from the vantage point of its early modern formation and subsequent evolution until the appearance of the constitutional state.[6]

In the following pages I begin by outlining the essential features of Loughlin's state-centred conception of the political and fundamental law which is based on a set of pairs of concepts, that is, on the political and politics, on *potestas* and *potentia*, and on *societas* and *universitas* (2). I also discuss the grounds for such distinctions (3). Subsequently, I allude to the dialectical structure and method of public law (4). With this background in view I attempt to show why the history of public law is necessarily a history of decline and fall (5). Notwithstanding this history of fateful destiny, in the conclusion I argue for the continuing relevance of Martin Loughlin's dualist structure of public law (6).

2 The Structural Dualism of Martin Loughlin's Approach to Public Law

I have already stressed the importance that the distinction between the political and politics assumes in Martin Loughlin's thinking. But this distinction, in turn, refers to the relation of the sphere of the political, as a strand of human experience, to religion. This same relationship is emphasized by Loughlin when he recognizes that, despite the development of the modern state as a process of secularization, this should not lead us to any illusions about the possibility of "a complete separation of political and religious questions". On the contrary, since "religion provides us with fixed points of guidance and offers guarantees of certainty and permanence", its

[5]Cf. Schupmann (2017), pp. 34–35; see also, Loughlin (2017b), pp. 573–574.

[6]As he himself acknowledges in the preface to *Political Jurisprudence* (2018a), p. 1, "I have recently been writing about constitutions, but the preliminaries keep getting in the way. By this I mean the most basic elements that establish the authority of the office of government".

continuing influence should not come as a surprise, "even if it is often disregarded in a rationalistic and secularized modern age".[7]

The importance of religion in the sphere of politics is emphasized by Claude Lefort, to whom we owe an in-depth distinction between *the political* and *politics* to which Loughlin alludes.[8] *Politics* refers us to the practices and institutions integrated in the general system of society as subsystem, and as such can be delimited by a criterion that distinguishes between what is political and what is non-political, and rather is economic, social, legal, aesthetic or religious. On the contrary, *the political* is a domain that does not simply result from methodological criteria, but rather refers to the principles that generate society, or different forms of society.[9] Politics concerns competition for power within a society, while the political is concerned with the way a society "represents its own unity before itself as a collectivity".[10] To that extent, politics is, in relation to the society in which it takes place, a constituted activity, while the political is a constitutive element of the society itself. It is understandable, therefore, the proximity between the political and the domain of religion, since both "govern symbolic access to the world and through their internal articulations determine the way of being of society".[11]

To a certain extent we can draw a parallel between Carl Schmitt and Claude Lefort when it comes to thinking the political, since both authors seem to admit the existence of an unavoidable link between the elaboration of a political form and the elaboration of a religious form. There would be, at least in Schmittian terminology, a structural analogy between political and theological concepts. Both authors seem to be "carrying theologico-political problematics over the epochal threshold into modernity" (Steinmetz-Jenkins 2009, p. 117). But while for Schmitt the legitimacy of modernity lies in the theological roots of modern political concepts, such as the state and sovereignty,[12] for Lefort modern democracy views the representation of

[7]Cf. Loughlin (2010), p. 48.

[8]It is not by chance that Loughlin quotes Claude Lefort precisely in the context of considerations of the persistence of religion in secularized societies referred to in the text: cf. Loughlin (2010), p. 48, note 169.

[9]Cf. Lefort (1986), pp. 279–280; Lefort (1988), pp. 216–217. Claude Lefort's claim that "the domain known as 'the political' does not result from methodological criteria alone" (cf. *op. cit.*, p. 279) seems to contradict Schmitt's famous thesis according to which the political is founded on the distinction between friend and enemy. It seems that "politics" according to Lefort corresponds to "the political" according to Schmitt. This is not the case: as clarified by Loughlin, when Schmitt says that the political is founded on the distinction between friend and enemy he is not concerned with conflict or the practices of politics—which Loughlin calls "the second order of the political"—but with a "first order phenomenon: the concept of the political itself". The important point here is to stress that the political points to the most intense and extreme antagonism as an inescapable aspect of the human condition: see Loughlin (2003), p. 33.

[10]Cf. Minkkinen (2018), p. 54.

[11]Cf. Steinmetz-Jenkins (2009), p. 105.

[12]According to Schmitt, "All significant concepts of the modern theory of the state are secularized theological concepts not only because of their historical development- in which they were transferred from theology to the theory of the state, whereby, for example, the omnipotent God became

power as an empty place, in which there is an irreversible distance between the symbolic and the real.[13] To be sure it is still the case in modernity that only the reconstitution of the relationship between religion and politics can give meaning to the latter, as Schmitt intended. However, this reconstitution became, according to Lefort, impossible with the advent of modernity.[14]

The way Martin Loughlin views the political seems to reveal greater affinities with Schmitt than with Lefort. The concepts through which he articulates his understanding of the state ultimately result from a distinction between what constitutes the political community and what is constituted by it. The same is true regarding his understanding of the distinction between the political and politics. The difficulty in maintaining the priority of what is constituent over what is constituted, notwithstanding its urgency, can be explained considering the famous affirmation by Machiavelli (1984), p. 465; Book III, chap. I, according to which there is no "thing more necessary in a common life, or sect or kingdom or republic that it is, than to render to it that reputation which it had in its principles".[15] This implies the belief in the capacity of a political community to structure itself in terms that correspond to the recognition that "cultures are formed only once a group is able to define itself in contrast to some other which they are not" (Loughlin 2003, p. 35). It also means that the ability to exercise control over those in charge of government depends on the ability to generate a sense of common identity thus establishing a political association.

It is this basic distinction between what constitutes and what is constituted that lies at the basis of Martin Loughlin's understanding of the political and public law and is unfolded in the concepts through which it expresses itself. Among these, special reference must be made to the notions of *potestas* and *potentia*, the notions of *societas* and *universitas*, and also to the distinctions between constituent power and constituted powers, fundamental law and constitutional legality. I will now deal with the first two pairs of concepts; I will deal with the latter distinctions in the next section.

---

the omnipotent lawgiver-but also because of their systematic structure, the recognition of which is necessary for a sociological consideration of these concepts. The exception in jurisprudence is analogous to the miracle in theology": cf. Schmitt (2009), p. 43.

[13]Cf. Lefort (1986), p. 291: "We have for a long time concentrated upon this singularity of modern democracy: of all the regimes of which we know, it is the only one to have represented power in such a way as to show that power is an empty place and to have thereby maintained a gap between the symbolic and the real".

[14]Cf. de Brito (2014), p. 334. Schmitt seems sometimes to acknowledge this impossibility, as when he says that "In the struggle of opposing interests and coalitions, absolute monarchy made the decision and thereby created the unity of the state. The unity that a people represents does not possess this decisionist character; it is an organic unity, and with national consciousness the ideas of the state originated as an organic whole. The theistic as well as the deistic concepts of God become thus unintelligible for political metaphysics" (cf. Schmitt 2009, p. 49).

[15]"cosa piú necessaria in uno vivere comune, o sètta o regno o republica che sia, che rendergli quella riputazione ch'egli aveva ne' principii suoi".

The difference between *potestas* and *potentia*—which we could also express through the words "*jus*" and "power"—performs two functions in Martin Loughlin's thought: first, it is the key to his understanding of the political, at least in the his more recent works; secondly it structures his narrative of the current decline of public law, which is patent in the degradation of *potestas*/*societas* and the continuous expansion of *potentia*/*universitas* (Dyzenhaus 2013, p. 215).

According to Loughlin (2018b, pp. 23–24), "the essence of the political rests in the relationship between *potestas* and *potentia*". *Potestas* refers to the power generated "by drawing people together in a common undertaking". This is the power "generated by the conviction that the association forms a unity, a collective singular: 'we the people'". There is no power in this sense without a cultural, historical, or linguistic identity that becomes a political identity.

Differently, *potentia*, refers to power "deployed by government to control and regulate conflict, to maintain order, and to promote the public welfare". For Loughlin (2018b, p. 24) *potentia*, as a domain that involves the exercise of physical force, corresponds to the "distributive aspect of a political power generated through *potestas*".

In *Foundations of Public Law*, the roots of this distinction are attributed to Spinoza's thought, for whom *potestas* would be the legitimate power of a ruler, his authority to command, while *potentia* would refer to the actual physical power that stems from the control of material resources.[16] Although *potestas* involves an absolute right to govern, the power of the sovereign would be weakened if it acted oppressively or inappropriately this could even lead to the collapse of the political regime.[17] According to Spinoza (2007), p. 200, in fact, sovereigns "retain the right to command whatever they wish only so long as they truly hold supreme power. If they lose it, they at the same time also lose the right of decreeing all things, which passes to the man or men who have acquired it and can retain it. This is why it can very rarely happen that sovereigns issue totally absurd commands. To protect their position and retain power, they are very obliged to work for the common good and direct all things by the dictate of reason; for no one has maintained a violent government for long, the Seneca says".

Loughlin, in drawing up the distinction between *postestas* and *potentia* in Spinoza's thinking, considers—following approaches such as that of Étienne Balibar or Edwin Curley—that at issue is neither the justification of a legitimate power, nor the defense of the claim that "might is right", but the very functioning of public law.[18] Correspondingly, the limitations to sovereign power are prudential rather than moral. The importance of the distinction between the two concepts for the idea of

[16]Cf. Loughlin (2010), p. 104.

[17]Cf. Loughlin (2010), p. 106.

[18]Cf. Balibar (2005), p. 72: "La question n'est pas en effet de donner une justification du droit, mais de former une idée adéquate de ses déterminations, de la façon dont il opère. Et la formule de Spinoza signifie d'abord, à cet égard, que le droit de l'individu inclut tout ce qu'il est effectivement capable de faire et de penser dans des conditions données". See also, Curley (1995), p. 322.

fundamental right can be understood in this context: the distinction reflects "the image of an all-powerful sovereign who issues orders, while recognizing that the ordering arrangements of the public sphere impose significant limitations on that formal jurisdictional authority" (2010, p. 106).

Another important distinction, which largely coincides with that which separates *potestas* and *potentia*, is the one Loughlin establishes—this time seeking inspiration in the thought of Oakeshott (1990), pp. 199 ff, 231 ff—between the state as *societas* and as *universitas*. In the first case, the state appears as an order of rules of conduct endowed with authority; in the second, as a corporate entity aimed at the pursuit of specific purposes. In the first case, the state is seen as a civil association that expresses a moral relationship between its members and whose conditions of association are expressed through a legal system. In the second case, the state is seen as a business association that brings together a group of people with a common purpose. It is not possible to conceive the state considering only one of these two images, but it is indispensable to negotiate the intrinsic tensions that they generate in the field of politics.[19] This is the task of the fundamental law.

We are now in position to understand the importance that the above-mentioned distinctions acquire in the narrative of the current decline of public law, as Loughlin presents it. This decline results precisely from the impossibility of maintaining on a secure basis the priority of the political over politics, of *potestas* over *potentia*, of *societas* over *universitas*. This impossibility manifests itself in the growth of administrative power, or *potentia*, especially through police powers, and in the emergence of what Loughlin (2010), p. 450 calls the "*new ephorate*", i.e. the proliferation of independent public entities that are not elected and increasingly undertake executive and regulatory functions.[20] Under these conditions it is increasingly difficult for the state to remain a realm aimed at the promotion of citizenship and freedom. The risk is for the state to convert into a domain of servants, as Rousseau had already pointed out.[21]

The categories above presented undoubtedly reveal a dualist structure in Loughlin's thought. In addition, the affinity between the pairs of concepts above mentioned becomes clear: *potentia* is the activity developed by the state when it acts as *universitas*; *potestas* refers to the foundation of authority that is generated by public law and is revealed in the establishment of a civil association, or *societas*. There remains however the question of the meaning of this duality of concepts. Does the distinction between *potestas* and *potentia* developed by Loughlin shows any correspondence with Spinoza's philosophy?

It would be tempting to look at the dualistic structure of Loughlin's thought as an attempt at exploring the tensions between an Aristotelian vision of the political, which portrays the human being as a social animal and is based on the idea of a common good, and a Hobbesian view, who sees politics in individualistic terms.

---

[19]Cf. Loughlin (2010), p. 160 ss.; idem (2018b), p. 23.

[20]Cf. Loughlin (2010), pp. 432, 448, 463.

[21]Cf. Loughlin (2010), pp. 12–13, 428.

These tensions, as we shall see, make it extremely difficult to integrate in a coherent manner the contrasting requirements of both visions.

3 Explaining the Dualist Structure of Public Law

3.1 The Influence of Carl Schmitt

In order to answer these questions, it is necessary to look at the relationship between Martin Loughlin's thinking and that of Carl Schmitt. Loughlin explicitly acknowledges an inspiration in Schmitt's thought on the autonomy of the political, a thinker he considers to be "one of the leading modern scholars of political jurisprudence" (2017b, p. 586). This poses the question as to how the liberal character that fades in Schmitt's political-constitutional thinking is preserved in Loughlin's construction of fundamental law. The difference between the two thinkers arises in a clear way in Schmitt's conception of democracy, which Martin Loughlin considers unacceptable, arguing that the "materialization of 'the people-as-one' leads to totalitarianism" (2017a, p. 166).

Notwithstanding this unequivocal difference, the truth is that almost all the central concepts in the theory of the constitution developed by Carl Schmitt, including the importance of the identity of a people for building a political community, also play an important role in Loughlin's thought. Furthermore, the way Schmitt relates to Spinoza's political thought is certainly enlightening in the perspective of understanding the distinction between *potestas* and *potentia*.

Spinoza's influence on Schmitt is ambivalent. On the one hand, Spinoza's distinction between *natura naturans* and *natura naturata* "helped to shape Schmitt's 'irrationalist' absolutist conception of an infinite *pouvoir constituant*". On the other hand, "Spinoza was one of the key figures in the historical turn from transcendental theism towards 'immanence-pantheism', and consequently he was in Schmitt's eyes co-responsible for the destruction of the 'person' of the worldly sovereign" (Koekkoek 2014, pp. 335–336).[22]

Spinoza's influence on Schmitt's thought thus lies in two aspects that cannot be easily harmonized. On the one hand, the importance that democracy as a people's identity assumes in Schmitt seems to be confirmed by the "Spinozist-Sieyesian account of 'constituent power' as an all-powerful principle that resists being constitutionalized" (Koekkoek 2014, p. 337).[23] At the same time, Schmitt was aware of the

[22]As noted by Koekkoek (2014), p. 335 Schmitt's condemnation of Spinoza arises particularly impressively in the assertion that "The most audacious insult ever to be inflicted upon God and man, and which justifies all the synagogue's curses, lies in the 'sive' of the formula: Deus sive natura". Cf. Schmitt (2015), p. 22.

[23]See also Del Lucchese (2016), pp. 188–189. The parallelism between Spinoza and Sieyès is expressly established by Schmitt, when the latter states that "In some of Sieyès's writings, the 'pouvoir constituant' appears in its relationship to every 'pouvoirs constitués' as a metaphysical

difficulty Spinoza's immanent metaphysics posed to the possibility of subjecting democratic power to political representation. In fact, as Schmitt (2010), p. 205 acknowledges, no state can waive all structural elements of representation. It is not only the formula "*Deus sive natura*" that renders Spinoza's thought problematic in Schmitt's eyes but also, and foremost, the formula "*jus sive potentia*".[24] If there is no transcendent God beyond nature, there cannot be neither a right beyond nature, nor a constructed people beyond the real existing multitude. To this extent, it is possible to affirm that the legacy of Spinoza appeared to Schmitt as essentially dilemmatic (Koekkoek 2014, pp. 348–350).

We know that Schmitt solved this dilemma by appealing to a plebiscitary conception of democracy, following a path already opened by Max Weber.[25] As mentioned, this is not Martin Loughlin's way. However, Loughlin appears to share Schmitt's refusal to destroy the person of the secular ruler or, in Lefort's terminology, to conceive of the political as an empty place. In fact, he claims, explicitly alluding to Lefort, albeit contradicting Lefort's understanding of modern democracy, that "the transcendent belief in divine authority might be effaced but that space remains. The transcendent figure of the sovereign is lost, but the space of sovereignty is retained. This is the space of the political, an autonomous domain which, despite its uncertainties, expresses a distinctive way of being that is revealed in its logic of action and singular conception of power" (Loughlin, 2014b, p. 228).

In this sense, the distinction between the political and politics is projected and prolonged in the distinctions between *potestas* and *potentia*, between *societas* and *universitas*. The dualist structure that is present in all of them performs the same function, which consists precisely in preventing the place of power from becoming empty. The way to ensure this goal is to establish priority of the political over politics, of *potestas* over *potentia*, of *societas* over *universitas*. However, this is not a simple normative priority, but rather the existential priority of the constituent over the constituted. But precisely this existential priority is nevertheless threatened by an inverse priority in the order of visibility and proximity, or in the order of what is more immediately perceptible and palpable. Indeed, the greater visibility of the institutional practices in which politics manifests itself (as compared to the ineffable character of the political) cannot be doubted, nor can the immediate presence of the effective physical power based on the control of the material resources to which *potentia* refers (as opposed to the symbolic dimension inherent in all *potestas*), or the

---

analogy to the 'natura naturans' and its relationship to the 'natura naturata' of Spinoza's theory. It is an inexhaustible source of all forms without taking a form itself, forever producing new forms out of itself, building all forms, yet doing so without form itself (cf. *die Diktatur*, p. 142). But it is necessary to distinguish the positive theory of the constitution-making power, which inheres in every constitutional theory, from the pantheist metaphysic. They are in no way identical with one another. The metaphysic of the potesta constituens as well as that of the analogy to the natura naturans is part of the theory of political theology": cf. Schmitt (2010), pp. 79–80; Schmitt (2008), p. 128.

[24]Cf. Spinoza [2008, pp. 80–81, 83 (Cap. II; 4-5, 8)].

[25]Cf. de Brito (2000), p. 383.

immediate perception of the advantages that are withdrawn from the understanding of the state as *universitas* (as opposed to the immaterial character of the state viewed as *societas*).

The problem for Loughlin is to assert this priority in a way that avoids materializing what is constituent, while at the same time aiming to ensure its continuous presence, with the function of challenging the performance of the instituted powers. In other words, while Schmitt advocates an effective and substantive occupation of the political space by the people represented by its leader, Loughlin proposes a symbolic occupation. Later on, with regard to the distinction between the constituent power and the constituted powers, we shall have occasion to develop this difference.

Schmitt, on his part, appears sometimes to be a reluctant dualist (hence the appeal Spinoza has to him): the tension found at the heart of the *Verfassungslehre* between the *Rechtsstaat* and the political components of the modern constitution always seems ready to be undone in favor of the political. In Schmitt's characteristically incisive terms, "no state without a people, no people without an acclamation" (2014, p. 52). On the contrary, the distinction between *Rechtsstaat* and the political is an irreducible feature of Loughlin's constitutional theory.

But is it really the case that democracy (albeit in its plebiscitary version) underlies Schmitt's concept of the political? Indeed, we may ask whether the conception of democracy is not just one of the several stages in which Schmitt successively (and, in a sense, opportunistically) re-elaborates the concept of the political. In a first phase, in *Politische Theologie*, the political appears in the idea of the sovereignty; in a second phase, which corresponds to the *Verfassungslehre*, the political manifests itself in democracy and the constituent power; finally, in a third phase, corresponding to *Der Nomos der Erde*, the political is (re)elaborated according to the idea of *nomos*.

In this third incarnation, however, the political loses its connection with the democratic idea that is at the heart of the concept of constituent power in the *Verfassungslehre*. What is now essential is not, in fact, democracy, but the idea of establishing a political order, understood as an existential rather than a normative reality. Loughlin (2015a, p. 72) precisely clarifies this when stating that, for Schmitt, "Nomos is an expression of the constituent power to establish order through an original act of appropriation and division".

According to Schmitt, "the Greek noun *nomos* derives from the Greek verb *nemein*, and, in common acceptance, *nemein* has three main meanings: these are (in German) *nehmen* (to appropriate), *teilen* (to divide) and *weiden* (to pasture)".[26] In its first meaning, it signifies a taking, i.e. a land appropriation; the second meaning of *nomos* is the action and process of division and distribution; finally, the third meaning of *nomos* or *nemein* "is *weiden* [literally, pasturage]. This is the productive work that normally occurs with ownership. The commutative right of buying and selling in the market presupposes ownership as well as production deriving from the

---

[26]Cf. Loughlin (2015a), p. 70; see also, Schmitt (1985), p. 491 ss. [this text is included in the English translation of Schmitt (2003), p. 326 ss.].

primary division: *divisio primaeva*. This third meaning of nomos derives from the type and means of production and manufacture of goods" (Schmitt 1985, pp. 491–492; Schmitt 2003, p. 327).

Notwithstanding this linguistic explanation, Loughlin (2015a, b, p. 70) leaves the third meaning relatively unattended: "*Nomos* is an expression of the constituent power to establish order through an original act of appropriation and division". In this sense *nomos* is the fundamental law of the political.[27] But this is not the only way Schmitt himself envisages *nomos*. On the one hand, Schmitt (1985), p. 493; Schmitt (2003), pp. 328–329 says that "all known and famous appropriations in history, all great conquests – wars and occupations, colonizations, migrations, and discoveries – have evidenced the fundamental precedence of appropriation before distribution and production". On the other hand, Schmitt (1985), p. 500; Schmitt (2003), pp. 334–335, after reviewing the views on the question of precedence of the three meanings of *nomos* implicit in imperialism, liberalism, and socialism, states, somewhat ironically and provocatively, that "We should abolish all appropriation, because it is inhuman and historically obsolete. We also should limit problems of distribution, because it is too difficult to find not only general principles, but persuasive measures and legally viable procedures. There remains only production".

In another text, Schmitt says that "just as division precedes production, so appropriation precedes division; it opens the way to apportionment. It is not division – not the *divisio primaeva* – but appropriation that comes first. Initially, there was no basic norm, but a basic appropriation" (2003, p. 345). However, he clearly admits the contrary possibility of the precedence of production in the present times. His words are certainly worthy of extensive reproduction:

> Everything on earth based on progress and development, in both East and West, now contains at its core a concrete and precise creed, whose principles of belief proclaim that the industrial revolution leads to an immeasurable increase in production. As a consequence, appropriation becomes outmoded, even criminal, and division is no longer a problem, given the abundance. There is only production, only the problem-less fortune of pure consumption. No longer are there wars and crises, because unchained production no longer is partial and unilateral, but has become total and global. In other words, like the bees, mankind finally has found its formula in the beehive. Things govern themselves; man confronts himself; wandering in the wilderness of alienation has ended. In a world created by man for himself – a world of men for men (and unfortunately sometimes against men) – man can give without taking.[28]

According to Schmitt analysis, it appears that the same idea of *nomos* that is the very origin of the sovereign state is also the distant foundation of the self-regulating free market. This means that the space of the political and the "new ephorate" pertain

---

[27]Cf. Loughlin (2015a), p. 76. See, also, Loughlin (2017b), p. 582: "In *The 'Nomos' of the Earth* he [Schmitt] shows the distinctive contribution that *nomos* makes to the establishment of political order. The most basic claim is that law is tied to space, that is, to a defined and bounded territory that distinguishes inside and out- side. Without this boundary, there can be no domain of the political. In this respect, it might be said that nomos is constitutive of the political".

[28]Cf. Schmitt (2003), p. 347.

to the same intellectual history. As we know, this is the hypothesis of a "double paradigm" of secularized theology developed by Giorgio Agamben, according to which, not only the political, but also the economy could be a secularized theological paradigm. According to that hypothesis "the living being who was created in the image of God in the end reveals himself to be capable only of economy, not politics, or, in other words,. . .history is ultimately not a political but a 'managerial' and 'governmental' problem, [it] is nothing but a logical consequence of economic theology" (Agamben 2009, p. 15). The religious past is as much inherent in the political as in our present claimed unpolitical condition. The question that remains unanswered by Schmitt concerns the relationship between democracy—that is, real and not acclamatory democracy—and the political.

3.2 The Troubling Legacy of Spinoza

Further ahead I shall have the opportunity to return to the merits of the dualist structure as the key to understanding the modern state. For the moment it is important to evaluate to what extent it can legitimately claim the legacy of Spinoza. In this context, it is necessary first to ask whether Schmitt abuses or distorts Spinoza's ideas for his own purposes. In the light of Spinoza's immanent metaphysics, it is not possible to extract from *natura naturans* "the ontological model for a sovereignty thought as a vestige of a transcendent power and, at the same time, as a recovery of the personal element that normativism would seek to dilute in the meanderings of a constitution" (Aurélio 2000, p. 286). Be that as it may it seems undeniable the appeal that *natura naturans* presents to thinking democracy as an all-powerful political principle that resists being constitutionalized.

As seen, Schmitt recognizes the origin of the concept of constituent power in Spinoza's thought. But, as also seen, the latter argued for a radical equivalence between right and power, according to the well-known formula *jus sive potentia*. In this context, Filippo Del Lucchese puts the right questions: "If the right of each individual, both singular and collective, is for Spinoza its power, in a relation of co-essentiality, how can constituent power derive from his thought? How can a power that, by definition, is pre-ordered and super-ordered vis-à-vis right fit in Spinoza's scheme? Is not this anteriority and superiority of power over right incompatible with the immanence advocated by Spinoza?".[29]

[29]Cf. Del Lucchese (2016), p. 188. It is however doubtful whether he gives the right answers. According to Lucchese, "Spinoza actually maintains a radical and original idea of constituent power, an idea that provides a solution for the paradox implicit in its modern definition. Spinoza's concept of *jus sive potentia* implies a redefinition of the relationship between factual and normative whereby it is not possible to imagine a relationship of priority or superiority between constituent power and constituted power. It is only through a radical immanence that one can confront the law's claim to obliterate constituent power. Spinoza's philosophy allows to clarify the paradox implicit in the traditional definition of constituent power". As he further says, "the only way to avoid violent

Even more so, it is necessary to question the extent to which Loughlin's distinction between *potestas* and *potentia* is actually embedded in Spinoza's thought. In fact, instead of this Spinozist distinction being mobilized in the sense of a dialectical tension at the root of any meaningful understanding of the political, it actually points to an equivalence or co-extension between the *potestas* and the *potentia* of the individual[30]: "*jus sive potentia*".

Spinoza, on the other hand, does not fail to explicitly affirm this equivalence when he argues that the natural right of the individual (his *potestas*) "extends as far as his desire and power extend" (2007, p. 11). This same principle also governs the right of a political society, which according to Spinoza resides in the *potentia multitudinis*: "the law of the city is determined by the power of the multitude" (2008, p. 97 [Ch. III, 7]). It is thus possible to conclude that for Spinoza "individuals are the only things that have *potentia*; other things do not. People do have *potentia*; the state does not" (Barbone 2002, p. 104). This conclusion certainly points to the radically democratic and individualistic character of Spinoza's political thought, but it makes it extremely difficult to consider his use of *potestas* and *potentia* as the basis for elaborating a theory of the political that assigns any meaningful role to instituted powers. On the one hand, the subjects for which the two concepts point are not exactly identical. While *potestas* can refer to the state or to the individual, the *potentia* is exclusive of the latter. On the other hand, and more importantly, Spinoza's *potestas* has no priority over *potentia*.

Spinoza's appeal to Schmitt was already mentioned. We can see now that it ultimately results from the overpowering force the latter attributes to the democratic basis of constituent power. It is far more difficult to understand Spinoza's appeal to Loughlin: it is doubtful whether Spinoza thinks of the concepts of *potestas* and *potentia* according to the dualist structure that is present in Loughlin's thought. The willingness of the latter to acknowledge the democratic principle the central importance which Spinoza attributed to it is also doubtful.[31]

revolutions is to maintain a state of permanent revolution, namely a situation in which the juridical does not detach itself from the factual from which it arises, but instead gives it life, in and through collaborative and conflicting relationships among subjects" (2016), pp. 188, 200. As one can see, in Lucchese's account Spinoza does not exactly solves the paradox of constituent power, as eliminates it, by denying any meaningful role to the constituted powers.

[30]Cf. Mignini (2000), p. 406.

[31]This importance seems undeniable, even if one rejects the extreme points of view defended by such authors as Antonio Negri: cf. Aurélio (2014), p. 379 ff.

3.3 *An Ambiguous Genealogy? Political Theology and the Distinction Between* **Potentia Absoluta** *and* **Potentia Ordinata**

Even if the foundation of Loughlin's dualist structure of the political in Spinoza's thought seems in need of revision, one could be tempted to anchor it in the distinction established by medieval theologians between *potentia absoluta* and *potentia ordinata*. However, it should be noted that he distinction between the two concepts has two very different understandings in this context. According to a traditional theological understanding, present in thinkers as diverse as St. Thomas Aquinas and William of Ockham, the *potentia absoluta* regards the divine power and is thus unrelated to its action and will; differently in *potentia ordinata* divine power is seen in the perspective of its decrees, of its revealed will. In this context, *potentia absoluta* is certainly not a model for describing a divine intervention, direct and destabilizing, in the world; it's not intended at undermining the possibility of human knowledge of the real, nor even the stability of a natural moral and political order. Its meaning is only to make it clear that God did not act according to necessity, that he could do things differently from the way he chose.[32]

Alongside this understanding, there is also an "operationalized" and juridical understanding of the distinction, developed by authors such as Duns Scotus, within which the *potentia absoluta* is understood as an immediately acting power of God, against which the natural order instituted by *potentia ordinata*, does not offer any guarantee. In light of this understanding the distinction is established in terms analogous to those of the distinctions between the normal and the occasional, the ordinary and the extraordinary, the regular and the exceptional.

It is possible to contrast the two understandings of the distinction in light of the distinction *de iure/de facto*. According to this view, Duns Scotus established a parallel between *potentia absoluta* and possibility of fact and, correlatively, between *potentia ordinata* and *ius*. This means that "the phrases of *potentia ordinata* and of *potentia absoluta* no longer simply characterized two different senses of *posse*; they now affirmed two different forms of action, one in conformity with the law and one outside and above the law" (Courtenay 1984b, p. 13). On the contrary, a more traditional understanding of the distinction would approximate *potentia ordinata* to the *de facto* dimension, since it designates the domain of what was already realized (Randi 1987, pp. 54–55).

First, it is necessary to bear in mind that when he refers to the theological origin of the concepts of modern state theory Schmitt does not have directly in mind the distinction between *potentia absoluta* and *potentia ordinate*.[33] His point of reference seems to be instead the contraposition between theists and deists in the seventeenth and eighteenth centuries, and the exclusion of the possibility of miracles which the

[32]Cf. Courtenay (1984a), pp. XI: 37–38; idem (1990), p. 120; Randi (1987), pp. 74–75.

[33]Despite some suggestions to the contrary: cf. Milbanks (2010), p. 28.

latter advocated by thinking of God as the engineer of a machine that has been operating on its own since its creation.[34]

But whatever the interpretation of the medieval theologians adopted,[35] it seems difficult to use their thought to invert the sense of the analogy established by Carl Schmitt and to hold that "rather than being a secularized theological notion, the constitution-making power is a theologized juristic notion".[36] On the contrary, the same analogy seems to express a constant proximity between religion and the political, to which medieval theology also bears witness.

Probably the best terms to describe such a proximity are the ones used by anthropologists:

> There are kingly beings in heaven even where there are no chiefs on earth.
>
> It follows that the state of nature has the nature of the state. Given the governance of human society by metaperson authorities with ultimate life-and-death powers, something quite like the state is a universal human condition.
>
> It also follows that kings are imitations of gods rather than gods of kings – the conventional supposition that divinity is a reflex of society notwithstanding.[37]

The human way of modeling power on earth is bound by religious experience and this feature is not likely to disappear.

4 The Dialectics of Public Law

Martin Loughlin's contribution to the concept of constituent power is to emphasize how its exercise can never be considered a closed question in a given constitutional order. It is not because there is a constitution in force, approved according to the most demanding democratic standards, that the constituted powers may disinterest themselves from the constituent power. Reacting simultaneously to Schmitt's decisionism and the current reigning normativism, Loughlin (2017a, pp. 171–172) refuses, against the former, the idea of an effectively acclaiming people and, against the latter, the possibility of the constituent power being fully absorbed into the constituted order and equated with some founding norm. Reacting to both conceptions, Loughlin's proposal lies in his concept of the relational character of sovereignty and constituent power. The relational approach replicates the dualist structure of the essential concepts of public law. Its basis is the claim that "the political space must be recognized as incorporating an unresolved dialectic of determinacy and

---

[34]Cf. Schmitt (2009), p. 52: "Der Souverän, der im deistischen Weltbild, wenn auch außerhalb der Welt, so doch als Monteur der großen Maschine geblieben war, wird radikal verdrängt. Die Maschine läuft jetzt von selbst".

[35]For more developed references on this matter, cf. de Brito (2007), pp. 137–141, esp.139, note 106; Castrucci (2016), p. 25 ff.; Oakley (2002), p. 14; Diamantides (2012), p. 333 ff.; Traversino (2012), p. 35 ff.

[36]Cf. Ojakangas (2012), p. 515. For a critical appraisal, see Yelle (2019), pp. 50–52.

[37]Cf. Graeber and Sahlins (2017), pp. 2–3, 23.

indeterminacy, of closure and openness" (Loughlin, 2014b, p. 228; Loughlin 2017a, pp. 166–167).

If the continuing existence of the political depends on not letting its space becoming empty, Loughlin (2014a, b), pp. 233–234; Loughlin (2017a), p. 174 seems to admit the impossibility of filling it in effective terms, when he states that "the question of who represents the people remains the indeterminate question of modern politics. The function of constituent power is to keep that question open, not least because 'the people-as-one' is the hallmark of totalitarianism".

Instead, the relevance of constituent power in a constitutional order goes through two aspects: *(1)* on the one hand, constituent power means the continuous projection of the dimension of the symbolic representation of the people as a unity (as opposed to the multitude); *(2)* on the other hand, it expresses the dialectical nature of the fundamental law by seeking "constantly to irritate the institutionalized form of constituted authority". As a result, through the constituent power "the people in their non-instituted manifestation irritate the instituted power in a dialectical engagement through which real political will results" (2017a, pp. 169, 173).

There is inherent in public law a dialectical structure that Loughlin (2018b, p. 27) openly assumes, and not only in what concerns constituent power. The dialectical method of fundamental law still seems to be very much present regarding situations of exception. Agamben (2003, p. 19) identifies a division in the legal traditions of Western states, which would be clear in terms of principles, but more imprecise in its implementation, between jurisdictions that regulate the state of exception and jurisdictions that do not explicitly regulate the question.[38] What is truly important is not so much the existence, or not, of a constitutional provision concerning the state of exception, but the existence, or not, of statutes of law regulating its operation. It is in this latter dimension that the distinction between the two traditions acquires full meaning: according to one of them (the Lockean tradition of the executive's prerogative) the law is used to suspend the law and only after restoration to normality the performance of the executive power developed with the objective of this reestablishment can be evaluated by the representatives of the people; according to the other (the continental tradition of legalizing emergency powers), the executive's performance in situations of exception is itself subject to legal regulation which amounts in a certain extent to the dissolution of the exception amid the strictures of law.

The option seems to be either to confront openly the existence of black holes in the law, or to accept the irreplaceable existence of gray holes. On another level, the question may be asked to what extent states of exception should be viewed in the light of Kelsen's identity thesis that the state is totally constituted by law (Dyzenhaus 2006, p. 199). It is at this point that Loughlin's conception of the fundamental law acquires its deeper meaning: states of exception are subject to fundamental law, but

[38]See also Keller (2008), p. 43 ff. The difference between these two kinds of attitude regarding states of exception also coheres with Loughlin's distinction between negative and positive constitutionalism; cf. Loughlin (2015b), pp. 8–9.

not to constitutional or administrative law. In Loughlin's own words "positive law recedes, but *droit politique* remains" (2010, p. 401). This statement has its clear parallel in Schmitt's formulation, according to which in the state of exception "the State remains, whereas law recedes".[39] The apparent difference in formulations conceals a substantial convergence of perspectives: in the state of exception there is an order, but not a legal order, and that order is accessible to legal knowledge insofar as not only the norm, but also the decision, remains within the framework of the juridical.[40]

The fundamental law is, therefore, a type of right whose object is the decision and no longer the norm. But the dialectical dimension of public law is also present here insofar as states of exception are marked by an action aiming to restore the normal situation. Loughlin (2010), p. 401 quotes in this context the words of Mark Tushnet: "legal black holes may be law-free zones, but they are not rule-of-law free zones, because they are created and sustained in part by a moralized politics".

5 Expanding Constitutional Legality and Losing Public Law

At the end of his review of Loughlin's *Foundations of Public Law* Dyzenhaus (2013), p. 326 complains of the omission of any reference to Kelsen's essay on "the nature and value of democracy". Although the omission of an in-depth treatment of democracy is a conspicuous feature of Loughlin's thought, the truth is that this observation demonstrates the incommensurability of both authors' thinking. While Dyzenhaus is one of the current heralds of Kelsen's thesis of the identity between law and state, Loughlin argues for the existence of an asymmetry between the two realities, at least if we understand by law the set of positive norms in a particular order. There is a dimension of the state that positive law does not regulate, nor could regulate. This means that the fundamental law as an expression of this reality consists in a blending of political and legal reason whose relationship with the law as we know it is problematic, to say the least. The same is true regarding its relationship with the democratic principle.

It is precisely at this point that the specificity of Loughlin's treatment of the state is revealed. To understand this specificity, the most fruitful starting point is undoubtedly the opposition between Schmitt and Kelsen on the concept of democracy. As is well known, while Schmitt establishes a radical opposition between democracy and the constitution, Kelsen argues for the essential compatibility between the two (de Brito 2015, p. 93 ff.). However, Loughlin's concept of democracy, or at least the way he sees the articulation between democracy and the Constitution, seems closer to Kelsen than to Schmitt. As Loughlin expressly states, "democracy and

[39]Cf. Schmitt (2009), p. 18: "der Staat bestehen bleibt, während das Recht zurücktritt".

[40]Cf. Schmitt (2009), p. 19. See also, Loughlin (2017b), p. 579.

constitutionalism are not contradictory movements" (2003, p. 112). This seems to bring him closer to the idea of a "co-originality" of law and democracy. And yet, Loughlin unequivocally rejects Kelsen's thesis on the identity of the state and law.

Herein lies the essential question: if the political does not find its materialization in democracy (as an immediate presence of the people with itself or as a presence of the people in its acclaimed leader) and, at the same time, if the political is not exhausted in the structures of positive constitutional law, where can it be located? There is no doubt that Loughlin rejects Schmitt's plebiscitarian democracy, according to which the will of the people is most effectively reflected in the political process through public acclamation given by a substantially homogeneous people, in response to precise questions formulated by the head of the executive power.[41] But even if he condemns Schmitt's inability, or lack of will, to "conceive the maintenance of the political domain without the constant presence of a determinate sovereign", Loughlin does not accept the idea of the political becoming an empty space in modernity (2014b, p. 228; 2017a, pp. 166–167).

But how can that space be occupied without admitting the constant presence of a determinate sovereign? Loughlin's answer can be found in his pure theory of public law. Purity is to be understood here in terms that, despite everything, retain a certain parallelism with the Kelsenian project: it means an autonomous legal discipline "stripped of political ideology" (2003, p. 4). In analogous terms, Loughlin's project consists of "present[ing] 'political right' in its own terms" (2016, pp. 59–60). Simply put, rather than finding a *Grundnorm* at the basis of this project as a mechanism for identifying positive law, Loughlin envisions a "*Grundakt*" (in the sense of founding deed) that brings a collective association into existence, this being consistent with his reading of *nomos*. In this context, the purity of public law points to its characterization as a form of practical reason that adheres to the law for reasons of prudential necessity and finds its most finished expression in the early modern category of the reason of state.[42] Less clear, however, is the relationship between this form of practical reason and democracy.

According to Loughlin the reason of state is a historically determined concept that was gradually eclipsed with the establishment of the modern state,[43] rather than being a "relative constant, having been in continuous usage since Machiavelli's time".[44]

This happens because of the radical foreignness of the concept of reason of state in the face of a legal reason regarded as a normative project that intends to measure all government activity in the light of abstract principles. The consolidation of constitutional legal reason (in Loughlin's saying "constitutional legality" or "superlegality") with the development of modernity corresponds to the eclipsing of early modern reason of state. It is the observed impossibility of the reason of state

[41]Cf. Schmitt (2010), pp. 83, 276, 352; idem (2014), p. 48 ff.

[42]Cf. Loughlin (2003), p. 163.

[43]Cf. Loughlin (2018a), p. 142.

[44]Cf. Poole (2015), p. 4 *apud* Loughlin (2018a), p. 142, note 3.

to maintain itself in the face of the expansionist tendency revealed by this juridical reason—which is today the reason at the center of all constitutional systems—that explains its temporally limited character. In this context, Loughlin (2018a, p. 165) rightly accentuates the difference between the concept of reason of state and the concept of constitutional reason of state. The latter corresponds simply to the institutionalization and normalization of the reason of state. Needless to say, with this transformation, the reason of state loses its own prudential character.

The decline of reason of state finds its most finished expression in the current definitive overcoming of Otto Mayer's well-known statement: "constitutional law passes by, administrative law stands".[45] Today, in times of constitutional legality, for this sentence to make sense its terms would have to be inverted: "constitutional law stands, administrative law passes by". The difference, which is not insignificant, is that the constitutional law that Mayer had in mind was still essentially a constitutional law of a political nature, while in the new formula administrative law is conceived as applied constitutional law in accordance with the mentioned normative project: stability at the top is a condition of accelerated mutability at the base. The exponential effects that this change entails are correctly expressed by Luhmann (1990, p. 196): "the political system should be bound to the law for the sake of inhibiting the misuse of political power. But now it founds itself entangled in the law by the fact that the law is at its disposal". The state founded on law is as much an instrument to limit power as to exercise and increase it.

The continuous erosion of political law is therefore a process that develops in terms that are inversely proportional to those of the expansion of constitutional legality. And, in fact, it should be remembered that this double process is, after all, what explains the growth of administrative power, or *potentia*, especially through police powers, and the emergence of the "*new ephorate*". Writing today the history of public law, as Loughlin understands the concept, is admittedly equivalent to writing the "chronicle of a death foretold". This would be the death of public law at the hands of legality.

But is this, all things considered, a necessarily bad outcome, at least compared with the one that existed in the golden times of the reason of state, at the dawn of modernity? Admittedly public law could help to avoid some excesses of legalism—as seen in the later distorted view of states of emergency, or in its incapability of understanding the function of constituent power—but can it positively determine its own content in a way that is still relevant to contemporary public life? In adopting a polemic position against the theory of constitutional pluralism, Loughlin asserts the domain of the political as a condition in which the collective association which possesses ultimate political authority presents itself as "a unitary entity able to take extreme collective action whenever its way of life is threatened" (Loughlin 2014a, p. 30). Even if I conceive states as collective associations with ultimate political

[45]Cf. Mayer (2004, Vorwort zur dritten Auflage): "Verfassungsrecht vergeht, Verwaltungsrecht besteht". Loughlin also cites this passage from Otto Mayer but in a different context, as a confirmation of Dicey's apprehension by the rise of administrative law (2010), p. 443, note 34.

authority, I find it difficult to conceive of a threat to the way of life of a European state that is not, at the same time, a threat to every other one.

6 Conclusion

Martin Loughlin's ideas on fundamental law are an invaluable resource for claiming to the liberal canon some categories previously developed in pre-liberal or even illiberal contexts. These categories, such as the state, sovereignty, constituent power and reason of state, which form the bulk of fundamental law, are the ones that alone can guarantee the presuppositions that nourish the liberal, secularized state.[46] But can fundamental law discharge this guarantying function in today's social, political and economic conditions? Here I can only briefly sketch *(a)* a likely scenario that denies this possibility, *(b)* the critical role that, notwithstanding, fundamental law could assume by inhibiting the substantiation of that scenario, and *(c)* the importance of acknowledging the continuity between divine authority and secular democracy.

The first thing to stress concerns the affinity between the category of the political and the persistence of the state and the political system as manifestations of segmental social differentiation, according to Luhmann's social theory, in a world in which the differentiation of social systems prevailingly takes place in a global setting in accordance with functional criteria.[47] At the same time, it is questionable to what extent this characteristic of the political system is not affected by the growing assertion of "constitutional legality" and the correlative erosion of political right. The dissolution of the mixture of political reason and legal reason at the center of political right is certainly consistent with the differentiation between the legal system and the political system, but also with the growing (self-)presentation of both systems as world systems. This same process is evoked by Loughlin when he notes that "it is said that Aristotle's Lyceum could specify 158 different types of political constitution but, as Sheldon Wolin notes, de Tocqueville 'was convinced that the political world, insofar as it was becoming modernized, was being reduced to one'".[48]

[46]The text obviously alludes to the famous Ernst-Wolfgang Böckenförde's *dictum* (2006), p. 112.

[47]In comparison, it seems to me less relevant Emilios Chistodoulidis's observation that the autonomy between the legal and political systems in Luhmann's perspective [see Luhmann (2004), p. 364] is called into question by a concept of State, such as the one Loughlin has in mind, that is both political and legal [cf. Chistodoulidis (2008), p. 38]. As noted by Loughlin, *The Idea of Public Law* "presents a modern account of the discipline", and if this account has been overcome by the late-modern world along the lines described by Luhmann this requires "a radical shift in thought about government, power, regulation and agency" [cf. Loughlin (2016), p. 60]. In fact, one could even claim that this shift is precisely the consequence of Loughlin's diagnosis of the decline of public law in the transition from modernity to late-modernity.

[48]Cf. Loughlin (2018a), p. 167. The reference to the work of Sheldon Wolin is to his book *Tocqueville Between Two Worlds: The Making of a Political and Theoretical Life* (2001), p. 97.

The loss of political diversity is an indication that the political system is not immune to processes of social differentiation according to functional criteria. This transformation, in turn, manifests itself in the following aspects, which characterize the so-called European constitutionalism, but are becoming increasingly present in the constitutionalism of states: *(1)* a foundational act is absent as a manifestation of constituent power, in the context of so-called post-foundational constitutionalism; *(2)* the ultimate integrative force of the (welfare-)state lies not in politics but in economics; *(3)* the essential substance of the constitution does not come from the unitary organization of political power, but from the constitutionalization of certain areas of law, or "constitutional objects", which allows us to speak of "sectoral constitutions" in the terminology of Kaarlo Tuori,[49] in line with the phenomenon of fragmentation in international law; *(4)* the idea of sovereignty is replaced by that of governance[50]; *(5)* democracy assumes a problematic relationship with the concept of people[51]; *(6)* the courts and executive bodies assume the preponderance in public life, to the detriment of parliament; *(7)* finally, there is a clear tendency towards the standardization/normalization of states of exception.[52] These developments are, in a way portrayed by Loughlin (2015b, p. 24) when he speaks of the emergence of a form of positive constitutionalism "shorn of most of its utopian features", which is still built on a rights foundation, but becomes "highly attuned to what has been called the 'governmentalization of the state'".

Fundamental law, however, is not necessarily a posthumous concept, so to speak. It can still play a meaningful role in the context of the current overcoming of the historical conditions that determined its flowering, or in times of expansion of the "new ephorate". I believe that despite these developments the notion of political right can still play an important critical function.

In fact, the prudential dimension of action and discourse proper to political right may find a critical substitute in the context of constitutional legality. This substitute consists in the subordination of constitutional argumentation to a "togetherness principle" extracted from Kantian critical philosophy and according to which one can affirm that the mobilization of constitutional normative principles without a

[49]Cf. Tuori (2015), p. 21 ff., who recognizes Luhmann's influence.

[50]On the concept of governance and its disposition to thinking about politics as an area of administration and management, cf. Wendy Brown (2015), p. 122 ff.

[51]This problematic relationship is expressed by Everson and Eisner (2007), p. 27, as follows: "European integration has heralded the passing of majoritarian politics, or conventionally legitimated democracy, not simply because it has introduced elements of technocratic rule within its supranational governance structures, but because it has dispensed with demos and thus has equally dispensed with the very foundation for legitimizing political representation". Instead, what would be at stake would be a democracy based on the opening of the political decision-making process to the manifestation of all relevant interests [see, also, Zielonka (2006), p. 117 ff.]. According to these conceptions what seems to await us is "protestation after the event, not representation before it, as the future political norm" [cf. Anderson (2009), p. 117].

[52]I identified these traits and tried to develop their theoretical foundations in de Brito (2016), pp. 825–826.

community frame of reference is empty, as this frame is blind without the appeal to the said principles.

This principle would assume the function of submitting to a critical analysis every constitutional discourse simply based on "some transcendental legal yardstick against which to measure government practices" (Loughlin 2016, p. 52), without considering the specificities of the political community that is supposed to be ruled by such principles. Hilary Putnam puts this point nicely when he states, in the context of discussing the option between patriotism and universal reason, that "tradition without reason is blind; reason without tradition is empty".[53]

The real crux of Martin Loughlin's constitutional thought lies, I believe, in his assertion of a transcendent background to the political. I have already alluded to the relation between religion and the political in the thought of Claude Lefort, whose terms appear to be very different from those underlying the thought of both Schmitt and Loughlin. In the present historical moment, Lefort (1986), p. 329; Lefort (1988), p. 255 puts the following question: "rather than searching in democracy a new episode in the transfer of the religious into the political, should we not assert that the old transfers from one register to the other were intended to ensure the preservation of a form which has since been abolished, that the theological and the political became divorced, that a new experience of the institution of the social began to take shape, that the religious is reactivated at the weak points of the social, that its efficacy is no longer symbolic but imaginary and that, ultimately, it is an expression of the unavoidable – and no doubt ontological – difficulty democracy has in reading its own story – and of the difficulty political or philosophical thought has in assuming, without making it a travesty, the tragedy of the modern condition?"

In the end the real question is not whether the theological and the political became divorced, as claimed by Lefort, but whether instead of simply celebrating this divorce and the break with transcendent forms of authority, and the subsequent advent of freedom and popular sovereignty, we should acknowledge the continuities between those forms of divinely cautioned authority and secular democracy.

As is clear from the foregoing discussion, Schmitt is one of the authors who best expresses this latter attitude. Hannah Arendt, by contrast, is undoubtedly one of the deepest defenders of the possibility of a purely secular politics, especially in her work *On Revolution*. This is certainly not the place to develop the contrast between the two opposing attitudes and the way in which Schmitt and Arendt's thought illustrate them.[54] But there is an important aspect to stress when understanding this

[53]Cf. Putnam (1996), p. 94. I have discussed this point in somewhat different contexts: see de Brito (2001), pp. 896–900; de Brito (2017), p. 486. For a concretization of the same idea regarding the concepts of the justice and the good, see Ribeiro (2019), p. 44. See also Loughlin (2017b), p. 583.

[54]Cf. Moyn (2008), p. 71 ff. I have tried to present that contrast in de Brito (2000), p. 99. Lefort appears to side with Arendt, and against Schmitt, on this issue, [in this sense see Steinmetz-Jenkins (2009), p. 112]. But this is not entirely clear as made evident by Lefort's recognition of the affinity between the political and the religious in what concerns the presence of the symbolical [see Lefort

contrast: while Arendt believed in a politics based on the participation of all members of the community, as shown by her somewhat anachronistic and unrealistic insistence on the potentialities of society's spontaneous forms of organization,[55] Schmitt understood the impossibility of suppressing representation from politics, even if it were the representation performed by the charismatic leader before the acclaiming people. It is precisely the impossibility of suppressing representation from politics that leads us to recognize its foundational character in the construction of the state and its people,[56] and it is this foundational character which in turn imposes the recognition of the continuity between forms of divine authority and secular democracy.[57]

Nietzsche already admitted that the decline of religion involves the "death of the state".[58] Martin Loughlin's thoughts on the state and the constitution suggest that working toward this objective is not necessarily a liberating move.[59]

References

Agamben, G. (2003). *Stato di Eccezione*. Torino: Bollati Boringhieri.
Agamben, G. (2009). *Il Regno e la Gloria. Per uma Genealogia Teologica dell'Economia e del Governo, Homo Sacer, II, 2*. Torino: Bolatti Boringhieri.
Anderson, P. (2009). *The new old world*. London: Verso.

(1986), pp. 286, 292]. What seems more problematic, to my view, is the rapprochement between Schmitt and Arendt tempted by Loughlin (2015a), p. 91 ff.

[55]Cf. Arendt (1990), p. 255 ff.

[56]Cf. Loughlin (2003), p. 70.

[57]This is not to deny that it also appears to exist, as I have mentioned in the text, a continuity between divine authority and governmental rationality.

[58]Cf. Nietzsche (1995), p. 254: "To briefly repeat what I have said: the interests of tutelary government and the interests of religion go hand in hand with each other, so that if the latter begins to die out, the foundation of the state will also be deeply shaken. The belief in a divine order of political things, in a mystery concerning the existence of the state, is of religious origin: if religion vanishes, the state will inevitably lose its ancient Isis veil and no longer arouse reverence. Seen from nearby, the sovereignty of the people also serves to scare away the last traces of magic and superstition from this realm of feelings; modern democracy is the historical form of the decline of the state".

[59]As was also suggested by Nietzsche. Although he affirmed that the prospect of the decline of the state is "not in every respect an unhappy one" (1995, p. 254), he also cautioned: "To work toward the diffusion and realization of this idea is admittedly something else: we would have to be quite arrogant about our rational capacity and hardly understand history halfway to put our hand to the plow right away—at a point when nobody can yet exhibit the seeds that later are to be strewn upon the rended earth. Let us therefore trust to 'the cleverness and self-interest of human beings' that the state will still persist for a good while yet and that the destructive experiments of over-zealous and premature half-knowers will be repelled!" (1995, p. 255).

Arendt, H. (1990). *On revolution*. London: Penguin Books.
Aurélio, D. P. (2000). *Imaginação e Poder: Estudo sobre a Filosofia Política de Espinosa*. Lisboa: Edições Colibri.
Aurélio, D. P. (2014). *O Mais Natural dos Regimes: Espinosa e a Democracia*. Lisboa: Temas e Debates – Círculo de Leitores.
Balibar, É. (2005). *Spinoza et la Politique, 3éme édition*. Paris: Presses Universitaires de France.
Barbone, S. (2002). What counts as an individual for Spinoza? In O. Koistinen & J. Biro (Eds.), *Spinoza: Metaphysical themes*. New York: Oxford University Press.
Böckenförde, E.-W. (2006). Die Entstehung des Staates als Vorgang der Säkularisation. In E. W. Böckenförde & F. Staat (Eds.), *Studien zur Rechtsphilosophie, Staatstheorie un Verfassungsgeschichte*. Frankfurt am Main: Suhrkamp.
Brown, W. (2015). *Undoing the demos: Neoliberalism's stealth revolution*. New York: Zone Books.
Castrucci, E. (2016). *On the idea of potency: Juridical and theological roots of the Western Cultural tradition*. Edinburgh: Edinburgh University Press.
Chistodoulidis, E. (2008). Public law as political jurisprudence: Loughlin's "Idea of Public Law". In E. Chistodoulidis & S. Tierney (Eds.), *Public law and politics: The scope and limits of constitutionalism*. London: Routledge.
Courtenay, W. J. (1984a). Nominalism and late medieval religion. In *Covenant and causality in medieval thought: Studies in philosophy, theology and economic practice*. London: Variorum Reprints.
Courtenay, W. J. (1984b). The dialectic of divine omnipotence. In *Covenant and causality in medieval thought, studies in philosophy, theology and economic practice*. London: Variorum Reprints.
Courtenay, W. J. (1990). *Capacity and volition: A history of the distinction of absolute and ordained power*. Bergamo: Pierluigi Lubrina Editore.
Curley, E. (1995). Kissinger, Spinoza, and Genghis Khan. In D. Garrett (Ed.), *The Cambridge companion to Spinoza*. Cambridge: Cambridge University Press.
de Brito, M. N. (2000). *A Constituição Constituinte: Ensaio sobre o Poder de Revisão da Constituição*. Coimbra Editora: Coimbra.
de Brito, M. N. (2001). O Patriotismo como Civilidade: Egas Moniz, Maquiavel e as Nações Europeias. *Revista da Faculdade de Direito da Universidade de Lisboa, XLII*(2), 835–902.
de Brito, M. N. (2007). *A Justificação da Propriedade Privada numa Democracia Constitucional*. Almedina: Coimbra.
de Brito, M. N. (2014). Reflexões sobre a Persistência da Religião na Política das Sociedades Secularizadas. *Revista Portuguesa de Filosofia*, 327–342, Ano 70, Fasc. 2-3.
de Brito, M. N. (2015). Schmitt's Spectre and Kelsen's Promise: The polemics on the guardia of the constitution. In L. P. Coutinho, M. La Torre, & S. D. Smith (Eds.), *Judicial activism: An interdisciplinary approach to the American and European experiences*. Cham: Springer.
de Brito, M. N. (2016). A Face Obscura do Constitucionalismo Europeu. In *Estudos em Homenagem ao Conselheiro Presidente Rui Moura Ramos* (Vol. I). Almedina: Coimbra.
de Brito, M. N. (2017). The harm principle, legal moralism, and the 'Disintegration Thesis': On Lord Devlin being unable to keep playing the smuggling game. *San Diego Law Review, 54*(2), 465, Spring.
Del Lucchese, F. (2016). Spinoza and constituent power. *Contemporary Political Theory, 15*(2), 182–204.
Diamantides, M. (2012). God's political power in Western and Eastern Christianity in comparative perspective. *Divus Thomas, 115*(2), 333–381, Anno 115.° - maggio/Agosto.
Dyzenhaus, D. (2006). *The constitution of law: Legality in a time of emergency*. Cambridge: Cambridge University Press.
Dyzenhaus, D. (2013). The end of the road to serfdom? *University of Toronto Law Journal, 63*, 310.
Everson, M., & Eisner, J. (2007). *The making of a European Constitution: Judges and law beyond constitutive power*. Oxford: Routledge-Cavendish.

Graeber, D., & Sahlins, M. (2017). *On kings*. Chicago: Hau Books.
Keller, A. (2008). In A. Bianchi & A. Keller (Eds.), *Constitutionalising emergency powers in Modern Europe: The English and the Roman Model Counterterrorism: Democracy's challenge*. Oxford: Hart Publishing.
Koekkoek, R. (2014). Carl Schmitt and the challenge of Spinoza's Pantheism between the World Wars. *Modern Intellectual History, 11*(02), 333–357. August.
Lefort, C. (1986). Permanence du Théologico-Politique? In *Essais sur le Politique, xixe-xxe Siècles*. Paris: Éditions du Seuil.
Lefort, C. (1988). The permanence of the theological-political? In *Democracy and political theory* (David Macey, Trans.). Cambridge: Polity Press.
Loughlin, M. (2003). *The idea of public law*. Oxford: Oxford University Press.
Loughlin, M. (2009). In defense of Staatslehre. *Der Staat, 48*(1), 1–28.
Loughlin, M. (2010). *Foundations of public law*. Oxford: Oxford University Press.
Loughlin, M. (2014a). Constitutional pluralism: An oxymoron? *Global Constitutionalism, 3*(01), 9–30. March.
Loughlin, M. (2014b). The concept of constituent power. *European Journal of Political Theory, 13* (2), 218–237.
Loughlin, M. (2015a). Nomos. In D. Dyzenhaus & T. Poole (Eds.), *Law, liberty and state: Oakeshott, Hayek and Schmitt on the rule of law*. Oxford: Hart Publishing.
Loughlin, M. (2015b). The constitutional imagination. *The Modern Law Review, 78*(1), 1–25, January.
Loughlin, M. (2016). Reflections on the idea of public law. In E. Chistodoulidis & S. Tierney (Eds.), *Public law and politics: The scope and limits of constitutionalism*. London: Routledge.
Loughlin, M. (2017a). On constituent power. In M. W. Dowdle & M. A. Wilkinson (Eds.), *Constitutionalism beyond liberalism*. Cambridge: Cambridge University Press.
Loughlin, M. (2017b). Politonomy. In J. Meierhenrich & O. Simons (Eds.), *The Oxford handbook of Carl Schmitt*. Oxford: Oxford University Press.
Loughlin, M. (2018a). *Political jurisprudence*. Oxford: Oxford University Press.
Loughlin, M. (2018b). Political jurisprudence. In M. A. Wilkinson & M. W. Dowdle (Eds.), *Questioning the foundations of public law*. Oxford: Hart.
Luhmann, N. (1990). *Political theory in the welfare state* (Introduced by John Bednarz Jr., Trans.). Berlin: Walter de Gruyter.
Luhmann, N. (2004). *Law as a social system* (Klaus A. Zieger, Trans.). Oxford: Oxford University Press.
Machiavelli, N. (1984). *Discorsi sopra la prima Deca di Tito Livio. Introduzione di Gennaro Sasso, note di Giorgio Inglese*. Milano: Rizzoli.
Mayer, O. (2004). *Deutsches Verwaltungsrecht, Band I, unveränderter Nachdruck der 1924 erschienenen 3. Auflage*. Berlin: Duncker & Humblot.
Mignini, F. (2000). Le Dieu-Substance de Spinoza comme potentia absoluta. In G. Canziani, M. A. Granada, & Y. C. Zarka (Eds.), *Potentia Dei. L'Onnipotenza Divina nel Pensiero dei Secoli XVI e XVII*. Milan: FrancoAngeli.
Milbanks, J. (2010). In J. Milbank, S. Žižek, C. Davis, & C. Pickstock (Eds.), *Paul against biopolitics, Paul's new moment: Continental philosophy and the future of Christian theology*. Grand Rapids: Brazos Press.
Minkkinen, P. (2018). The tragic politics of public law. In M. A. Wilkinson & M. W. Dowdle (Eds.), *Questioning the foundations of public law*. Oxford: Hart.
Moyn, S. (2008). Hannah Arendt on the Secular. *New German Critique, 105, 35*(3), 71–96. Fall.
Nietzsche, F. (1995). *Human, all too human, I. Translated, with an Afterword, by Gary Handwerk*. Stanford: Stanford University Press.
Oakeshott, M. (1990). On the character of a Modern European State. In *On human conduct*. Oxford: Clarendon Press.
Oakley, F. (2002). *Omnipotence and promise: The legacy of the scholastic distinction of powers*. Toronto: Pontifical Institute of Mediaeval Studies.

Ojakangas, M. (2012). Potentia Absoluta et Potentia Ordinata Dei: On the theological origins of Carl Schmitt's theory of constitution. *Continental Philosophical Review, 45*, 505–517.
Poole, T. (2015). *Reason of state: Law, prerogative and empire*. Cambridge: Cambridge University Press.
Putnam, H. (1996). Must we choose between patriotism and universal reason? In J. Cohen (Ed.), *For love of country: Debating the limits of patriotism. Martha Nussbaum with Respondents*. Boston: Beacon Press.
Randi, E. (1987). *Il Sovrano e l'Orologiaio. Due Immagini di Dio nel Dibattito sulla «Potentia Absoluta» fra XIII e XIV Secolo*. Firenzi: La Nuova Italia Editrice.
Ribeiro, G. D. A. (2019). *The decline of private law: A philosophical history of liberal legalism*. Oxford: Hart Publishing.
Schmitt, C. (1979). *Der Begriff des Politischen. Text von 1932 mit einem Vorwort und drei Corollarien*. Berlin: Duncker & Humblot.
Schmitt, C. (1985). Nehmen/teilen/Weiden: Ein Versuch, die Grundfragen jeder Sozial- und Wirtschaftsordnung vom Nomos her rightig zu stellen (1953). In *Verfassungsrechtliche Aufsätze aus den Jahren 1924-1954: Materialien zu einer Verfassungslehre, Dritte Auflage*. Berlin: Duncker & Humblot.
Schmitt, C. (2003). *The Nomos of the Earth in the international law of the Jus Publicum Europaeum*. Translated and Annotated by G. L. Ulmen. New York: Telos Press.
Schmitt, C. (2007). *The concept of the political, translation, introduction, and notes by George Schwab*. Chicago: The University of Chicago Press.
Schmitt, C. (2008). *Constitutional theory*. Translated and edited by Jeffrey Seitzer. Duham: Duke University Press.
Schmitt, C. (2009). *Politische Theologie. Vier Kapital zur Lehre von der Souveränität, Neunte Auflage*. Berlin: Duncker & Humblot.
Schmitt, C. (2010). *Verfassungslehre, zehnte Auflage*. Berlin: Duncker & Humblot.
Schmitt, C. (2014). *Volksentscheidund und Volksbegehren. Ein Beitrag zur Auslegung der Weimarer Verfassung und zur Lehre von der unmittelbaren Demokratie*. Berlin: Duncker & Humblot.
Schmitt, C. (2015). In G. Giesler & M. Tielke (Eds.), *Glossarium: Aufzeichnungen der Jahre 1947–1958. New enlarged, corrected and commented edition*. Berlin: Duncker & Humbolt.
Schupmann, B. A. (2017). *Carl Schmitt's state and constitutional theory: A critical analysis*. Oxford: Oxford University Press.
Spinoza, B. (2007). In J. Israel (Ed.), *Theological-political treatise* (Michael Silverthorne & Jonathan Israel, Trans.). Cambridge: Cambridge University Press.
Spinoza, B. (2008). *Tratado Político. Translation, introduction, and notes by Diogo Pires Aurélio*. Lisboa: Temas & Debates.
Steinmetz-Jenkins, D. (2009). Claude Lefort and the illegitimacy of modernity. *Journal for Cultural and Religious Theory, 10*(1), 102–117.
Traversino, M. (2012). The Mediaeval distinction of God's Potentia Absoluta/Ordinata as an archaeology of the early modern investigation of power. *Divus Thomas, 115*(2), 35–82, Anno 115.° - maggio/Agosto.
Tuori, K. (2015). *European constitucionalism*. Cambridge: Cambridge University Press.
Wolin, S. (2001). *Tocqueville between two worlds: The making of a political and theoretical life*. Princeton: Princeton University Press.
Yelle, R. A. (2019). *Sovereign and the sacred: Secularism and political economy of religion*. Chicago: The University of Chicago Press.
Zielonka, J. (2006). *Europe as Empire: The nature of the enlarged European Union*. Oxford: Oxford University Press.

Miguel Nogueira de Brito is Associate Professor at the University of Lisbon's School of Law and senior researcher at CIDP—Lisbon Centre of Research in Public Law where he coordinates the area of Constitutional Law. He worked as a law clerk at the Portuguese Constitutional Court. His publications include *A Justificação da Propriedade Privada numa Democracia Constitucional* (Coimbra, 2007) e *As Andanças de Cândido* (Lisboa, 2011).

Part II
A Political-Theological Dimension

Decision and Legal Interpretation

Paul W. Kahn

Contents

Abstract What is the relationship of interpretation to decision? Many scholars believe that decision marks the limit of law, the point at which doctrine no longer determines judicial outcomes. Others believe outcomes are the result of political contests between sociologically identifiable groups. Theorists seem to have to choose between legal apologetics and political critique. Rejecting both views, this article argues that decision is a necessary condition of interpretation. It engages with Carl Schmitt's claim that "Every political idea in one way or another takes a position on the 'nature' of man and presupposes that he is either 'by nature good' or 'by nature evil.'" The decision of law is not about the state of the soul, but about the narrative frame. Legal interpretation begins with a choice between project and system. A project locates the origin of order in the deliberate act to realize an idea; a system believes order to be spontaneous and immanent. Writing a constitution is a project; the common law is a system. To interpret law as a project is to see man as naturally evil, for absent a plan we will have only the chaos of the state of nature. To interpret law as a system is to see man as naturally good, for he need only be himself for the regularities of law to emerge. This is the decision that grounds interpretation and, therefore, lies behind every legal claim and legal theory.

P. W. Kahn (✉)
Yale Law School, New Haven, CT, USA
e-mail: paul.kahn@yale.edu

© Springer Nature Switzerland AG 2020

M. Nogueira de Brito, L. Pereira Coutinho (eds.), *The Political Dimension of Constitutional Law*, https://doi.org/10.1007/978-3-030-38459-3_4

1 The Puzzle of Disagreement Within the Law: The Jurisprudential and Political Challenges

More than 30 years ago, Ronald Dworkin began *Law's Empire* with the puzzle of disagreement within the law (Dworkin 1986). Equally knowledgeable jurists regularly come to different conclusions about the meaning of a legal norm. They are not disagreeing about the facts; they are reading a common text. Yet, they come to different conclusions when they resolve a legal controversy. Such disagreements are not exceptional. Disagreement about the meaning of the law is institutionalized in legal practices, ranging from the parties' submission of briefs to the courts' reporting of dissents. Reading the majority and dissenting opinions in a Supreme Court case, and not knowing the actual distribution of the vote, one cannot distinguish between them as one might distinguish a right from a wrong answer with regard to a mathematical problem or a problem in the physical sciences. Opinions—judicial or otherwise—are always various, that is, we expect differences in opinions.

Observation of such disagreements poses a jurisprudential puzzle and a potentially explosive political situation.[1] The jurisprudential challenge is to understand the nature of legal interpretation as a practice that supports disagreement within some sort of unity.[2] What exactly is that unity and how much difference can it tolerate? These are genuine questions today as our politics threatens belief in the autonomy of law. The political challenge is to defend the democratic legitimacy of judicial decision-making in the face of disagreement. If judges choose between competing interpretations of the law, should they be held accountable to electoral politics? These two challenges can reinforce each other: the more we acknowledge interpretive pluralism, the more we will demand a democratic check. Conversely, solving the jurisprudential puzzle may help to ease the political challenge. At least, it may help to ease the self-doubt among judges, who are themselves uncertain of their own political legitimacy.

2 Disagreement and the Problem of Decision

These jurisprudential and political puzzles arise out of the unsettled relationship of the rule of law to rule by the people: how can a constitutional democracy simultaneously express commitment to both? Our ordinary political intuition offers a reconciliation with a simple formula: the democratic warrant for the rule of law is grounded in the origin of law in representative institutions. Democratic institutions make laws; judges apply them. Yet, if judges disagree on the meaning of law, this

[1]The politics of this issue of jurisprudential disagreement exploded into view just 1 year later with the hearings on Robert Bork's nomination to the Supreme Court in the fall of 1987.

[2]That unity, in the first instance, is the lawsuit itself.

model will not get us very far. Disagreeing on the content of the law, we disagree on what exactly the voters—through their representatives—did.

Moreover, the simple model of reconciliation fails as a description of judicial reasoning, particularly in constitutional cases. Judges spend far less time worrying about what the voters intended and far more time reasoning from precedents. They attempt to identify the immanent principles that organize the cases. A controversy over the meaning of freedom of speech, for example, asks what the necessary speech conditions are for a flourishing democracy. The courts work out the meaning of that freedom through an interpretation of prior cases that have dealt with similar issues.

Interpretation introduces disagreement, for different judges will understand the principles for which the cases stand differently. What appears as principled decision-making to a judge can appear to the public, or at least to some substantial part of the public, as an illegitimate political intervention. It surely does not look as if the courts are applying a law given to them by the representative, political branches. When controversies arise, the losing party asks why it should be bound by the views of a majority of Justices on the Supreme Court. The question becomes even more compelling when that party believes it has the support of a sufficient number of voters to win a political contest.

Two generations of American constitutional-law scholars labored at the intersection of these jurisprudential and political puzzles, labelling it "the counter-majoritarian difficulty."[3] Why should a 5-4 vote on the Supreme Court determine policy on such politically controversial issues as access to abortion, affirmative action, or religion's place in the schools and public square? Are such controversies properly settled, in a democracy, by the vote of a single, unelected Justice? Does that not make law look entirely contingent, and is not contingency the domain of politics? Absent a convincing response to these questions, political actors will inevitably attempt to control judicial outcomes—a consequence that Alexander Bickel foresaw (Bickel 1962, pp. 111–199). That response can take various forms, including jurisdiction stripping or legislative work-arounds. Today, the dominant form of response is through the appointments process: if law is nothing more than the outcome of a vote among the Justices, politicians will work to control who votes.

After several decades of controversy over the legitimacy of a judge-led constitutional revolution in the meaning of equality and liberty, we find ourselves far down this path of political reaction. Our deeply polarized political process often focuses on appointments to the Supreme Court. Presidential campaigns organize around this theme; hearings on nominees can erupt into occasions for national protest.

Politics may have eclipsed theory by this point. There is little the theorist can do to overcome the deep sense of political difference that now extends to the work of the courts. Indeed, theory has itself polarized, such that each side in the debates now relies on its own theorists. Political differences are translated into different methods of interpretation. No one believes there is a neutral point from which "to do law." The familiar sources of interpretation—text, history, precedents, structure, policy—

[3]The term comes from Alexander Bickel (Bickel 1962).

have all taken on a political cast. Under these conditions, theory sets itself an impossible task if it believes it can respond to the counter-majoritarian difficulty in a way that will satisfy the demands of popular politics. Nevertheless, the theorist must do his or her best to understand the structural forces at work within the polity and the particular way in which the jurisprudential and political puzzles surface.

Judges too experience this tension between the rule of law and rule by the people. They write openly of a worry about their own democratic legitimacy; they accuse each other of usurping political power that belongs with the people. Doing so, they accept the critique of themselves offered by popular politics.

The counter-majoritarian difficulty arises when we fail to distinguish ordinary, electoral politics from the political work of the popular sovereign. It arises when we equate popular sovereignty with electoral politics, as if democracy extends no further than the last election. If that is what we mean by rule by the people, we will never understand the democratic legitimacy of the Constitution. It will appear as the dead-hand of the past, even if that hand is manipulated today by the Justices on the Court. So too will most of our statutes, for they too come to us from a past that precedes the last election. Measured by politics, the work of the Court will always pose a puzzle. The problem, however, lies in the measure.

A democratic political identity is created and sustained only in part through the ordinary politics of the ballot box. Competing with ordinary politics is the extraordinary politics of the Constitution. At stake is the difference between identifying oneself as a Democrat or Republican, and identifying oneself as an American. To be American is to see oneself as part of a people who see their history as an expression of self-government. To be a Republican or Democratic is to take a position within that larger process. The Court's distinctive role is to draw us toward our American identity.

The particular burden of the American practice of writing judicial opinions has been to try to bridge the gap between politics and law (Kahn 2016, pp. 46–87). The Justices on the Supreme Court, in particular, must not only explain their decisions as grounded in law; they must also make clear the democratic source of that law. The ambition of an opinion is to persuade citizens to see the law as an expression of popular sovereignty. The ideal reader comes away from an opinion persuaded not only that the Court has given voice to the meaning of the Constitution but that the Constitution is the product of a national project of which each citizen is a part. She imagines herself as a part of this intergenerational project; it is her political identity that is at stake. Listening to the Court, she is to understand the law as something that we—"We the People"—have done together. An unsuccessful opinion fails to convince the reader that it expresses anything other than the Justices personal views.

Looking at the law through the prism of the opinion, we are to see ourselves as members of an intergenerational, collective subject: the popular sovereign. We are to think of the Constitution as something we authored and together maintain. The burden on the courts—and on the Supreme Court in particular--is to persuade us to see ourselves in and through law; it is not to decide in our place. If all that we see is the vote among the Justices, we will inevitably believe the Court is intruding into the sphere of politics.

There is, however, reason to doubt that the Court is capable of sustaining its burden of persuasion today. Fewer and fewer citizens believe that the Court acts on grounds different from those of ordinary politics. They see the frequent 5-4 decisions as simply another iteration of the unending political contest that occupies the nation's attention. If citizens actually read the opinions, they are likely to be confirmed in this view, for the Justices regularly accuse each other of putting politics before law. For example, Chief Justice Roberts closes his dissent in the case extending constitutional protection to gay marriage with the accusation that the majority decision is a victory for a political faction, which has "nothing to do" with the Constitution (Obergefell 2015, p. 2626).[4] It is politics, rather than interpretive disagreement. If that is so, why should the dissenters or, for that matter, citizens respect the decision? Not surprisingly, we find widespread resistance to the decision, including on the Court itself.[5]

If the contemporary Court is less capable of bearing the rhetorical burden of persuading us of its democratic legitimacy, the source of the problem is not a decline in the legal abilities of the Justices. Rather, there has been a larger failure of faith in the idea of the popular sovereign as a collective, transgenerational subject. The public and the Court too quickly identify popular sovereignty with electoral politics. They assign constitutional authorship to the "Framers," rather than to We the People. They are uncertain what links the latter to the former. They cannot easily answer the question of why we should be governed by "dead white men." Absent a theory of constitutional legitimacy, they too stumble over the fact of disagreement among the Justices, producing statements like that of the Chief Justice in *Obergefell.*

Absent a faith in a transgenerational popular sovereign, and in the face of relentless pressure from ordinary politics, judges will fall into a fear of judging. They will constantly find themselves on the defensive politically. They will not know how to defend themselves beyond the repetition of claims that few any longer believe—for example, that they are "sticking to the text" or to an "original intention." They too will be confused by interpretive disagreement, thinking it a continuation of the political polarization of the broader society. They too will think that unanimity is the measure of a persuasive decision, but they will have no idea of how to reach unanimity other than through the appointments process.

3 The Difficulty of Theorizing the Decision

While theory cannot resolve our political problems, it can help us to understand the fundamental sources of interpretive disagreement. Until we understand that, we remain largely defenseless against the political critique of judicial outcomes. The issue of disagreement will constantly be posed as one of "who decides?" We can

[4]See also *Boumediene* (2008).

[5]See *Masterpiece Cakeshop* (2018).

begin to make some progress by examining more closely the nature of the decision. Justices and scholars constantly stumble over the relationship between interpretation and decision. They assume that a good decision is one that follows upon interpretation, as if the decision is the conclusion of an argument. The ideal judge, on this view, withholds decision until she has read and listened to the arguments of the opposing parties. She will be persuaded by the logic of one side or the other. Focusing on the end of this process of deliberation, however, is not the answer, but a repetition of the problem. It models the judicial decision on the same process of deliberation and choice that every thoughtful citizen and representative should deploy.

Scholars and judges often seem trapped within an antinomy in which either the decision fails to appear at all or it is all that appears. On the first view, no decision ever need be made because there is no gap between doctrine and outcome. Dworkin's figure, Hercules, captures the effort to eliminate the decision from legal reasoning. Hercules resolves the case through reasoning up toward first principles. There is never a moment in which legal resources are exhausted and a decision is required to resolve the case.[6]

Other scholars write as if the judicial outcome is the result of a political contest between sociologically identifiable groups.[7] On this view, doctrine is not doing any work independent of political interests and social movements. An entire discipline of positive social science studies judicial outcomes as if they are to be explained independently of the legal reasoning put forward by parties and judges (Gillman 2001). What matters is how judges vote, not what they say. Patterns of voting are to be explained by identifying their causes in interest-group politics, not by looking at post-hoc rationalizations.

If the first view never leaves the domain of doctrine, the second never leaves that of politics. Theorists seem to have to choose between legal apologetics or political critique. The decision seems either to make no appearance or it is all that we see. The first group wants to speak of doctrine working itself out; the second wants to count votes. The *Obergefell* decision, for example, was either immanent in the constitutional doctrine of equality or it was a victory for a political movement.

These contemporary disputes over the place of decision are a replay of older disputes. Dworkin began writing in the 1960s in response to the legal positivists, who did indeed think that often a judge has to decide (Hart 1961). On their view, when the law gives no clear answer, the judge must engage in an act of law-making. Deciding, he is exercising a political function. To this, Dworkin responded that when the sources of law are properly understood, the law never gives out before judgment is reached. Both sides of this dispute agree that the appearance of a decision marks the limit of law. They disagree about the reach of the legal sources, not about the relationship of law to decision. Casting back a little further, we see the legal realists argued that law actually decides very little; we never leave the sphere of politics,

[6]Famously, Dworkin argued that there are right answers even in hard cases (Dworkin 1978).

[7]On popular constitutionalism, see Siegel (2008), Kramer (2004) and Tushnet (2006).

because a decision is always required (Holmes 1897; Frank 1930). They were, in turn, responding to the formalists who thought no decision was ever necessary because law could resolve controversies through the application of practical syllogisms from general principles (Grey 1983). Again, it seems that the decision either makes no appearance or it has no limits.

Perhaps the modern theorist who gave the most prominent place to decision was Robert Cover. But he assigned the decision to the imperial, jurispathic character of the state (Cover 1983). Cover himself embraced the jurisgenerative forces of interpretation—a sort of disorderly legal pluralism. For him, interpretation is the life of the law and of a community. Law is a rich source of multiple narratives. The decision kills law. Its source is in power, that is, in politics.

We need a better account of the role of the decision in law—an account that helps us to understand interpretive pluralism. We need, in short, to rethink the way in which decision and interpretation relate to each other. Decision, I will argue, is not an exogenous intervention in the process of interpretation, but neither is it a product of interpretation. Decision is better thought of as a transcendental condition of interpretation.

4 Decision as a Condition of Interpretation

To explore these matters, I am going to engage with Carl Schmitt. Schmitt's Weimar writings struggled with the issue of where and how law figures in the meaning of the political (Schmitt 1932). Most importantly, Schmitt put the decision at the center of his work. Famously, he wrote, "Sovereign is he who decides on the exception." (Schmitt 1922, p. 51). Less famously, he wrote, "a decision in the broadest sense belongs to every legal perception," and "the juristic deduction is not traceable in the last detail to its premises" (Schmitt 1922, p. 30). Schmitt argued that not only does law depend upon decision, but absent the decision we could not imagine law as a free practice (Kahn 2011). Freedom is not or not only giving oneself a rule, as Kant argued (Kant 1785). It is deciding. It is a matter of will, as much as of reason. At issue, then, is what sort of a free practice is at stake in the rule of law. Schmitt was correct to associate sovereignty and decision. The first decision, however, is not quite that of the exception; rather, it is the decision that locates the popular sovereign.

My engagement with Schmitt will focus on a single passage in the last chapter of his *Political Theology*. He writes, "Every political idea in one way or another takes a position on the 'nature' of man and presupposes that he is either 'by nature good' or 'by nature evil'" (Schmitt 1922). This claim certainly appears counter-intuitive to a contemporary reader. While the assertion might be relevant to a discussion of the reactionary, eighteenth and nineteenth century, political theories of Donoso Cortes or of Joseph de Maistre—the context within which Schmitt makes the statement—why would anyone think the claim had to be true in general? Why should it play a part in a political theology of the modern, democratic state?

Anarchists might, as Schmitt suggests, implicitly assume the natural goodness of man. At least, they do not think a catastrophic return to the state of nature will result from undermining political authority. While anarchy is hardly a plausible political position today, libertarianism is and it shares this faith. Conversely, the justification for a Hobbesian sovereign might ultimately appeal to a belief that man is evil by nature. Surely, Hobbes's state of nature suggests that whatever man is *by* nature, he will act poorly *in* nature. This observation might ground the Hobbesian sovereign, but the modern Rechtsstaat is no closer to that sovereign than it is to anarchy.

Schmitt's comment is part of his critique of what he describes as the politically indecisive character of liberalism. His critique, however, fails to recognize that liberals won't take a position on this question because they reject Schmitt's alternatives—good or evil? Instead, they believe that man is *good enough* for politics, by which they mean that his tendencies toward evil are capable of being controlled by well-constructed institutions. Not only do they believe this position to offer a viable political psychology, but they think that resolving the question of original sin has no place in a secular politics. That question raises a matter of faith upon which reasonable people can disagree without undermining the possibility of political order.

Schmitt's critique of liberalism may not be convincing, but by pressing the question, he helps to identify a problem that generally eludes liberal political theory. That issue is not the necessity of an Augustinian confrontation with original sin, but rather that of the relationship of legal interpretation to decision. Indeed, to think of the issue as the Augustinian problem of sin is to misunderstand the role of political theology in the modern nation state. That state, grounded on popular sovereignty and organized under the rule of law, has no use for political theology, if we mean by that a set of normative political claims that follow from a sectarian faith (Lilla 2007). The role of political theology today lies rather in the exploration of the belief conditions of our political practices (Kahn 2011). The modern social imaginary is a structural, not a doctrinal, heir to the Western religious imaginary.

If Schmitt's dramatic claim about good and evil is to be useful to a modern political theology, it is by helping us to see something about the social imaginary that otherwise fails to appear (Taylor 2003). The work of the imagination can fall from view in two different ways. First, some things are not seen because the theorist avoids looking at them. The violence of the state is like this. Violent sacrifice—killing and being killed—has been central to the construction of political meaning in the modern nation-state (Kahn 2008). Yet, political theorists continue to follow Hobbes in imagining violence as that which the state leaves behind in the state of nature. What the state actually leaves behind is murder, not violence. The state substitutes sacrifice for murder.

Second, some imaginative phenomena are not seen because they are aspects of the frame or horizon of our perception. The nature of political space—territory—and political time—history—are like this (Kahn 1999, pp. 43–65). Accounts of political actions, agents, and norms assume a background order of history and territory as if this is the natural field within which narratives are constructed. Once the categories come to our attention, however, we see that they are themselves contingent constructions of the imagination. There is nothing natural about them.

Schmitt's claim about good and evil is misunderstood if seen as an effort to raise a problem of the first sort, asking us to look at some object or phenomenon we had been avoiding. To that claim, it is appropriate to respond that there is no such object, because the secular state need have no position on original sin. Schmitt's assertion, however, is better understood in the second way: it forces us to see what otherwise slips from view as part of the horizon of explanation. Pressing the question of good or evil, he draws our attention to the decision that is a condition of interpretation.

The political order as a form of social life is sustained in the narratives deployed by citizens. We use these narratives to understand ourselves and to persuade others to see as we do (Kahn 2016, pp. 1–17). Without them, we would be as speechless before political claims as we are before an unknown, ancient artifact. We can describe its appearance and analyze its composition. But we cannot take it to-hand in the way of those for whom it had meaning—perhaps as a part of a religious ritual or as an element in a game. Narratives provide the common ground that is necessary to make sense of our political past and to plot a future.[8] Making sense, here, does not mean agreement. Appealing to the narratives in circulation does not tell us what to think about any particular event, act, or agent. There are always alternative narratives available. There are, for example, an indefinite number of ways to write a history of the nation. We might think of them sharing family resemblances (Wittgenstein 1953, sections 66–67).

Popular sovereignty, too, is a product of narrative. The popular sovereign is not something we can discover in the world. There is not a truth of the matter upon which we are all converging. Rather, the popular sovereign figures in political claims and political accounts. It is sustained only in the narratives that we construct and the ways in which those narratives are put to use. It has no other life. Even a claim to the revolutionary presence of the popular sovereign is only that—a claim. If the revolution fails, the claim of presence will be denied. No one believes that the Greek gods were once present, but have since departed. That observation does not diminish the power that claims about the gods had for the Greeks. The popular sovereign is like those gods: it does not predate the narrative of its existence and it does not outlive those narratives.

Someone—a politician or a judge—who claims to speak *for the people* is not setting forth a proposition that has a truth-value apart from the way in which the claim figures in the practices and beliefs of the community. There is no right narrative apart from the interpretive practices of the community. The truth of a narrative lies in the way in which it is put to use. Again, think of the way in which a particular historical narrative can move from being a common way of organizing experience to one that no one would think to deploy. This is why there is never a

[8]Thus, the importance of truth and reconciliation commissions as elements of a transition from authoritarian to democratic regimes. They are collective efforts to reconstruct the narrative (Minow 1998).

final, definitive account. Interpretive practices are not settled by facts because we have no separate access to the facts these practices describe.

When we look at American public law narratives over the course of the long nineteenth century, we find contest and a general direction of change. The century begins with a reliance upon an imaginative structure of *project*; it ends with that of *system*. Project and system differ in their representation of the origin of order. For a project, form comes from without. Order comes to a project through the intentional act of a conscious subject. For a system, order is immanent in the phenomena. A system does not depend upon a person or group setting forth an idea as the object of an intentional act. In a system, we have order without intention; in a project, order is evidence of intention (Kahn 2019).

Both of these frameworks imagine law as the successful ordering of politics. They might even agree on the content of particular legal rules. They disagree on the kind of narrative within which we explain—and so argue about—law. They disagree on what counts as an explanation. When we offer an account of law, where do we look and what do we look for? A persuasive interpretation on one view may seem merely anecdotal to the other. Each draws the line between law and politics at a different point. For the systemic view, any project to create law may seem a political intervention; for the project view, any assertion of system may seem a political defense of the status quo.

In the narrative of project, politics is a matter of constructing laws and institutions based upon abstract concepts. Theory precedes practice. We reason out the project in advance; projects follow blueprints in order to realize deliberate goals. Because modern politics begins as a revolutionary project, the modern era has been an age of political theory. Revolutionaries never lack for theory. Or, perhaps the relationship is the other way around: modern political theory—particularly the idea of a social contract—created the possibility of a new popular politics of projects. Causal claims are beyond the purview of hermeneutics. Narratives of project link constitution to theory, and theory to constitution.

Contra wise, the narrative of system does not depend upon the intentions of any of those subjects whose actions are constitutive of the system. System figures in our ordinary experience of an organism: it has a form, which means that it develops and maintains itself according to an immanent order. That order, however, is not the consequence of its own intention. The oak develops from the acorn as system, not as project. The spontaneity of order is one way to characterize life.

None of us could account for ourselves without appealing to both system and project, but there is not some sort of natural boundary to each. We want to make of our lives a project for which we are accountable. We want also to realize our nature as we grow into that which we already are. The first value speaks to "authenticity;" the second to "self-discovery."

To the mythical imagination, the order of nature is God's project. The difficulty of imagining order without intention explains not just archaic myths but the continuing turn to creationism. Order must be grounded in representation because only a consciousness can link the future to the present. That linkage is called a "plan" or, in popular theology, a "design." That God has a plan for us in what otherwise appears as a system is the idea of general providence (Viner 1972). Projects always have final, as well as formal, causes.

The rise of the social sciences across the nineteenth century represents the extension of the narrative of system to social phenomena. The sciences of the social seek to explain the immanent order that is constitutive of the forms of society. The social sciences are organized around the idea that collective human behavior exhibits order without intention. Strikingly, 1776 marked not only the appearance of a revolutionary politics of project in the American Declaration of Independence, but also the appearance of Adam Smith's *Wealth of Nations*, the founding text of modern economics and the paradigm of systemic analysis of the social.

The laws of the economic order are not put into practice through deliberate intentions. They emerge spontaneously from our natural inclination to truck and barter, as Adam Smith puts it (Smith 1776; 2003, p. 22). Early economists were amazed and liberated by the working of system, for it permitted them to understand how public good could arise from the pursuit of private interests (Grewal forthcoming). In a project, this is a much more difficult idea, for intentions reflect character—a public good can only emerge from publicly minded citizens (Washington 1796). An economic system, on the other hand, is not dependent upon the character of those engaged in individual transactions because its order does not depend upon their intentions. Indeed, economics offers a new theodicy: the immanent principles of market order will themselves produce the best possible world (Mandeville 1729).[9]

For system theorists, accounts that look at particular intentions are only anecdotal. They no longer belong in a rigorous, scientific explanation. The anecdotal account, for example, may portray the capitalist as doing something malevolent to the worker, while the systemic account naturalizes the relationship as the immanent order of an economy that will produce the public good. That can be a hard lesson for workers, but so is Darwin hard for the religious believer. Of course, workers need not accept this lesson. They can take up a project of political redistribution of wealth, insisting that the only legitimate political order is that which emerges from a democratic project.

Early American constitutionalists not only theorized politics as a project, they remembered taking part in that project. This was the narrative form by which they understood drafting and enacting a constitution. Project ideas continued in the invention of judicial review. Chief Justice Marshall understands the Court to be applying the same abstract principles as the Founders (Kahn 1992, pp. 22–31). By the time of the Civil War, however, the project narrative was failing. Books began to appear that spoke of an unwritten constitution (Fisher 1862). That constitution was no one's project; it converged with the immanent order of the common law. The new accounts of law imagined an order that would emerge spontaneously wherever the Anglo-American race was allowed the freedom to develop without external constraint (Tiedeman 1890). This sounds a good deal like what Smith had to say about "perfect liberty" creating the conditions for the realization of an immanent economic

[9]Today, we speak of the pareto optimal point.

order. This unwritten law was to be the object of a new legal science. Taking this point of view, theorists came to think that the generation of the founders had been naïve—relying on anecdote—in their belief that a legal order could be the product of a project.

By the end of the century then, legal order was thought of less as a project and more as a system. Popular sovereignty does not precede law as in a project, but is bound to law in the same way that an individual is bound to his or her body. Law emerges, develops, and grows in a systemic way.[10] Strikingly, the Revolution as an event in the American project of law creation disappears in the new narrative of law as system. Thus, the newly appearing American casebooks are full of British cases (Langdell 1879; Thayer 1892). If law is an immanent order of system, it no longer makes a difference from which side of the Atlantic the cases come. To think otherwise would be like thinking it matters where the laboratory that does an experiment is located. Compare this with Thomas Jefferson's presidential campaign of 1800 in which he attacked the recently created federal courts for applying the British common law. For Jefferson, the drafter of the Declaration of Independence, these courts had failed to understand the significance of the Revolutionary project (Kahn 1997, pp. 49–52). British law was not our project.

Turning to system does not render legislative institutions irrelevant. The legislative function for the systemic imagination is declarative or remedial. A well-wrought statute or constitutional provision, on this view, must be declarative of the law actually at work in the immanent order of society. Positive law that is not declarative will simply fail, in which case it was not really law at all. In addition, a remedial role remains, for even a natural system can develop pathologies. This, for example, is the way in which many economists think of intervention in the market: a response to market failures. The systemic order of law too may be subject to pathologies and thus in need of remediation.

If we ask whether project or system gives the better account of law, we are asking a nonsensical question. The right inquiry is to explore the conditions under which one narrative or the other persuades. Law just is an interpretive practice. To quote Schmitt again, the decision between the two narratives turns on "philosophical-historical or metaphysical conviction." (Schmitt 1922, p. 7). Schmitt's comments on original sin should be interpreted in this light.

This is the key point: the choice upon which Schmitt insists—between man as good or evil—is identical to the choice between project and system. The interpreter of law must make a decision, because only after that choice does she know what sort of narrative to construct. Indeed, before that decision, she does not know what she is doing at all. This decision, then, is not the product of legal inquiry, but the condition

[10]Constitutional law is no different from contract and tort, which were the subjects of the new American law school, founded at Harvard by Christopher Langdell in 1870. The aim of the discipline is to set forth the immanent principles that informed the cases, where "[l]aw, considered as a science, consists of certain principles or doctrines. . . . Each of these doctrines has arrived at its present state by slow degrees . . . . This growth is to be traced in the main through a series of cases . . . ." (Langdell 1879, p. viii).

under which it can begin. Interpretation does not determine the decision; rather, interpretation follows from the decision.

To decide that law is a project is to imagine man as fundamentally fallen. It is fallen man's responsibility to bring order to his disordered world. Outside of Eden, he is on his own. He must re-form his world according to an idea that is not yet realized and that will not be realized unless he pursues it as his own. He must bring to this formless world an idea of order. That is project's invitation to theory. The mythical representation of this thought is the memory of Eden.

Thinking of politics in the abstract as a project won't tell us what the character of that project should be. It will not decide between the ideas of Hobbes and Rousseau; it will not tell us the content of the social contract. It surely will not tell us whether to construct a presidential or a parliamentary order; neither will it tell us the best way to structure the tax code. It will, however, tell us that we have to turn to theory and decide for ourselves. It tells us that ends as well as means are for us to decide, for the good is our burden to achieve. Accordingly, to think of constitutionalism as a democratic project opens a space for political theory inside of our political practices.

The narrative of project tells us that man must work to achieve the good. He cannot rely on the spontaneity of a natural order. Neither can he look to the world for a paradigm of order, as if there is some necessary relationship between being and the good. Every project is a free act by a subject capable of making his thoughts the objects of his intentions. The politics of projects creates order and then works to maintain that order against the forces of disruption and dissolution—forces that arise from man himself.

Projects can be misconceived; they can also be undermined by changes in circumstances. Eventually, all political projects must fail. This idea of the life cycle of a project in a fallen world is expressed in the Declaration of Independence: "whenever any Form of Government becomes destructive of [unalienable rights], it is the Right of the People to alter or abolish it, and to institute new Government, laying its foundation on such principles and organizing its powers in such form, as to them shall seem most likely to affect their Safety and Happiness." They can and must do this, for law is their project.

If law is the result of a political project, then it always has an experimental quality. Not surprisingly, Federalist Number One describes the American project of constitutional construction as a vast experiment that will determine whether men are capable of organizing themselves on the basis of "deliberation and choice." (Hamilton 1781; 1961, p. 33). Deliberation points to theory; choice to intentionality. Together they describe a politics of projects.

The narrative of political project puts at its center not only a theory of justice, but a representation of the actor whose project it is. In the modern era, the political project of law creation is always that of the sovereign people. We get things backwards if we imagine the popular sovereign as a subject/author who grounds the form of the project narrative; rather, that narrative form opens the space for this idea of the popular sovereign. The best definition of the popular sovereign may simply be that subject whose project is the constitution. This idea provides a norm by which to judge judicial performance: the opinion must persuade citizens to see themselves as authors of the law. If the law appears as someone else's projects, the rule of law and rule by the people have split apart.

In American history, a particular controversy over the locus of popular sovereignty—the nation or the states—dominated constitutional disagreement in the first half of the nineteenth century. This began as a theoretical debate over the appropriate narrative by which to speak of the authorship of the project, but came to a point of existential conflict in the Civil War. That War did not so much resolve this question as suggest the need for a new way of thinking about political order. The original project had failed; it had led to civil disorder rather than to peace. Lincoln begins to respond to that failure when, near the end of the War, he appeals to a theodicy: "The Almighty has His own purposes." God's project appears as a system to man, for it realizes immanently the good that is God's design. Thus, Lincoln speaks of God's providence acting through the destruction of battle, for through war the offense of slavery will come to an end (Lincoln 1865). The meaning of American history is beyond our individual intentions: our acts are elements of a larger system of which we are not the authors.

The War is a sort of inflection point in the move from project to system. Just as the War and the economy operate to achieve an order independent of intentions so does law. The real constitutional order is now imagined as an order of legality that emerges spontaneously from within national political practices, including Lincoln's wartime practices. Law is now tied to practices, not to intentions. It is no longer authored; it need not be written.

A narrative of system imagines law as an immanent order that develops on its own, i.e., without deliberate direction. An immanent order, accordingly, does not generate any concerns about whether man is adequate to sustain and support that order. The Founders' concern for project had included a worry about the citizens' moral character. Washington and Hamilton thought that a democratic political order needed a supplement in the form of sectarian faith, for only religion could support morality, and citizens in a democratic political project had to be moral. By the end of the century, even as jurists easily write of America as a Christian nation, they no longer think of religion as a supplement to the political project.[11] There is no need for such a supplement, because Christian faith is imagined as the end point of a natural development. America is a Christian nation because it is a civilized nation. Christianity, civilization, and reason are now all the products of history itself (Rana 2015). Indeed, they all express the same systemic conception of man's natural goodness. This goodness will realize itself under proper conditions—the conditions of late nineteenth century America. The American legal order is now a model for the world, not because it is the finest achievement of the new era of political theory in the age of Enlightenment. It is a model because it has fully realized the natural goodness of man's political nature. One hundred years before Francis Fukuyama declared "the end of history," American constitutionalists thought they had arrived there.

[11]See the Court's definition of the United States as "a Christian nation." (Church of the Holy Trinity 1892, p. 471).

This idea of a legal system takes form right alongside nineteenth century economic thought. The immanent order that arises from "perfect freedom" *is* Lochnerian constitutionalism with its protection of contract and property. This is the realization of the truth of man's free nature, not a project imposed on that nature. Freedom simply is contract, and its realization is property. Citizens are the natural beneficiaries of this immanent order for they are its bearers. They need only be that which they are by nature; they have no need to re-form themselves. The role of government is not to create order but only to remove those pathologies that prevent the natural order from emerging among free, rational agents (*Lochner* 1905).

The turn to system accounts for the remarkable convergence of American constitutional law and British common law at the end of the nineteenth century, and the convergence of both on a laissez-faire economic order. The Social Darwinists contributed to this systemic view of legal order, but it would be a mistake to think of the new constitutionalism as attributable only to their influence. They are part of a larger shift in the narrative frame.[12] This same shift toward system is powering the entry of the law school into the university. The laws of society and the laws of nature are not far apart; social science will develop alongside natural science. Both are systemic and immanent.

That the free acts of individual agents can themselves express an immanent order was the idea behind the emerging techniques of statistics (Sheehan and Wahrman 2015). The order of law, however, was not merely statistical; it was normative. That such a normative order could be understood as immanent points back toward ideas of general providence. The mystery of God's order was precisely the way in which it worked through individual free will. For Blackstone, the whole system of the common law cannot make sense without this ground (Blackstone 1765, p. 39). Today, we might compare Roberto Unger's claim that legal theorists become "Right-wing Hegelians" when they interpret the law (Unger 1996, p. 72). They too interpret law as if it is objective reason working itself out in an immanent system. That objective reason is another way of speaking of the popular sovereign. It is its appearance within the systemic imagination.

That the imagination of law as immanent order traces back through natural theology to ideas of general providence makes clear the alternative theological predicate of this imagination structure. Order no longer depends upon a memory that survives the fall and is put to work in man's labor. Man need not labor to create the good. Rather, a well-functioning polity reveals God's good work. By the late nineteenth century, God's work is also the work of reason. By the twentieth century, God is dropped, but the systemic work of reason remains. So too does the natural goodness of man, for law is not asking him to reform himself, but only to pursue his interests.

[12]Speaking of legal theory in 1890, Pollock states, "The doctrine of evolution is nothing else than the historical method applied to the facts of nature; the historical method is nothing else than the doctrine of evolution applied to known societies and institutions." (Pollock 1890, pp. 37–41).

That the systemic account simultaneously expresses the new science of the social and a belief in general providence—of reason and revelation—helps explain how it comes to support American imperialism (Rana 2015). At the turn of the century, Americans believe they have both a civilizing and a Christianizing mission. Imperialism is imagined not as a political *project* of hegemony, but as an effort to bring about those conditions under which other peoples can realize the immanent principles of order within their own polities. All of the word would become America, not because of the strength of our project but because there is an immanent order that will realize itself once the proper conditions are established (Thayer 1899). When Locke had written 200 years earlier that all the world was once America, he was suggesting the need for political projects (Locke 1689). By the time of Teddy Roosevelt, all the world is to become America because of the immanent system of order.

The systemic view supported hegemony abroad, even as it had a substantial disabling effect on popular, democratic politics at home. That citizens are natural beneficiaries of immanent order does not mean they are all naturally capable of ordering themselves. Ordinary citizens, left to their own, may fall into pathology. Science—including a science of law—requires expertise. Judges now claim authority against popular majorities because they know the true content of public opinion, which is not the actual beliefs of the community. The judge—or the treatise writer—speaks for the popular sovereign, while a democratic majority may speak only with the voice of a mob. Accordingly, for voters to believe that politics is subject to their own ideas of the good is a dangerous democratic pathology. It would displace system by project.

That we have to decide between project and system does not mean that we always make the same decision or that we are not in need of both narratives. The narrative of project founds our idea that a legitimate order is one in which we give the law to ourselves. That is an essential idea of democratic freedom. We must collectively raise ourselves up from the disordered character of our own natures. The narrative of system founds our idea that the legal order is a single whole that develops in a progressive, i.e., reasonable, direction. This belief grounds our idea that there is always more law to be found and that law is never exhausted in the particularity of our intentions. Absent this idea, even the best of political projects would become, over time, a sort of prison of arbitrariness. Freedom within law requires appeals to both project and system, even if they cannot be reconciled in a single narrative. In theological terms, we might say that we need an account of both the fall and of providence to make sense of ourselves.[13]

In American constitutional theory, we see repeated clashes between these narrative forms. Today, both narratives are regularly deployed. The contemporary appeal

---

[13]Instead of project and system, Giorgio Agamben speaks of "transcendence" and "immanence." (Agamben 2011). Nothing turns on the choice of terms. Transcendence and immanence capture the distinct forms of political narrative. Project requires a subject who transcends any particular commitment; system is always an order of immanence.

to the narrative of project often takes the form of originalism: the meaning of law is exhausted in the intentions of those who had the authority to make law. Ironically, the potentially liberating idea of a political project is thereby inverted to become an instrument of interpretive constraint. Opposed to originalism are claims for an immanent order of reason working itself out through an evolving public opinion. Thus, Justice Kennedy, writing in *Obergefell*, speaks of the society learning, over time, the true meaning of constitutional freedom. The Court's judgment supporting gay marriage is, he argues, only declaratory of a meaning already immanent in our practices (Obergefell 2015, pp. 2602–2603).

One might think that I have, over the course of my argument, moved from politics to metaphysics. Can it be that the necessary decision at the origin of interpretation requires an entire metaphysics of project or system? That law depends on a metaphysical choice seems different from saying it depends on political choices. But that is a mistake of our secular age. The decision for project or system is not the end point of a philosophical reflection on man's essential nature. Law is not philosophy. This decision for law reflects rather all of our other beliefs, values, interests, and relationships. It reflects opportunities and circumstances, that is, it depends upon judgments about what forms of rhetorical address will work here and now. We must decide for ourselves, and about ourselves. The decision is both necessary and ungrounded, meaning it is a free choice. If this is metaphysics, it is its political face.

Schmitt's mistake was to think that one had to decide between good and evil, as if one stood at judgment day itself. Law is not like that. We do have to decide before we can begin to argue, but we face the need to decide constantly. We create a narrative every time we make a legal argument; every narrative represents a choice between good and evil, between system and project. At issue is how and where we see ourselves in and through the popular sovereign. That decision is the condition of interpretation, for until we make it, we do not know where to look, what to say, or even who we are.

References

Agamben, G. (2011). *The kingdom and the glory: For a theological genealogy of economy and government* (Lorenzo Chiesa, Trans.). Stanford: Stanford University Press.

Bickel, A. (1962). *The least dangerous branch: The supreme court at the bar of politics* (2nd ed.). New Haven: Yale University Press.

Blackstone, W. (1765). *Commentaries*. Oxford: Clarendon Press.

Boumediene v. Bush, 553 U.S. 723 (2008) (Roberts, C.J., dissenting).

Calder v. Bull, 3 U.S. (3 Dall.) 386 (1798) (Iredell, J., concurring).

Church of the Holy Trinity v. United States, 143 U.S. 457 (1892).

Cover, R. (1983). The Supreme Court, 1982 Term—Foreword: Nomos and narrative. *Harvard Law Review, 97*, 4–68.

Dworkin, R. (1978). *Taking rights seriously*. Cambridge: Harvard University Press.

Dworkin, R. (1986). *Law's empire*. Cambridge: Harvard University Press.

Fisher, S. G. (1862). *The trial of the constitution*. Philadelphia: J. B. Lippincott & Co.

Frank, J. (1930). *Law and the modern mind*. New York: Brentano's.
Gillman, H. (2001). Review: What's law got to do with it? Judicial behavioralists test the "Legal Model" of judicial decision making. *Law and Social Inquiry, 26*, 465–504.
Grewal, D. S. (forthcoming). *The invention of the economy*. Cambridge: Harvard University Press.
Grey, T. (1983). Langdell's orthodoxy. *University of Pittsburgh Law Review, 45*, 1–53.
Hamilton, A. (1781). Federalist No. 1. In C. Rossiter (Ed.), *1961. The Federalist Papers: Alexander Hamilton, James Madison, John Jay*. New York: Signet.
Hart, H. L. A. (1961). *The concept of law*. Oxford: Oxford University Press.
Holmes, O. W. (1897). The path of the law. *Harvard Law Review, 10*, 457–478.
Kahn, P. (1992). *Legitimacy and history: Self-government in American Constitutional Theory*. New Haven: Yale University Press.
Kahn, P. (1997). *The reign of law*. New Haven: Yale University Press.
Kahn, P. (1999). *The cultural study of law*. Chicago: University of Chicago Press.
Kahn, P. (2008). *Sacred violence: Torture, terror, and sovereignty*. Ann Arbor: University of Michigan Press.
Kahn, P. (2011). *Political theology: Four new chapters on the concept of sovereignty*. New York: Columbia University Press.
Kahn, P. (2016). *Making the case: The art of the judicial opinion*. New Haven: Yale University Press.
Kahn, P. (2019). *Origins of order: Project and system in the American legal imagination*. New Haven: Yale University Press.
Kant, I. (1785). *Grundlegung zur Metaphysik der Sitten*. Berlin: Verlag von L. Heimann. English Edition: Kant, I. (1873). *Groundwork of the metaphysics of morals* (Thomas Kingsmill Abbott, Trans.). New York: Green and Company.
Kramer, L. (2004). *The people themselves: Popular constitutionalism and judicial review*. New York: Oxford University Press.
Langdell, C. C. (1879). *A selection of cases on the law of contracts* (2nd ed.). Boston: Little, Brown.
Lilla, M. (2007). *The Stillborn God: Religion, politics, and the Modern West*. New York: Vintage Books.
Lincoln, A. (1865). *Second inaugural address*.
Lochner v. New York, 198 U.S. 45 (1905).
Locke, J. (1689). *Two treatises on Civil Government*. London: George Routledge and Sons.
Mandeville, B. (1729). *The fable of the bees; or, Private vices, Publick benefits*. London: Penguin Books.
Masterpiece Cakeshop, Ltd. v. Colorado Civil Rights Comm'n, 138 S. Ct. 1719 (2018).
Minow, M. (1998). *Between vengeance and forgiveness: Facing history after genocide and mass violence*. Boston: Beacon.
Obergefell v. Hodges, 135 S. Ct. 2584 (2015).
Pollock, F. (1890). *English opportunities in historical and comparative opportunities, Oxford lectures and other discourses*. London: Macmillan.
Rana, A. (2015). Constitutionalism and the foundations of the security state. *California Law Review, 103*, 335–386.
Schmitt, C. (1922). *Politische Theologie. Vier Kapitel zur Lehre von der Souveränität*. Berlin: Duncker & Humblot. English Edition: Schmitt, C. (2005). *Political theology: Four chapters on the concept of sovereignty* (George Schwab, Trans.). Chicago: University of Chicago Press.
Schmitt, C. (1932). *Der Begriff des Politischen*. Munich: Duncker & Humblot. English Edition: Schmitt, C. (1996). *The concept of the political* (George Schwab, Trans.). Chicago: University of Chicago Press.
Sheehan, J., & Wahrman, D. (2015). *Invisible hands: Self-organization and the eighteenth century*. Chicago: University of Chicago Press.
Siegel, R. (2008). Dead or alive: Originalism as popular constitutionalism in Heller. *Harvard Law Review, 122*, 191–245.
Smith, A. (1776). *The wealth of nations*. New York: Bantam Classics.

Taylor, C. (2003). *Modern social imaginaries*. Durham: Duke University Press.
Thayer, J. B. (1892). *A selection of cases on evidence at the common law*. Cambridge: Harvard University Press.
Thayer, J. B. (1899). Our new possessions. *Harvard Law Review, 12*, 464–485.
Tiedeman, C. G. (1890). *The unwritten constitution of the United States*. New York: G. P. Putnam's Sons.
Tushnet, M. (2006). Popular constitutionalism as political law. *Chicago-Kent Law Review, 81*, 991–1006.
Unger, R. M. (1996). *What should legal analysis become?* London: Verso.
Viner, J. (1972). *The role of providence in the social order: An essay in intellectual history*. Princeton: Princeton University Press.
Washington, G. (1796). Farewell address. In V. H. Paltsits (Ed.), *Washington's farewell address, in facsimile*. New York: New York Public Library.
Wittgenstein, L. (1953). *Philosophische Untersuchungen* (English edition: Wittgenstein, L. (1953). *Philosophical investigation* (G. E. M. Anscombe, Trans.)). Oxford: Blackwell.

Paul W. Kahn is Robert W. Winner Professor of Law and Humanities at Yale Law School. His publications include *Legitimacy and History: Self-Government in American Constitutional Theory* (Yale University Press, 1993) *The Reign of Law* (Yale University Press, 1997), *The Cultural Study of Law* (University of Chicago Press, 1999), *Putting Liberalism in Its Place* (Princeton University Press, 2005), *Political Theology—Four New Chapters on the Concept of Sovereignty* (Columbia University Press, 2011), *Making the Case: The Art of the Judicial Opinion* (Yale University Press, 2016) and *Origins of Order: Project and System in the American Legal Imagination* (Yale University Press, 2019).

An Alternative Political Theology: The Negative and Anticipatory Significance of the Constitutive Concepts of Constitutional Law

Luís Pereira Coutinho

Contents

Abstract This chapter explores the dimension of constitutional law composed of constitutive concepts, such as *national sovereignty*, *the people* and the concept of *Constitution* itself. That dimension can be considered as a political-theological dimension in the sense that constitutive concepts are analogous to theological concepts. Both have a negative and anticipatory significance, bearing in mind their understanding in the light of negative theology. In this light, political theology is not to be understood in the terms proposed by Carl Schmitt.

1 Introduction

There are different layers in constitutional law. There is a superficial dimension formed by norms, and then there is a deep dimension formed by constitutive concepts, such as *national sovereignty*, the *people*, and the concept of *Constitution* itself. They are constitutive in the sense that there wouldn't be a "law" that could be predicated as "constitutional" without implicit or explicit reference to them, at least

L. P. Coutinho (✉)
Lisbon's School of Law, Lisbon University, Lisbon, Portugal
e-mail: lpcoutinho@fd.ulisboa.pt

© Springer Nature Switzerland AG 2020
M. Nogueira de Brito, L. Pereira Coutinho (eds.), *The Political Dimension of Constitutional Law*, https://doi.org/10.1007/978-3-030-38459-3_5

in the continental tradition shaped after the French Revolution. Taken together, they structure a given juridico-political system—the system of national sovereignty—within which national sovereignty is expressed in the Constitution, outside which no ruling people is conceivable.[1]

At issue in this article is whether that deep dimension of constitutional law is a political-theological dimension. This inevitably leads us back to Carl Schmitt's famous dictum according to which "all significant concepts of the modern theory of the state are secularized theological concepts" (1985, p. 36). However, it is important to point out from the start that the idea of political concepts as theological-political concepts (or as analogous to theological concepts) does not have to be understood in the rather imprecise terms proposed by Schmitt.

It is difficult to deny that, understood in Schmitt's terms, political theology endorses, or at least permits, a sort of mystical coercion in those concepts he considers to be "secularized theological concepts". Indeed, in Schmitt, those concepts seem to be mere covers for political caprice or arbitrariness, i.e., mere instruments of "false consciousness". In this way, Hans Blumenberg (1985, p. 89) holds that Schmitt—who takes "at its word secularized stylistic means"—sanctions a (supposed) transferal of the "linguistic means" of "theological absolutism" to the theory of the state. As a result, the corresponding structures and actions become "familiar and sanctioned" at the level of consciousness, being "accepted fatalistically" regardless of their arbitrariness in rational terms. That is, "through cunning, the political sphere acquires an appearance of legitimacy…[which] renders the caprice of its actions invisible".[2]

However, and *pace* Blumenberg, to question Schmitt's particular understanding does not necessarily mean to abandon the idea of political theology altogether: one may conceive the analogy between political concepts and theological concepts in different terms. The point is that Schmitt's understanding builds around an analogy to what may actually be bad theology in the first place (i.e., the sort that allows for "theological absolutism"). I'm referring to non-negative theology, i.e. positive theology, spuriously applied to core scriptural concepts in spite of the limits of human understanding—those concepts actually demanding, given those limits, the way that is proper to negative or apophatic theology. It is considering the latter that it becomes possible to consider an alternative political theology.

At issue in *negative* political theology is the *the specific mode of significance of constitutive political concepts*. Pointing precisely in this direction, Fernando Atria (2016) recently drew attention to the impact negative theology could have on the

[1]The notion of "constitutive concepts" was developed by Troper (2018, p. 78). Constitutive concepts shape a given political system: in the case of the modern state, the concept of "sovereignty" and the concept of the "state" itself are constitutive concepts, i.e., in the absence of such concepts, there would be no "state" (in Troper's terms, there would be no "game" that could be considered as the "game of the state").

[2]The last quote is from Schmitz (2016, pp. 719–720) who develops Blumenberg's thesis on Schmitt.

clarification of the modern legal and political concepts. The basic idea is that, as in the case of core theological concepts, their mode of significance is negative and anticipatory. That is: core modern political concepts, as core theological concepts, are *not aimed, at least primarily, at informing us on actualizations. On the contrary: they are aimed at preventing false actualizations corresponding to forms of idolatry, transferred self-worship or fanaticism.*

It is considering this that I am not convinced by Blumenberg's thesis that theology, political or otherwise, inevitably leads to "absolutism" or implies "false consciousness". Bearing in mind negative theology, it is indeed questionable to consider that an analogy between the "linguistic means" of pre-modern theology, on the one side, and of modern politics, on the other, always renders (or is aimed at rendering) caprice or arbitrariness invisible. Even if Schmitt's political theology may have actually deserved that remark.

2 Negative Theology and the Doctrine of the Trinity

As mentioned, the constitutive political concepts I'll address here are primarily those that still structure continental constitutional discourse after the decisive contributions of the Abbé Sièyès and the French Revolution, i.e. the concepts of *national sovereignty*, *the people* and the *Constitution*. In order to explore the analogy that exists between those concepts and theological concepts—namely, those which compose the doctrine of the Trinity—one must begin by exploring the "negative way" (*vis negationis*) in which the latter were understood in negative theology.

Applying that negative way to the First Person of the Trinity, Thomas Aquinas asserted the impossibility for humans beings, given the limits of their understanding, to access positive descriptions of God, at least univocal ones (i.e. not merely analogical).[3] According to Aquinas, the divine essence is inaccessible to created knowledge.[4] Thus, if meanings can be attributed to the concept of "God", they are essentially negative.[5] The first and essential meaning is that there are no gods.

It is true that God is described by Scripture as the Creator of "all things that are in heaven and that are on earth, visible and invisible". But in negative theology, that should not be read as a positive description of God. It should be read instead as an affirmation of the world as "created" and therefore as filled with meaning. Not having a positive knowledge of God means not to be able to determine that meaning in arbitrary or idolatrous ways—least of all in "decisionistic" ways.

It is also true that the First Person unmistakably is a personal God. But the paramount meaning of that indication is also negative. The point is that God is not to be understood as an impersonal force, i.e., as an Aristotelian "first motor".

---

[3]On this see Pannenberg (1992, p. 372 ff).

[4]*S.T.* I, 12,7.

[5]See Atria (2016, pp. 437–438).

Regarding Christian theology in particular, the *vis negationis* is not compromised by the doctrine of the Trinity. On the contrary, considering that "the mystery of the Trinity can only be understood in the divinity itself, not in the creature" (Peterson 1999, p. 95). Moreover, the presentations (including the "self-presentations") of the Second and the Third Persons of the Trinity have a paramount *negative* meaning, very much aware of the limits of human understanding and its vulnerability to idolatry or fanaticism.

Indeed, the Second Person (that is, Jesus Christ) affirms that "no one comes to the Father except through me".[6] The "Son" therefore excludes those "ways" to "the Father" which do not pass through him as "the way, the truth and the life".[7] In the words of Karl Barth (2004, p. 152) referred to the Second Person, "it is in the particular fact and the particular way that Jesus Christ is very God, very man, and very God-man that he works, and he works in the fact and *only in the fact that He is this One and not another*".

As to the Third Person, the Holy Spirit, it has also a paramount *negative* meaning. It is true that through the gift of the Holy Spirit, it becomes possible for human beings to be redeemed in the affirmation that "Jesus is the Lord". But what is really meant is that no one can say that "Jesus is the Lord" and thus achieve redemption except through the Holy Spirit.[8] The Holy Spirit is therefore a negative concept which means that the people of Christ, the Christian community, exists only in sacramental form, in anticipatory form. To assume otherwise is to challenge the core of Christian eschatology, i.e., it means a heretical "de-eschatolization" of Christianity.

With this brief explanation of Trinitarian concepts, I intended to illustrate their negative and anticipatory mode of significance. As said, the point to explore in this paper is that the core concepts of the system of national sovereignty reproduce that negative and anticipatory mode. The result is the rationalization of political structures and political action—and perhaps paradoxically their desacralization. But before I go there, I should point out that from a theological perspective—at least one informed by the church fathers—a political theology in the Schmittian terms is a grave irregularity, even an impossibility.

3 The Irregularity of Schmitt's Political Theology

Christianity lives in anticipation, its *imperator* is no *Caesar*, His kingdom is not of this world. To be sure, after Constantine's conversion, there were attempts—most importantly, by Eusebius of Caesarea—at conceiving the *Pax Romana* as a providential design or the Roman Empire as a divine monarchy but these were shattered

[6]John 14:6.

[7]*Idem.*

[8]1 Cor. 12, 3.

by Augustine. In Erik Peterson's words (1999, p. 93 ff.) "the doctrine of the divine monarchy had to fall before the Trinitarian dogma and [Eusebius's] interpretation of the *Pax Augusta* had to fall before Christian eschatology". What actually results from a proper theological perspective in the Christian tradition is an imperative of "eschatological reserve" before any political instance.

Peterson takes Augustine's rejection of Eusebius's political theology as exemplary for the whole problem of political theology, which he believes to be "impossible". In *Political Theology II*, Schmitt (2008a, p. 65 ff.) defended his thesis, claiming that political theology is a "polymorphous phenomenon" to be understood in its own terms even if it escapes the boundaries of dogmatic theology. In this direction, Schmitt recovered non-Christian "political theologies", namely Jewish, Islamic and pagan, including "the *theologia politica* or *civilis* of Graeco-Roman antiquity", in which "political theology is part of the *nomos* and constitutes the public sphere through the worship of the gods, rites of sacrifice and ceremonies. It belongs to the political identity and continuity of a people".

One may infer from this defense that Schmitt's thesis on political theology implies an acknowledgement of forms of "political paganism"—both ancient and modern—which are wrongly (for Schmitt) unacknowledged by Peterson. One may also infer that Schmitt's thesis on political theology has no consequences at the proper theological level, being indifferent to the thesis whether the "political theologies" it acknowledges are heretical or not from the perspective of Christian theology.

However, such inferences may be hasty. Schmitt's defense is not exhausted by the claim that there are political theologies which have nothing to do with Christianity and that can be envisioned from a theoretical perspective that has nothing to do with dogmatic theology. The real reason why, for Schmitt, the epoch of the Roman Empire and the case of Eusebius is not to be taken as exemplary is different. The esoteric meaning of *Political Theology II*—which appears to be also Schmitt's defense, as a Catholic who had supported Nazism, before Peterson's accusation of heresy—seems to be that heresy may be endorsed as long as it is justified in a context of attack on Christianity by "de-theologised" forces.

In this direction, Schmitt (2008a, pp. 63–64) dismissed the idea of Eusebius's case as exemplary *even regarding Christianity in particular*. That since "in the case of Constantine the Great [whose "divine monarchy" Eusebius's political theology endorsed] we are dealing with the relation between the Christian church and a powerful Christian...Furthermore we are dealing with an almost intra-Christian struggle".

What is thus suggested is that the theological considerations that may be applicable in the context of an "intra-Christian struggle"—a context in which political theology may dispensed with, so to speak—"cannot be transferred either to the theoretical or to the political relation between the Christian church and non-Christian, antichristian or even irreligious and completely de-theologised opponents". In this situation—considering that the church of Christ "is *in* this world" even if "not of this world"—political theology may be justified if necessary to face political enemies, their "de-theologised" character allowing for the political "side" of the question to take precedence over strict theological considerations. According to Schmitt (2008a, p. 89), in such a situation a "Catholic lay person" may be "politically active in the interest of the church without having to become theological in a dogmatic way". And that is the sort of situation he claims he has faced, one in which—in the words by Böckenförde he cites (2008a, p. 46)—"one cannot circumvent the political by retreating to a neutral position, to some pre-political natural law or to the pure proclamation of the Christian gospel" even if that means to endorse a "decision" in which the theological is overwhelmed by the political.

One may say that this justification of political theology made in 1970 was already present in Schmitt's *opus* from 1922—which should not be read therefore as a mere book on the structural identity of theological and juridical concepts. Most revealingly, the book culminates in the recovery of Donoso Cortés's anticipation of "the last battle". In the last paragraph of the last chapter of *Political Theology*, the unmistakably "de-eschatolizing" point is that "the moment of the last battle [has] arrived; in the face of radical evil the only solution is dictatorship".

I should clarify that such description of the esoteric meaning of Schmitt's political theology does not mean, by any means, an endorsement. But a full rejection of it can only be made from the internal point of view of Christian theology and is thus beyond the scope of this paper. For our purposes it is sufficient to say that, this being the true meaning of Schmitt's political theology, it amounts to an endorsement of political cunning through mystifying concepts. Blumenberg's diagnosis is therefore confirmed by Schmitt's defense before Peterson's accusation of heresy. In this sense, Schmitt's political theology is a Machiavellian devise, whose conceptual means are taken to be justified by pseudo-theological ends.

The main point here is that Schmitt's political theology justifies—and not merely describes—those mystifying concepts through which a dictatorship can be legitimized. One other important point is that a *positive* political theology thus conceived for legitimating purposes paradoxically ends up failing to understand actual historical examples of political theology, namely those explored by Kantorowicz (1957). Indeed, if the latter, namely the doctrine of the "king's two bodies", managed to circumvent a theological imperative of "eschatological reserve" before any political instance—thus escaping the orthodoxy of dogmatic theology—one cannot say with certainty that they were aimed at transferring forms of "theological absolutism" to the political sphere and thus at legitimating just any form of political ruling.

The contrary may be true, actually. One may say that, in those examples, the purpose was negative and anticipatory. In the doctrine of the "king's two bodies", the concept of the "political body" of the king is there to signal *what the natural body is not*. And if that is the case, the purpose of the concept is not to endorse the caprice of political action, or to render it invisible, but at isolating negatively what is "political" as being different from what is capriciously "natural".

So not even "proper" theological-political concepts are so in the terms proposed by Schmitt and accurately criticized by Blumenberg. Nor are their immediate secular successors. What is said about the "political body" of the king (as a rationalizing, non-merely legitimating concept in a bad sense) could be said about the secular concept that takes its place in Hobbes's theory of the state.

I'm referring to the concept of the sovereign-representative as an artificial person, to be distinguished from the natural person of the sovereign. That concept actually is a rational and restraining concept. It frames the political structure of the sovereign state as a unified structure in a way that necessarily implies the rationality of the actions of the sovereign (a rationality that is very different from the pre-modern one, it should be stressed[9]).

In this reading of Hobbes's concept of the sovereign-representative person I am contradicting Schmitt's theological-political reading. Schmitt unmistakably emphasizes the alleged elements of "transcendence" present in Hobbes's theory of the state. The result is the presentation of Hobbes's sovereign as he "who brings peace and security to people tormented by anguish, who transforms wolves into citizens and through this miracle proves himself to be a god". Correspondingly, Schmitt condemns those conceptions of the Hobbesian sovereign as a rational sovereign-representative person who animates a correspondingly rational "mechanism". Against such creature of "technology"—who is ultimately unable to secure unity and peace—Schmitt envisions the recovery of a sovereign whose "transcendence" makes him the analogous to an omnipotent God. For Schmitt (2008b, p. 31), only a "god", i.e. the political sovereign as "god", can represent and secure the state as "something more than and something different from a covenant concluded by individuals".

In Schmitt's reading of Hobbes, one can therefore confirm that the allegedly Hobbesian, actually Schmittian, concept of sovereignty carries a coercive irrational element. Moreover, one can confirm that the theological analogous to Schmitt's "sovereignty" is to be found in the *omnipotence of God*, as it was thought in absolutist, non-negative, theology, namely in nominalist theology.

That Schmitt's concept of sovereignty is only allegedly Hobbesian can be demonstrated if one accepts that Hobbes's theory of the state finds its motivation in the rescuing of man from the enormous pressure made upon him by the immediate worldly claims of non-negative theology. Regarding Hobbes's theory of the state one can make the same claim Blumenberg (1985, p. 196) made regarding Descartes: the claim according to which the latter essentially seeks a "guarantee" against the "ambushes set by the hidden absolute will" of the nominalist God, bringing to light in the process "the constants, the no longer touchable kernels"—in the case of Descartes, the *cogito ergo sum*.

Hobbes's political construction, before a world torn apart by the irrational and divisive claims of absolute theology, also seeks a guarantee against its ambushes, beginning from the constants and ending in rational and restraining concepts. In this context, to consider the Hobbesian concepts as mere succedaneums to the ways of absolute theology—and not as concepts pertaining to a different, non-mystical, rationality, capable of pacifying the world and allow for the worldly happiness of

[9]On the modern, instrumental nature of Hobbes's political rationality, see Loughlin (2012, pp. 5, 21).

men according to the corresponding constants—may mean to utterly subvert Hobbes's system.

Even if Hobbes's theory of the state looms in the background of this discussion—and a confrontation with Schmitt's reading of Hobbes cannot be avoided in our context—my main focus here is not Hobbes but modern political concepts as they were present in the French Revolution and as they still frame the continental constitutional discourse. And the point is that they are not theological-political in any sense, neither "proper", nor Schmittian.

However one can and should admit that their mode of significance is analogous to that of theological concepts. Most importantly, their purpose, as negative and anticipatory concepts, is not to confer an appearance of legitimacy to the political sphere "through cunning". Their purpose is to exclude idolatry (which in the political world inevitably culminates in fanaticism, most dangerously in the fanaticism of mobs). It is also to anticipate, to institutionalize political action and induce its rightfulness or rationality (even if that rightfulness or rationality may be very different in the context of Modernity from what it was in the pre-modern context).

It is precisely in this sense that those core political concepts can be taken to be concepts of a (now secular) form of right—constitutional right—whose mode of significance is analogous to that of theological concepts. In order to illustrate the analogy, I'll focus now on the system of national sovereignty.

4 The System of National Sovereignty

Article 3 of the 1959 French Constitution provides an accurate expression of the system of national sovereignty. It states that:

> National sovereignty shall vest in the people, who shall exercise it through their representatives and by means of referendum.
>
> No section of the people nor any individual may arrogate to itself, or to himself, the exercise thereof.

The text is cryptic, perhaps as cryptic as the doctrine of the Trinity. And the reason is precisely that the mode of significance of the core concepts explicit or implicit in that text is exactly the mode of significance of the core concepts that compose that doctrine. Moreover, the three concepts that compose the system of national sovereignty (which are national sovereignty, the people and the Constitution) perform exactly the same structural purposes the concepts of God, the Christ and the Holy Spirit perform in the doctrine of the Trinity.

Beginning with the concept of national sovereignty.

As we saw above, in theology the *negative* meaning of God is that:

- There are no gods;
- The world is something created
- God cannot be understood instrumentally as an impersonal driving force.

Well, in the system of national sovereignty, the meaning of national sovereignty is that:

- There are no sovereigns in the plural, being the sovereign nation *one*. In the terms of Article 3, paragraph 2, "no section of the people nor any individual may arrogate to itself, or to himself, the exercise of national sovereignty";
- The political world is something already created, i.e., instituted by that national sovereignty as a constituent power;
- The sovereign nation cannot be understood instrumentally.

Thus being, the meaning of national sovereignty is purely negative (as the meaning of the First Person of the Trinity is). Correspondingly, the nation who is sovereign cannot be described in positive terms (that is, non-negative terms). As such, it is incapable of appearance in the ordinary legal world, its "will" being exclusively manifested in the precise logic and strict boundaries of its single "act" (the Constitution).

As Pierre Brunet (2004, pp. 105–106) clarifies, explaining the concept of "nation" in Siéyès—which ultimately inspires the system—"the nation does not create the Constitution. . .but explains its existence. She is a reconstructed explanation and not a creative and irresistible natural force". This concept of nation would be reflected in Carré de Malberg's *negative* theory of the constituent power and also in Hans Kelsen's theory of the "basic norm"—to the degree in which it is conditioned by the conceptual structure of the constitutional state and may be understood as a *negative theory* of sovereignty.[10] In both cases, at issue is an anti-decisionistic "exclusion of the originarian", according to which it is not for the jurist to conceive a primordial power but only to presuppose it when attesting those powers that are already constituted.[11] The conclusion is that there is no "transcendent" power in the state, at least from a legal perspective. In Carré de Malberg's words (1922, p. 166) "the power of the state can only be conceived in the state. . .there is not in the state a power prior to that which is of the state itself".

Whether there is or not a "transcendent" power in the state—i.e. whether sovereignty should be treated as "transcendent"—is really the crucial question here. When affirming sovereignty as a theological-political concept, Schmitt was affirming its transcendence. What I am claiming on the contrary is that to treat sovereignty as a theological-political concept actually means to deny its transcendence. More precisely, it means to deny sovereignty as anything other than a reconstructed explanation for the rational immanence that the state exclusively is.

To further clarify this point it is necessary to go back to Schmitt's reading of Hobbes. Schmitt (1985, p. 34) accurately praises Hobbes for having determined the

---

[10]Carré de Malberg's negative theory of the constituent power is a central element of his theory of the state (1922, p. 490 ff). On Kelsen's theory as conditioned by the structure and arguments characteristic of the modern state, see Troper (2017). On Hans Kelsen's theory of the fundamental norm as a negative theory of sovereignty, see Bobbio (1998, p. 435 ff).

[11]The expression "exclusion of the originary" is due to Maulin (2003, p. 124).

representational character of political reality. The state is not a reality in the sense of the "natural sciences" but the "specific reality of legal life which pertains to the legal form". That is, the state is a representation composed by the concepts and forms which constitute it—the concepts and forms of modern political right.

I'm following Schmitt so far. But at this point a divisive question arises: why should one consider something non-naturalistic or non-empirical—the state as a representation, I mean—as also being transcendent and irrational?

The question is all the more pressing as I believe that to consider sovereignty as something irrational or transcendent betrays Hobbes. In Hobbes, the sovereign-representative person, established within a relation between protection and obedience, is not a suprarrational entity. On the contrary: it is a self-conscious representation. It definitely is so for those who rationally author the state and thus institute the sovereign actor. The original covenant is a moment of conscious rationality.

Schmitt does not deny that the covenant is a moment of conscious rationality. But he distinguishes two moments: the *ideal* moment of the covenant and corresponding institution of the sovereign-representative person, on the one side, and the actual moment of existence of the state on the other. For Schmitt (2008b, p. 33), the Hobbesian state is foundationally instituted as rational, conscious representation—when a "spark of reason flashes", in his words. But that same state cannot persist *afterwards* as a mere sum of individual self-conscious representations. The state has to be entrenched in the minds of men as more than the result of multiple authorships. It is in this way that Schmitt points to a *necessary* suprarrational nature of the actually existing Leviathan.

I understand that one cannot suppose the representation of the state—or the state as a representation—to be the mere sum of individual representations. The state, by definition, is a unified representation shared by citizens agglutinated in a common body. It pertains to collective or social rationality and not only to individual rationality.

However I believe Schmitt's reading of Hobbes implies a radical opposition that cannot be taken for granted. I refer to the opposition between *individual rationality*, on the one side, and *collective irrationality*, on the other. Thus as if rationality was necessarily only the strict rationality of individuals (being exhausted at the moment of the original covenant). In this line of reasoning, the post-contractual moment, since it necessarily corresponds to a collective representation, would unescapably be a moment of irrationality or transcendence. At that moment the sovereign would be "new god". The concept of sovereignty would be a political-theological concept in the exact "mystical" sense criticized by Blumenberg.

But should one accept a radical separation between the rationality of individuals, on the one side, and the forceful irrationality of persisting political collectivities, on the other?

Not necessarily. Beginning at a strictly interpretative level, it should be said that in Hobbes—contrary to what is claimed by Schmitt—there is no separation of that sort. In Hobbes, rationality (that is, the consciousness of the state as a human representation) is not exhausted at the moment of the covenant. It extends over time as a collective or social rationality. Only in this way can one understand the consideration of the sovereign as an artificial person whose actions cannot break the persisting relation between protection and obedience. It is undoubtable that if that strictly rational relation is broken, the representation of the state is dissolved.[12] *Ergo*, that representation is strictly rational.

In this reading of Hobbes, the covenant is not an original moment of individual rationality followed by collective irrationality. It persists as a reconstructed explanation for the state, i.e., as a place of representation of the state and its rational logic. In other words, the covenant persists as a rational place from which the institution of the sovereign as an artificial person bound by a relation between protection and obedience is continuously represented.

What is said about the Hobbesian covenant can be said about "national sovereignty" as a reconstructed explanation for the constitutional state, the latter being a legal person who cannot act but through the forms established by the Constitution in due respect of the rights of the citizens; the state being now identified with the Constitution—with a Constitution that strictly rationalizes the collective or social representation that the state is. One finds therefore in the constitutional state a completion of the Hobbesian conception of the state as a representation—a representation that is both *radically* non-empirical and *radically* non-mystical.

As we know, a full identification of the state with the Constitution was only made possible by the French Revolution. However, and *pace* Siéyès, it did not become possible *as a collective representation* immediately after. It only became possible at the moment in which the political language of the Revolution was converted into a "form of life" and thus into a positive language. It was that positive language that—more than 100 years after the Revolution—Carré de Malberg could take as his starting point when conceiving his *negative* theory of national sovereignty.

Carré de Malberg (1920, p. 3 ff) precisely envisioned a nation that is *not* sovereign—that is not even a nation—but at the moment in which it is personified by a state identified with the Constitution. In this light, the sovereign nation is a reconstructed explanation for the validity of the Constitution, i.e., it is a negative and anticipatory concept.

It was at that moment of completion of the modern state that a non-dissociation of collective or social rationality and individual rationality became fully possible. Collective or social rationality is the rationality of a nation personified by the constitutional state. Individual rationality is the rationality of those individuals (the citizens) who embody the nation—citizens who have internalized the political language of the Revolution.

Both rationalities, collective and individual, are not separable. On the one side, no nation or state "thinks" or "acts" on itself and by itself, thus independently of the conscious actualization of the representation that corresponds to it in the minds of citizens (namely citizens are the ones who interpret as acts of the state those acts

[12]In Hobbes's words "The Obligation of Subjects to the Soveraign is understood to last as long, and no longer, than the power lasteth, by which he is able to protect them", *Leviathan* (1651), XXI, § 14.

which are performed by the individuals and groups who are authorized by the Constitution to act as organs of the state).

On the other side, no citizen is, thinks or acts as a citizen outside the language that constitutes the state (the constitutive language that forms the political dimension of constitutional law). It is that language that allows him to be, to think and to act as a citizen. And it is also that language that constitutes the collective agent to which the citizen belongs.

That collective agent is the people, the agent on whom national sovereignty is "vested", using the terms of Article 3 of the French Constitution. The people is thus the "second person" of the system of national sovereignty. It occupies in this system the same structural place the Christ occupies in the dogma of the Trinity.

And if the people is the "second person", the Constitution with which the state identifies is the "third person". As no one can say that "Jesus is the Lord" except through the sacramental forms of the Holy Spirit, no one can say that "the people is sovereign" except through the sacramental forms of the Constitution, i.e., outside the boundaries of the Constitution no ruling people is conceivable.

Going back to the terms of Article 3 of the French Constitution if national sovereignty is vested in the people, the people can only exercise it in the forms provided by the Constitution, i.e., through representative institutions and by means of a regulated referendum.

Perhaps paradoxically, if the mode of significance of core political concepts is analogous to that of theological concepts, their "operation" does not result in the least in a limitless or arbitrary power. One confirms therefore that Blumenberg's criticism to political theology can only be understood as a criticism to bad political theology—i.e. to what actually are political analogies to bad theology.

The mode of significance of constitutive concepts—as analogous to theological concepts—does not result in capricious or limitless power. On the contrary, it results in the thorough institutionalization and rationalization of power. Moreover, it results in the desacralization of power, even if that may sound paradoxical.

The paradox is solved if one considers that the entities, or non-entities, described by constitutive concepts—namely, the sovereign nation and the people—are not *actual* entities able to appear in the world in contradiction with the proper mode of significance of the concepts which give them form. They are not reifications, but *self-conscious representations*.

Those who refer to the "sovereign nation" or to "the people" in speech are aware—must be aware—of the negative or sacramental character of the entities they are invoking. A negative character in the case of the sovereign nation, a sacramental character in the case of the people.

In case they aren't, they are consciously or unconsciously betraying the specific mode of significance of constitutive concepts as analogous to theological concepts, that is, as negative and anticipatory.

If it is inadequate to speak of heresy in this field, it may be adequate to speak of the perversion of constitutive concepts, which takes place when negative or sacramental entities (representational entities) are conceived as *actual* entities able to subsist outside the conceptual world.

Before such abuses (and still avoiding the expression political heresies) to clarify the analogy between theology and the political dimension of constitutional law, may precisely mean to pursue an exercise of demystification, contrary to what was believed by Schmitt (who actually promoted a sort of mystical coercion in political concepts).

Indeed, to clarify the analogy between theological concepts and constitutive concepts may mean to pursue an exercise of "epistemic anarchism"—to use Hans Kelsen's terms (2004, pp. 146–147). An exercise which takes place when those reifications covering for political caprice—or even worse, for political fanaticism—are exposed for what they are.

5 Final Remarks

Some qualifications are required before concluding.

In the first place, it is important to stress that to affirm an analogy between political concepts and theological concepts does not mean to consider the former as "pseudomorphs", as inauthentic forms of the "real thing" which is then believed to reside in proper theological concepts. Much of Blumenberg's anxiety regarding the "secularization thesis" concerned exactly this point. That is, he feared the de-legitimating effect for Modernity that could result from the consideration of its core concepts as succedaneums to theological concepts.[13]

In order to dissipate that anxiety, it should be clarified that secular concepts are not "pseudomorphs", but morphs in their own right—i.e. with their own rationality which is specifically modern. In our case, constitutive concepts are morphs in their own *constitutional right*. The similar negative and anticipatory significance of constitutive concepts—similar to that of premodern theological concepts, that is—does not diminish the fact that they structure a different world. They shape a desacralized, secular world, whose core is to be found in the citizen with rights. The point is that that world is not made worse by rational and restraining concepts.

Much to the contrary, I believe, and that considering the perennial nature of the dangers human beings are exposed to in their collective pursuits—both themselves and those many others who may fall victim to their different forms of self-worship and fanaticism, which inevitably take place in absence of negative and anticipatory meanings.

Given the continuous human exposure to those (mostly self-induced) dangers, the sort of needs or questions constitutive concepts answer to are not "residual needs"

[13]This is clarified by Blumenberg (1985, p. 17) when saying that, for those endorsing the secularization thesis, "the genuine substance of that which was secularized is "wrapped up in" what thus became worldly, and remains "wrapped up in" it as what is essential to it, as when, in the model instance developed by Heidegger for the hermeneutics of his school, "Dasein's understanding of Being" is essential to it and yet "in the first instance and for the most part" hidden and withdrawn from it. *I am almost inclined to say that that was what I was afraid of*" (Italics added).

which can be eliminated. Blumenberg (1985, p. 65) suggested this possibility censoring "the modern age's readiness to inherit a [heavy] mortgage of prescribed questions and to accept as its own the obligation to pay it off".

This suggestion cannot be accepted, even if only because political Modernity has already proven that it has its own heavy mortgage to pay—thus confirming that the "needs" at stake are not merely "residual"—and I see no other way of paying that mortgage except through negative and anticipatory concepts, thus analogous to the theological concepts it managed to emancipate from.

The suggestion by Blumenberg I'm referring to emerges within a discussion of the "secularization thesis"—of which Schmitt's thesis on political theology is taken to be one of many manifestations. As already pointed out, Blumenberg is skeptical regarding an historical succession between theological concepts and modern secular concepts. However, he adds an important proviso, in which probably resides his most important contribution to the discussion.

Indeed, Blumenberg (1985, p. 64) distinguishes between the "content" and the "function" of concepts. His skepticism regarding the "secularization thesis" did not prevent him from accepting a continuity between theological concepts and modern concepts with respect to their "function", although not with respect to their "content". He stated that "totally heterogeneous contents [can] take on identical functions in specific positions in the system of man's interpretation of the world and of himself".

As can be inferred from its last segment, this statement does not refer to political concepts, but to general ideas on the meaning of the world, of man and their purpose. Blumenberg was essentially addressing those thesis, namely Karl Löwith's, which considered modern ideas of historical progress to be secularizations of Christian eschatology. It was in this context that he admitted that the "functions" of both ideas were the same, even if the corresponding "contents" were different. And it was also in this context that he suggested the spurious nature of modern quests which impossibly pretend to offer answers to ultimate questions through the limited means of modern reason. Such questions simply belonged to a past world—as the ideas and concepts providing them with answers—and should not be "reoccupied" with new ideas and concepts.

Given what was already said about political Modernity's indebtedness to itself—and that considering its unsurmountable excesses—what may apply to general questions on the meaning of the world, of man and their purpose does not apply to political questions and consequently *different* negative and anticipatory concepts are still needed to provide persisting questions with answers.

But the point now is that nothing of the above said is intended at denying that the "contents" of core modern political concepts and those of Christian theological concepts are different. The point is that their mode of significance is the same. If one uses Blumenberg's distinction, one may say that they have the same "function".

Indeed, regarding the Trinity, on the one side, and the modern system of national sovereignty on the other, one can make a parallel with Blumenberg's thesis regarding Christian eschatology, on the one side, and the modern idea of progress, on the other.

In Blumenberg, the idea of progress "is viewed neither as a secularized Christian idea nor as a modern idea unaffected by Christianity...it is essentially modern in its content...but heavenly influenced by Christianity in the functions the content [performs]".

The same is valid regarding the system of national sovereignty, which should be viewed neither as a secularized version of the doctrine of the Trinity nor as modern idea unaffected by that doctrine. In this light, the system of national sovereignty is essentially modern in its content but heavenly influenced by the doctrine of the Trinity in the functions the content performs.

Those functions essentially are to settle the world as "constituted", to prevent idolatry (and its dangerous political manifestations) and, most importantly, to warn man against the inevitable frailties of his understanding and judgment—frailties which, in the political world, inevitably carry heavy consequences.

References

Atria, F. (2016). *La Forma del Derecho*. Madrid: Marcial Pons.

Barth, K. (2004). *The doctrine of reconciliation* (*Die Kirchliche Dogmatik – IV – Die Lehre von der Versöhnung 1*, G. W. Bromiley, Trans.). London/New York: Continuum.

Blumenberg, H. (1985). *The legitimacy of the modern age* (*Die Legitimität der Neuzeit* (1973), R. M. Wallace, Trans.) (2nd ed.). Boston: MIT.

Bobbio, N. (1998). Kelsen and legal power. In S. Paulson & B. Paulson (Eds.), *Normativity and norms: Critical perspectives on Kelsenian Themes* (pp. 435–450). Oxford: Clarendon Press.

Brunet, P. (2004). *Vouloir pour la Nation: Le Concept de Representation dans la Théorie de l'État*. Paris: Bruylant/LGDJ.

Carré de Malberg, R. (1920). *Contribution à la Théorie Générale de l'État* (Vol. I). Paris: Recueil Sirey.

Carré de Malberg, R. (1922). *Contribution à la Théorie Générale de l'État* (Vol. II). Paris: Recueil Sirey.

Kantorowicz, E. (1957). *The King's two bodies: A study in mediaevel political theology*. Princeton: Princeton University Press.

Kelsen, H. (2004). *Lineamenti di Teoria Generali dello Stato* (*Grundriss einer allgemeinen Theorie des Staates* (1926), A. Carrino, Trans.). Torino: G. Giapppichelli.

Loughlin, M. (2012). The political jurisprudence of Thomas Hobbes. In D. D. Dyzenhaus & T. Poole (Eds.), *Hobbes and the law*. Cambridge: Cambridge University Press.

Maulin, E. (2003). *La Théorie de l'État de Carré de Malberg*. Paris: PUF.

Pannenberg, W. (1992). *Teologia Sistematica*, I (*Systematische Theologie I* (1988), J. Martinez Camino, Trans.). Madrid: UPCO.

Peterson, E. (1999). *El Monoteísmo como Problema Politico* (*Der Monotheismus als politisches Problem* (1935), A. Andreu, Trans.). Madrid: Editorial Trotta.

Schmitt, C. (1985). *Political theology: Four chapters on the concept of sovereignty* (*Politische Theologie* (1934), G. Schwab, Trans.) (2nd ed.). Chicago: University of Chicago Press.

Schmitt, C. (2008a). *Political theology II – The myth of the closure of any political theology* (*Politische Theologie II* (1970), M. Hoelzl & G. Ward, Trans.). Cambridge: Polity.

Schmitt, C. (2008b). *The Leviathan in the state theory of Thomas Hobbes* (*Leviathan in der Staatslehre des Thomas Hobbes* (1938), G. Schwab, Trans.). Chicago: University of Chicago Press.

Schmitz, A. (2016). Legitimacy of the modern age? Hans Blumenberg and Carl Schmitt. In J. Meierhenrich & O. Simons (Eds.), *The Oxford handbook of Carl Schmitt* (pp. 719–720). New York: Oxford University Press.

Troper, M. (2017). *The structure of the legal system and the emergence of the state*. Straus Working Paper 01/12.

Troper, M. (2018). Souveraineté et Représentation. In Les Défis de la Représentation, ed. by Manuela Albertone and Dario Castiglione. Classiques Garnier, Paris, pp. 76-89.

Luís Pereira Coutinho is Associate Professor at the University of Lisbon's School of Law and senior researcher at CIDP – Lisbon Centre of Research in Public Law. His publications include *Teoria dos Regimes Políticos* (AAFDL, 2013), *O Estado como Representação* (AAFDL, 2019) and, as co-editor, *Eichmann in Jerusalem – 50 Years After* (Duncker und Humblot, 2013), *O Tribunal Constitucional e a Crise* (Almedina, 2014) and *Judicial Activism – An Interdisciplinary Approach to the American and European Experiences* (Springer, 2015).

Part III
Political Constitutional Law

Informal Constitutional Change and Political Law

Manon Altwegg-Boussac

Contents

Abstract Informal constitutional change refers to a change in the normative meaning of the constitution, which occurs without following the procedure for constitutional revision. Theories of informal constitutional change often bolster the argument for a political approach to constitutional law that is sometimes described as "political law"—with a certain degree of ambiguity. In that way, constitutional law cannot be reduced to the study of the written constitution and its interpretation by a judge. Indeed, political law consider the political practice and constitutional interpretation. However, the political approach to constitutional law can pursue very different, more or less prescriptive, objectives since it serves at once to define the constitution, and produce certain representations of constitutional law.

1 Introduction

Theories of informal constitutional change often bolster the argument for a political approach to constitutional law. The expression "political law" (*droit politique*) refers to a French line of doctrinal thinking that is reflected, in particular, in the editorial line of the journal *Jus Politicum*. The approach of "droit politique" stands in opposition to a tendency to reduce constitutional law to the text of the written

M. Altwegg-Boussac (✉)
Paris-Est Créteil University, Paris, France

© Springer Nature Switzerland AG 2020

M. Nogueira de Brito, L. Pereira Coutinho (eds.), *The Political Dimension of Constitutional Law*, https://doi.org/10.1007/978-3-030-38459-3_6

constitution and its interpretation by a judge. This political law approach stems from an observation that presents itself as "realistic", and according to which the meaning of the constitution can evolve outside of the rules provided for its revision.

The notion of informal constitutional change can be defined—starting with Jellinek's work *Verfassungsänderung und Verfassungswandlung. Eine staatsrechtlich-politische Abhandlung*—as "a modification of the constitution that, formally, leaves the text of the constitution unchanged, stemming from facts that do not necessarily derive from an intention to modify the constitution or an awareness of doing so" (Jellinek 1906, p. 3)[1] Informal constitutional change thus refers to a change in the normative meaning of the constitution, which occurs without following the procedure for constitutional revision.[2] The text of the constitution is therefore not altered, while its normative meaning is. A constitutional interpretation is thus deemed capable of altering the original meaning of the constitutional wording.[3]

Discourses regarding informal constitutional changes are highly heterogeneous in two respects. Firstly, they differ in terms of their conclusions. Sometimes, they are forbidden in the name of a formal, or normative, conception of the law. This is one of the predominant positions within cultures of written constitutionalism, and constitutes the more or less accepted view in the field of legal theory.[4] However, authors tend to use the expressions "violation of the constitution" or "political practice" to consider such constitutional interpretations outside the scope of law.[5] Kelsen's concept of "legal revolution" proves to be the only "borderline case" for the normativist approach which admits such informal constitutional changes. In other cases, conversely, such informal changes to the constitution are deemed valid. In other words, it is conceded that the constitutional norm can evolve outside the formal rules provided for the revision of the constitution. This is the line followed by advocates of a "political constitutional law": they are more likely to use notions such as constitutional customs,[6] constitutional conventions,[7] or indeed 'political law, and sometimes make use of a 'realistic' theory of law to support their conclusions.[8]

Secondly, such discourses differ depending on whether they consider constitutional changes initiated by jurisdictional actors or merely political ones. It is difficult to use the term "political" without loading it with the associated positive or negative ideologies and connotations. Two possible approaches present themselves. According to the first approach, only interpretations by actors deemed "political"

---

[1] "Jene Änderung der Verfassung, die die Texte unverändert bestehen lässt und durch Tatsachen hervorgerufen wird, die nicht von der Absicht oder dem Bewusstsein einer solchen Änderung begleitet werden müssen". Jellinek (1906). See Beaud (2001) and Jouanjan (2003).

[2] Altwegg-Boussac (2013).

[3] See Ackerman (1991, 1998), Amar (1994), Griffin (1996) and Levinson (1995).

[4] See Kelsen (1999), Tribe (2000) and Vile (1991). On "textualism", see Schauer (1995).

[5] See Carré de Malberg (2003).

[6] See Capitant (2004).

[7] See Avril (1997).

[8] See Troper (2001).

are pertinent in the context of an approach to "political law", excluding jurisdictional actors. Since they respond to a way of assuming power and a specific regulation of its exercise (election, political accountability), their constitutional interpretations concern the question of "political law".[9] According to the second approach, the problem of 'political law' affects any interpretation of the constitution, regardless of whether it comes from so-called "political" or "jurisdictional" actors. In the latter case, the focus is on interpretative capacity in institutional matters.[10] Even if the argumentative constraints differ, these interpreters of the constitution can put forward a meaning of the constitution that will have legal effects. Therefore, this concerns any actor likely to put forward an interpretation of the constitution. Certain contemporary theories of constitutional change, such as that of Bruce Ackerman, include both types of actors in their consideration of the "construction" of a constitutional change. The first approach has the merit of appealing to current understandings (distinguishing the political from the jurisdictional) and the major balances on which our legal systems are based, but it also tends to distinguish between two different spheres: the "political" and the "law proclaimed by a judge". The second approach uses the word "political" in a more abstract sense but has the merit of highlighting the issue of the interpretation of these actors (competing or constructive) as well as its effects on the meaning of the constitution.

Such constitutional changes produce an "unwritten" constitutional law, with the constitutional text remaining unchanged. When it comes to defending a specific approach to constitutional law—"political law"—what matters most is to ascertain its contribution to the study of constitutional law. Yet in this regard, the functions of these discourses are clearly very different.

We must therefore begin with an observation: informal constitutional changes are no longer understood as an anomaly in written constitution models (1), but rather as a mode of production of unwritten constitutional law (2). This gives rise to different concepts of "political law" (3), the functions of which vary according to their uses (4).

2 An Anomaly in Models of Written Constitutionalism

In cultures of written constitutionalism, constitutional change is traditionally conceived of as an anomaly. "Written constitutionalism" refers to a movement of ideas deriving from the liberal thinking in the eighteenth century underpinning the first modern constitutions in France and the United States. It draws the key principles concerning the limitation of power, representation, and rights guarantee from the British experience. However, unlike "unwritten constitutionalism", or British constitutionalism, cultures of written constitutionalism refer to a moment of

[9]See Waldron (2016).

[10]See Whittington (2001).

"constitutional foundation". This idea of a constitutional foundation in writing refers to four complementary aspects. Firstly, a foundation in history: constitutions relate to a political moment of rupture (revolution, independence). Writing resembles an act of "emancipation" from an earlier regime.[11] British constitutionalism, on the other hand, is somewhat hostile to this concept of foundation inasmuch as it presupposes a rupture.[12] Secondly, it concerns the foundation of a political "order". Written constitutions aim to institutionalise power over the long term. From this perspective, a constitution is not only a fragmented set of statements; it reveals a material unity (one thus speaks of the "spirit of the constitution", its "principle", "idea", or "substantial matter"). Thirdly, there is a legal foundation. A foundation in writing is also a legal foundation: the written form is regarded as the norm. The written constitution thus defines the legal capacities that underpin the exercise of power. Formally, it is considered as the supreme law. Fourthly, there is a political foundation. The written constitution is established *in the name of the people*. It is the expression of a "constituent power": the sovereign people. The distinction between constituent power and constituted powers established by Sieyès reveals the subordination of the latter to the will of the former.

Such a constitutional foundation thus sets itself apart from common law systems, which occur through history. It leads to the regulation of a specific legal timeframe by combining contradictory requirements: allowing the constitution to adapt to social evolution (in order to avoid violent ruptures) and guaranteeing the material stability of the constitution (in order to prevent its distortion). By establishing a special procedure for constitutional revisions, the "constituent power" in France and the United States seek to regulate constitutional change. In terms of form: unlike the unilateralism of constitutional review, the rigid procedure of constitutional revision combines different powers. In terms of content, a difference is established between the "revision", which is permitted, and the "abrogation" of the constitution, which is not: a revision of the constitution should not call into question any of its core substantive content. Indeed, eighteenth century constituents wished to limit the function of constitutional revision to *advancing* the revolutionary cause. In this regard, one might cite the first article of Title VII of the 1791 Constitution, which mentions the "right to amend any of articles whose drawbacks have been proven".

This model of constitutional foundation by means of a written constitution explains why constitutional change outside the procedure of constitutional review is not permitted within the rhetoric of legal actors. An authorised institution (political and jurisdictional actors) cannot explicitly declare that it unilaterally "changes" the meaning of the constitution outside the rules provided for its revision. The constitutional argument supporting controversial decisions is often more elaborate. One might consider the manner in which De Gaulle justified the use of Article 11 on the referendum based on formal arguments in 1962, or indeed the US Supreme Court's use of the theory of changes in circumstances, which is far subtler than that of a

[11]See Beaud (1994).

[12]See Baranger (2008).

change in meaning. It follows that the notion of constitutional change is essentially a doctrinal notion. It springs from observers of the law, who seek to offer an adequate, pertinent presentation of the constitution.

A formal, and radical, perspective denies the legal value of such constitutional changes. From the latter perspective, we are dealing with simple "facts", "violations of the constitution", "practices", or "political uses", which are not the be considered "valid law". According to Kelsen's normativism, there can be no constitutional "change" because the constitutional norm remains intact in the absence of a constitutional revision. The problem with such a discourse is that it can stand at odds with the "real" or "actual" constitution. To overcome this difficulty, more formalistic authors have found themselves obliged to construct a concept of "legal revolution": this concerns the case in which an interpretation contrary to the constitution is produced and accepted, the corresponding meaning not being in accordance with the original system of validity. However, above a certain threshold, the observer must recognise that its object has changed. Legally speaking, the norm exists in another system of validity, and Kelsen's basic norm is displaced (Kelsen 1999, p. 215). This adjustment to the facts reveals the heuristical limits of normativist theory: such constitutional interpretations are either denied or admitted as "valid law" provided we recognize a new legal system."[13]

Against such a reduction of constitutional law to written constitutional norms, the positions in favour of informal constitutional change occupy a field that might be described as "realistic" (the term "realistic" is understood in its common sense here and not in the sense of ontological realism), inasmuch as it claims to offer a "real" representation—that is, one in accordance with practice—of constitutional law.

3 Unwritten Constitutional Law: A "Realistic" Observation

Turning the formal vision of the constitution on its head, another approach does not envisage the constitution through the text, insisting instead on its historical, social or political dimension. From this perspective—which presents itself as "realistic"—the constitution is adopted through history and politics. In this context, the recognition of informal constitutional change essentially derives from an "observation" that claims to be "realistic" or "concrete". According to such an observation, there are major disparities between the text of the constitution and its interpretation by the actors concerned (political or jurisdictional).[14] The observer is not satisfied with merely describing the formal constitution, thus providing an erroneous image of constitutional law.

---

[13]See Pfersmann (2003).

[14]"My descriptive claim is that much-perhaps even most – of "constitutional" work in our legal system is in fact done by legal norms existing outside what we traditionally think of as "the Constitution"". Young (2007).

The observation of several political practices at odds with the balance sought by the constituent power and formalised in the written constitution reinforces this recognition of another constitution, which is unwritten but applied in practice. Whether one considers the transition to the Second Republic in Italy[15] or the reinforcement of the presidential office in the United States, it is this constitutional practice that leads authors to recognise phenomena of informal constitutional change. M. Tushnet, for example, believes that a "political constitution with emergency powers" exists, determined by the political forces: such changes are to be understood as constitutional and not simply "political".[16]

In France, several events led to these conclusions. The example of the 16 May 1877 crisis is revealing in this respect. On this occasion, authors used the expression "Grevy Constitution", a political, unwritten constitution. Indeed, the constitutional texts of the 3rd Republic (intended to be provisional pending the restoration of the monarchy) envisaged a dualist parliamentarianism, with a head of state holding significant powers (namely, right to dissolution, right to dismiss ministers). Mac-Mahon, President of the monarchist Republic, put forward a formal reading of the constitution. At variance with the Republican Chamber, he dismissed Jules Simon, who nonetheless enjoyed the confidence of the Chamber. This letter repudiating Jules Simon was at the origin of the "16 May crisis". The conflict between the Republican Chamber, which invoked its sovereignty, and the head of state, who cited his "responsibility to France", led MacMahon to call upon his right to dissolve the Chamber. After the victory of the Republicans at the legislative and then senatorial elections, MacMahon resigned and gave way for J. Grevy. Once in office, in a famous message addressed to the Chamber, the latter announced that: "*Submitting myself, with the utmost sincerity, to the great law of the parliamentary system, I will never place myself at odds with the will of the country, as expressed by its institutional bodies*". It was these few words that justified the designation "Grevy Constitution". This "actual" or "real constitution", which asserted the dogma of parliamentary sovereignty throughout the 3rd Republic, and even the 4th, was nonetheless unwritten.[17] Conversely, one could take the example of the current 5th Republic: outside of the texts that consider the head of State as an "arbitrator" and a government that "determines the politics of the nation", the political balance is largely in favour of the President of the Republic. The Prime Minister and other ministers are, informally, politically accountable to him.

Numerous examples of such disparities between the practice and the text of the constitution can be found. They suffice for these non-written constitutional practices to be taken seriously. Theoretical tools have thus been fashioned to conceptualise these phenomena of informal constitutional change from the standpoint of political law.

[15]See Rescigno (2000) and Ruggeri (2005).

[16]See Tushnet (2007).

[17]See Prélot (1950).

4 The Concepts of "Political Law"

Each approach to law has its own logic, assumes specific choices and pursues specific goals. Alongside the formal approach to constitutional law, certain conceptions of law also allow for the phenomena of informal constitutional change. The psychological approach to law encountered in authors such as Jellinek considers the ultimate basis of law to reside in the 'forum internum' of individuals. If the basis for the validity of law is psychological, the constitution also evolves in an invisible manner according to perceptions of what is "experienced" as obligatory.[18] Likewise, the sociological approach to law establishes a distinction between the social constitution and the normative one, which must be consistent, while a historical conception of the law, as encountered in Burke, notably, sees the law as "an experience". All such non-formal conceptions of the law allow a place for informal constitutional change.

The political approach to the constitution stands out inasmuch as it places the emphasis on the political principles at the heart of constitutional practice. Whether this concerns the principles of legitimisation or regulation of power (sovereignty of the people, political responsibility, parliamentarism or checks and balances, etc.), or rather the substantive principles that make up the material Constitution (i.e. a unitary content of substantive principles, which may relate to the form of the State—unitary or federal—to the relationship between the State and civil society, welfare State or limited, or to the nature of the political system), this approach denies a formal and disembodied vision of the constitution understood as a fragmented set of norms. Informal constitutional change is as relevant for the political approach as it reveals the gaps in the formal vision of the law. This approach has thus naturally delivered the key concepts that make it possible to grasp these phenomena of informal constitutional changes.

Three types of conceptualisations can be distinguished, each of which—in different ways—supports the existence of a political constitutional law.

The first involves establishing a fundamentally political concept of the material constitution. This sometimes draws on an institutional theory of the constitution found in authors such as Schmitt or Mortati. In Mortati, the concept of the material constitution is defined as the vital principle of the State. Strictly formal approaches are rejected.[19] The written constitution is the expression of a historical-political content. Thus, the rules do not derive from an arbitrary will, but are and *must be* the expression of the live of the people. It is a historical creation that is constantly evolving (Pierandrei 1965, pp. 29–80). The resemblance to Schmitt's theory of the State is striking at this level. Indeed, the same type of conceptualisation can be found in Schmitt (even though the legacy of German historical thought can also be detected). According to Schmitt, the constitution reveals the fundamental decision of a political people concerning the type and form of existence of the State (Schmitt

[18]See Jouanjan (2003).

[19]Mortati (1998).

1993, p. 160). Both Mortati and Schmitt agree that the superior material constitution defines political unity in its historical reality and underpins the validity of the law. It is at once *is* and *ought to be*.

This material definition of the constitution has consequences when it comes to the question of constitutional change. Mortati takes a more specific interest in this phenomenon than Schmitt. The material constitution can change through "constitutional mutations" (*mutamenti costituzionali*), defined as "*tacit modifications of the constitution, whereby the latter evolves imperceptibly in its institutional context, in accordance with historical-political necessities, even if the letter of the written text remains unchanged*" (Pierandrei 1965, p. 516). Consequently, the formal revision process is not exclusive; it is even considered as subsidiary. The formal constitution must adapt to the evolution of the material constitution, with or without revision. For Schmitt, the informal "decision" of the people occurs at a given moment: it can therefore be replaced with another decision on the political form of the State. Far removed from such decisionism, Mortati envisages the change to the material constitution somewhat unclearly. Its content varies depending on the movement of the dominant political forces. The constitution thus encompasses the "vital dynamic of the State; it is to be understood as a whole, which makes it possible to include the "normative force" of the facts" (Mortati 1998, pp. 176–179). This concept falls within political law by isolating the principles of a political constitution in relation to which the "constitutional normative enactments"—to use a Schmittian expression—must adapt. This leads to a clear separation—for the purpose of its accentuation—of the political constitution from the constitution as a set of written norms.

The second form of conceptualisation might be termed dual and moderate. It involves distinguishing first the "normative constitution", or written constitution, and secondly the "political constitution", also called the "working constitution" (Llewellyn 1962, pp. 237–240),[20] "political constitution" (Whittington 2001, p. 1), or even the "small-c constitution" (Levinson 2011, p. 700). This constitution is implicitly accepted by the political actors, who apply it on the assumption that it is binding. There is nonetheless a certain ambiguity in the relationships between these two constitutions: the written and unwritten one. Are they two hermetic constitutional worlds? That of norms grounded on writing and its jurisdictional sanction on the one hand, and of the political regulated by political principles on the other? Or does a form of hierarchy exist between the two constitutions: the one being the formal framework, the enabling framework of the other? In the first case, two distinct objects can be identified: normative constitutional law and political constitutional law. This "political" constitutional law is thus not the "real law", the "normative" law. Such an approach does not tally, then, with the approach to political law that

[20]"Let me attempt further to a seemingly unorthodox position unambiguous: the working Constitution is amended whenever the basic ways of government are changed [. . .] Indeed, amendment occurs typical by action of the relevant specialists along, and without alteration of the Document. Of their own motion they can, and of their own motion or under pressure from interested groups they do, change the manner of government vital aspects, widen it startlingly, ring out old pieces of the Constitution as bells ring out an Old Year". Llewellyn (1962).

stresses the juridical status of political law itself. In the second case, the hierarchy of the constitutions ultimately leads to an admittance of the formal approach: the written constitution is a "framework" that offers various political interpretations. This framework remains formally binding (Avril 1997, pp. 149–150). Moreover, while insisting on the "political" production of constitutional law, such a conceptualisation tends to preserve the model framework of the written constitution.

The third conceptualisation, which is audacious, formalises the conditions of an alternative norm of change, distinct from the written norm of constitutional revision. Bruce Ackerman's theory illustrates this particularly well. It is based on a meticulous reading of history and American constitutional practice, suggesting the existence of an alternative route to constitutional change. This alternative route includes different institutional stages, which range from the institutional conflict between a reformative institution and a conservative one, to the moment at which this conflict of constitutional interpretation is dissolved by the decision of the people. These stages are formalised by the author in very precise terms, beginning with the evolutions of "political regimes" since 1787. This approach revives "political" law in two respects. On the one hand, it formalises a "political" mode of production of constitutional law drawn from the American experience of the practice of power. On the other, these conditions of implementation include the political actors and the Supreme Court, which are both involved in production of constitutional law under the control of the people.[21]

These different conceptualisations draw on phenomena of informal constitutional change to form the basis of an approach to political law. This varies according to the concepts of constitution that are mobilised and the relationships that exist between such a political constitutional law and the written constitution. Furthermore, the functions of these discourses of political law are varied, heterogenous and not always explicit.

5 The Functions of a "Political" Approach

The political approach to constitutional law can pursue very different, more or less prescriptive, objectives since it serves at once to define the constitution, modify the way in which constitutional law is described and, frequently, produce certain representations of constitutional law. The prescriptive element is thus not always situated at the same level of discourse.

Firstly, it may serve to legitimise the exercise of power. The uses of the concepts of political law can provide a limitless resource for legitimising political practices which lack any constitutional basis. Arguments could be drawn from theories of constitutional customs, or from the political constitution, to base an authoritarian use of power in the field of constitutional and political law. It is no coincidence that

[21] Ackerman (1991, 1998).

certain concepts have also been used by authoritarian regimes. Any "violation of the constitution" would thus be dissolved into a "normal" practice of political power. This essentialisation of the "political" self-legitimised by concepts that confer a legal basis upon it can also pose serious problems for the analysis of the law. Indeed it could preclude any critical distance from the exercise of power and its strategies of justification. Therefore, the issue of a "political" approach depends entirely on the preservation of a critical distance through the distinction between several exercises of power: "valid" political law and the violation of the law. Concepts must thus be constructed that make it possible to distinguish uses of power that comply with political constitutional law from those that do not.

This second type of function might be described as "constructive". It is directed at establishing the conditions in which a constitutional interpretation could be qualified as a custom or convention of the constitution. Outside the *Common Law* tradition—and thus in systems that rely on the principle of the supremacy of the written constitution—legal actors rarely recognise the notion of a convention of the constitution. When doctrine does make use of such concepts (a convention of the constitution or constitutional custom), they are presented as descriptive of a mode of production of political law that would be accepted and recognised by the actors concerned. Two problems present themselves in this context. Firstly, these criteria are sometimes difficult to use. The example of the criterion of the acceptance of the rule presents serious difficulties depending on whether a subjective approach is adopted—subjective consent to the content of the rule—or rather an objective one—respect (or application) of the rule in practice. Furthermore, such a description is never truly removed from the prescriptive or dogmatic objective. The latter requires pertinent criteria to be devised that allow a distinction to be drawn between valid political law and non-law. While such criteria vary depending on the actors concerned, they also translate certain balances or principles inherent in constitutionalism: the focus might be on the sovereignty of the people and/or on the balance of power. Thus, the final decision by the people could endorse the new constitutional meaning by bringing to power the party or institution behind it. Nonetheless, this approval by the people,[22] often invoked, rarely suffices. Against a plebiscitary use of democracy leading to a situation wherein any violation of the constitution could be served by a people's vote, more sophisticated mechanisms for the separation of powers are generally considered. Thus, in Ackerman's theory, the people only intervenes following a conflict of interpretations between institutions, to decide on a constitutional issue.[23] Only such a conflict allows the constitutional issues at stake to be crystallised. These criteria, which one encounters for conventions of the constitution in terms of consent to the rule, make it possible to avoid an overly unilateral, deleterious approach to political constitutional law.[24] In the same way, the consideration of a certain threshold for the repetition of a practice has the advantage

[22]On decisionism see Schmitt (1988, 1993).

[23]Cf. Ackerman or Whittington, and the notion of "constitutional construction".

[24]On this issue, see Arato (1995, 2000) and Böckenförde (2000).

of privileging the duration of a practice and thereby guaranteeing a certain stability for political constitutional law. The same is true regarding the criterion (taken from British doctrine) of "a reason for rule",[25] which ensures consistency with the principles of political law.

It matters not if political constitutional law is produced independently of the rule of revision or if the major balances of constitutionalism are reproduced, whether this concerns procedural conditions (agreement, conflict, approval of the people) or the coherence of the rule with the political principles at the heart of the political constitution. This approach offers an attractive vision of political law and removes the fear of self-legitimating political practices. Nonetheless, such practices cannot rely on positive constitutional law, which does not explicitly recognise this mode of legal production. Such criteria are thus determined by doctrine, such that the existence of a political constitutional law is taken seriously, while still guiding a critical discourse. The difficulty lies in the fact that this prescriptive dimension is rarely accepted as such.

At another level of discourse, the functions of a political approach to constitutional law can be understood in terms of representational choices. The first function, probably the most important in contemporary discourse, involves acting upon the study and comprehension of constitutional law by repoliticising it. In this case, the political approach responds to a marked trend, notably in French culture, wherein the political side of constitutional law is abandoned in favour of a normative vision focused on the judicial interpretation of the constitution. The aim is to defend political constitutionalism in response to the model of legal constitutionalism. From this perspective, theories endorsing a "political constitution" make it possible to single out this object. The political constitution is written on a day-to-day basis, with its own rules and independently of the actions of the judge. It is based on standards and reasoning distinct from those employed by jurisdictions, inasmuch as they appeal to values (a "constitutional morality") and principles (representation and political accountability). The constitution thus needs to be "repoliticised" to bring it closer to the citizen, and to the political sphere.[26] This objective must be taken seriously before a form of negligence by one part of the doctrine vis-à-vis this "political" object of constitutional law. According to the latter, that object does not fall within real "law" understood as written law interpreted by a judge. This also

[25]"Something more must be added. As in the creation of law, the creation of a convention must be due to the reason of the thing because it accords with the prevailing political philosophy. It helps to make the democratic system operate; it enables the machinery of State to run more smoothly; and if it were not there friction would result. Thus, if a convention continues because it is desirable in the circumstances of the constitution, it must be created for the same reason. We have to ask ourselves three questions: first, what are the precedents; secondly, did the actors in the precedents believe that they were bound by a rule; and thirdly, is there a reason for the rule? A single precedent with a good reason may be enough to establish the rule. A whole string of precedents without such a reason will be of no avail, unless it is perfectly certain that the persons concerned regarded them as bound by it. And then, as we have seen, the convention may be broken with impunity". Jennings (1955, pp. 131–135).

[26]Waldron (2006).

explains the somewhat paradoxical proclivity of the doctrine towards an accentuated formalisation of concepts of political law.

At a very different, even more abstract level, the last function seeks to *deconstruct* the structures of power to better reveal the discursive modes involved in its exercise. As against an idealist, self-regulated vision of constitutional law, such an approach insists on the normative effects of any interpretation, whether it originates from political or jurisdictional actors. Accordingly, the "political" dimension is conceived, not merely as the object of constitutional law produced by political actors but concerns more broadly any form of exercise of power and thus any interpreter of the constitution capable of determining its meaning. Each interpreter of the constitution thus contributes to the shaping of constitutional law and might be described as "political" since each act of interpretation means an act of power which impacts directly on the meanings of the constitution (whether in relation to fundamental rights or to the major political balances of a specific regime). This approach might be termed "political" in that it takes the political practice of the constitution seriously, but also in a broader sense inasmuch as it calls into question the vision of a Hercules-judge or a judge who "declares the law" by exercising an interpretive activity dependent on knowledge. Often poorly understood, it has the merit of revealing the argumentative strategies and ideologies conveyed in support of such and such an evolution of constitutional law.

Engaging in a reflection on informal constitutional changes has thus allowed us to feed into the argument for "political law", assessing the conclusions that can be drawn from it in the light of different constitutional approaches. As seen, these different approaches to political law pursue very different strategies according to the functions they serve: while they all insist on the political side of the constitution, the focus is not always in the same.

References

Ackerman, A. B. (1991). *We the People: Foundations* (Vol. 1). Cambridge, MA, Londres: The Belknap Press of Harvard University Press.

Ackerman, A. B. (1998). *We the People, Transformations* (Vol. 2). Cambridge, MA, Londres: The Belknap Press of Harvard University Press.

Altwegg-Boussac, M. (2013). *Les changements constitutionnels informels*. Paris: Institut Universitaire Varenne, LGDJ.

Amar, R. A. (1994). The consent of the governed: Constitutional amendment outside Article V. *Columbia Law Review, 94*, 457–499.

Arato, A. N. (1995). Forms of constitution making and theories of democracy. *Cardozo Law Review, 17*, 202.

Arato, A. (2000). Carl Schmitt and the revival of the doctrine of the constituent power in the United-States. *Cardozo Law Review, 21*, 1739–1747.

Avril, P. (1997). *Les conventions de la Constitution, Normes non écrites du droit politique*. Paris: PUF.

Baranger, D. (2008). *Écrire la constitution non écrite: Une introduction au droit politique britannique*. Paris: PUF, Leviathan.

Beaud, O. (1994). *La puissance de l'État*. Paris: PUF, Leviathan.
Beaud, O. (2001). Les mutations de la Ve République ou comment modifier une Constitution écrite. *Pouvoirs, 99*, 19.
Böckenförde, E.-W. (2000). Le pouvoir constituant du peuple. In id. *Le droit, l'État et la constitution démocratique*. Bruxelles, Paris: Bruylant, LGDJ, La pensée juridique.
Capitant, R. (1929 reed. 2004). La coutume constitutionnelle. In *Écrits d'entre deux-guerres (1928–1940)*. Paris, Éditions Panthéon-Assas.
Carré de Malberg, R. (1922 reed. 2003). *Contribution à une théorie générale de l'État*. Paris: Dalloz.
Griffin, M. S. (1996). *American constitutionalism. From theory to politics*. Princeton: Princeton University Press.
Jellinek, G. (1906). *Verfassungsänderung und Verfassungswandlung*. Goldbach: Keip Verlag.
Jennings, I. (1955). *The law and the constitution* (4th ed.). Londres: University of London Press.
Jouanjan, O. (2003). Le problème du changement constitutionnel informel et ses perspectives théoriques dans l'œuvre de Georg Jellinek. In A. Viala (Ed.), *La constitution et le temps*. Lyon: L'Hermes.
Kelsen, H. (1962 reed. 1999). *Théorie pure du droit* (2nd ed.). Bruxelles, Paris: Bruylant, LGDJ.
Levinson, J. D. (2011). Parchment and politics: The positive puzzle of constitutional commitment. *Harvard Law Review, 124*, 657–746.
Levinson, V. S. (1995). How many times has the United States constitution been amended? (A) < 26; (B) 26; (C) 27; (D) > 27. In S. Levinson (Ed.), *Responding to imperfection. The theory and practice of constitutional amendment*. Princeton: Princeton University Press.
Llewellyn, N. K. (1962). *Jurisprudence: Realism in theory and practice*. Chicago: University of Chicago Press.
Mortati, C. (1940 reed. 1998). *La Costituzione in senso materiale*. Milan: Giuffré.
Pfersmann, O. (2003). De l'impossibilité du changement de sens de la Constitution. In *Mélanges en l'honneur de Pierre Pactet, L'esprit des institutions, l'équilibre des pouvoirs* (pp. 353–337). Paris: Dalloz.
Pierandrei, F. (1951 reed. 1965). Saggio sulla teoria della Costituzione. In F. Pierandrei (Ed.), *Scritti di diritto costituzionale*. Turin: Giappichelli.
Prélot, M. (1950). *Précis de droit constitutionnel*. Paris: Dalloz.
Rescigno, U. G. (2000). Una transizione verso una Constituzione non scritta ? *Rassegna parlamentare, 1*, 25–34.
Ruggeri, A. (2005). Revisioni formali, modifiche tacite della Costituzione e garanzie dei valori fondamentali dell'ordinamento. *Diritto e società, 4*, 454.
Schauer, F. (1995). Amending the presuppositions of a constitution. In S. Levinson (Ed.), *Responding to imperfection. The theory and practice of constitutional amendment*. Princeton: Princeton University Press.
Schmitt, C. (1988). *Théologie politique*. Paris: Gallimard, Bibliothèque des sciences humaines.
Schmitt, C. (1993). *Théorie de la constitution*. Paris: PUF, Léviathan.
Tribe, H. L. (2000). *American constitutional law*. New York: Foundation Press.
Troper, M. (2001). Une théorie réaliste de l'interprétation. In M. Troper (Ed.), *La théorie du droit, le droit et l'État*. Paris: PUF, Leviathan.
Tushnet, M. (2007). The political constitution of emergency powers: Some lessons from Hamdan. *Minnesota Law Review, 91*, 1451–1472.
Vile, R. J. (1991). Legally amending the United State constitution: The exclusivity of Article V's mechanism. *Cumberliand law Review, 21*, 274.
Waldron, J. (2006). The core of the case against judicial review. *Yale Law Journal, 115*, 1367.
Waldron, J. (2016). *Political political theory*. Cambridge, MA, London: Harvard University Press.
Whittington, E. K. (2001). *Constitutional construction. Divided powers and constitutional meaning*. Cambridge, Londres: Harvard University Press.
Young, A. E. (2007). The constitution outside the constitution. *Yale Law Journal, 117*, 408–473.

Manon Altwegg-Boussac is Professor of Public Law at the University of Paris-Est Creteil (Paris 12). Associate member of the Michel Villey Institute (Assas University, Paris 2) and of the Legal Theory Research Center (Nanterre University, Paris 10). Her publications include Les changements constitutionnels informels (Institut Universitaire Varenne, Paris, LGDJ, 2013), Le constitutionalisme global, quels espaces pour la disucssion? (Jus Politicum 19, http://juspoliticum.com, 2018), Le concours des organes politique et juridictionnel à la garantie des droits. Regard sur une modélisation alternative de la justice constitutionnelle (Jus Policitum 13: http://juspoliticum.com, 2014), and Le théoricien face aux déconvenues de son objet. Le cas des interprétations défaillantes de la constitution, (*Analisi e diritto ricerche di giurisprudenza analitica*, Torino, 2014).

“Liquid Constitutions” and Their Informal Changes

Carlos Blanco de Morais

Contents

Abstract Certain constitutional courts assign, “on shot” or step by step, normative content to constitutional provisions, modifying them without altering the text, under the pretext of interpretative activity. In consequence constitutional provisions tend to lose their normative identity as law decided by a constituent legislator, legitimized by popular vote and instead begin to assume different and even contradictory shapes determined by judicial rulings which generate the juridical uncertainty of a “liquid constitution”. Those rulings can be described as “impure” constitutional changes since they transpose the constitutional normative reservation, break the principle of constitutional rigidity, twist the limits and techniques of the interpretive function, and make political choices incompatible with the passivity and impartiality of a jurisdiction. In this context, this paper addresses some remedies or other forms of containment of impure informal changes.

C. B. de Morais (✉)
Lisbon’s School of Law, Lisbon University, Lisbon, Portugal
e-mail: cbm@meo.pt

© Springer Nature Switzerland AG 2020
M. Nogueira de Brito, L. Pereira Coutinho (eds.), *The Political Dimension of Constitutional Law*, https://doi.org/10.1007/978-3-030-38459-3_7

1 The Era of "Liquid Constitutions"?

The "liquefaction" to the point, even of evanescence of the normativity of the positive constitution in certain romanist or civil law legal orders refers to the mutability of the content of constitutional norms in the face of modern socio-political developments and the attendant need for judicial normative interpretation. It is one of the most delicate problems of the rule of law to arise since the late nineteenth century.

The phenomenon is linked less to a tendency for courts, and the constitutional courts in particular, to abstain from applying rules, but rather to the ways such courts apply constitutional norms that do not objectively flow from the Constitution. Indeed, the courts/judges frequently create norms under the guise of interpretation and gap filling in a way which amounts to political decision-making.

Here we refer to judicial rulings that denature the structure of the positive norm, distance themselves from the objectivity of the "constitutional program" and can at times be transformed to the extent they no longer reflect the will of the constituent power. The consequence is to plunge uncertainty in legal relationships and further to cast doubt on the role of constitutional courts, as custodians of the Constitution, within observance of the separation of powers. To this extent these courts or judges overstep a borderline and meddle in discretionary political-legislative decision-making.

Assuming that a Constitution is the statutory basis of political sovereign authority as well as the relations between society and that authority,[1] it becomes evident that social reality as the object of constitutional regulation interacts with the same Constitution. If, as the institutionalists maintain, when we find a "society" we find "law", and if the influences of a new sociopolitical dynamics in civil and political society impacts on substantive changes in ordinary laws and in the organization of the state, then it seems evident that such changes influence the Theory of the State and generate transformations in state constitutions.[2]

The expression "liquid constitution", used here figuratively, is to be understood in the light of recent transformations in civil and political society in the western democratic states. Such developments amount to a form of modernity which certain sociologists such as Bauman (2001) have called "liquid modernity".

The "liquid society", furrowed by the metamorphoses of the abovementioned modernity, would move on, contrary to the "solid" texture of twentieth-century society (the time of all emancipations, revolutions and myths), without following a guiding project, a design or an utopia: its members are predominantly mobilized by the disorderly pursuit of individual pleasure, in a free market economic order shaped on a global scale. Such "liquidity" would stem from the lack of a definite form or a

---

[1] See Burdeau (1956), p. 59 ff. Adopting this definition Miranda (2013), p. 25; de Morais (2018), p. 39.

[2] In general, see Kriele (2009), pp. 24 ff., 29 ff.

vertical structure, rendering it incapable of "solidifying", but rather seeking to assume the various forms that market dynamics oblige or induce.

For Bauman, the pre-existing "solid" universe begins to "melt" due to a set of factors, of which the following may be detailed:

i) traditional loyalties, rights, customary obligations and family structures (increasingly transformed into a category of scarce relevance or reference in people's lives) would dissolve (2001, p. 9); and the basis of society would begin to be founded on the empire of the economy and an increasingly individualized modernity;
ii) the territorial dimension of power would be lost in favor of a contraction of borders and the loss of national references, a situation fostered by the globalization of goods, capital, people and information, while real power assumes diffuse contours, and capital would "nomadize", without defined actors, control or fixed geographical centres;
iii) the state and the nation would lose their integrative role for society, as protector of the interests of its collectivities, exercising sovereign monopoly of the use of force, giving way to supranational orders, transmitting responsibilities both upwards and downwards, to the benefit of infra-state communities, corporate interests and disaggregated identities (2001, p. 125);
iv) the main political authorities would fade, since both global capitalism and the vertigo of hyper-control of the state public powers would lead to the multiplication of those same authorities. In consequence, each of them would smoothly be emptied of power and status, their powers of command weakening to be replaced by the art of seduction of those who choose them;
v) the search for a more just community would have given rise to a form of society that would consume itself in the hypertrophy/ of fundamental human rights of individual bias, locking the citizen into a psychological state of individual hedonism diluted in a global universe;
vi) the idea that working activity is the normal condition of mankind, increasing the wealth of nations and rendering the individual the 'master of their own fate' would fade, giving way to a disorganized society where the "marriage" of capital and labour would dissolve, robotization and labour redundancy would spread, workers would perform their functions outside the company, while protective structures such as unions would lose their role; the result would be a model of society where individuals would be exempted from working and would be entitled to a universal basic income (2001, pp. 155, 170–174);
vii) the dissolution of norms, with their increasing lack of clarity, would tend to create a framework of anomie and uncertainty, fostering a society ruled by case decision, lack of rational and integrative order, informal normative transformation, evolving towards to spongiform legal systems, with an absence of effective obedience to objectively identifiable legal rules (2001, pp. 11, 28).

2 Judicial Activism and Informal Changes in the Constitution from a Judicial Source

From a normative point of view, the "liquid constitution" absorbs the symptomatology of a "liquid society" which itself forms part of the object of constitutional regulation.

However, the dissolution of legal norms has a clear impact on the stability, rigidity and political programming of the Constitution. Constitutional provisions tend to lose their normative identity as law decided by a constituent legislator, legitimized by popular vote and instead begin to assume different and even contradictory shapes, meanings and contents distinct from of the original provisions. In other words, certain courts assign, "ex abrupto" or step by step, substantive content to constitutional provisions, modifying them without altering the text, under the pretext of interpretative activity.

The resulting loss of hermeneutical reference anchored in a science of law means that a constitutional provision will not infrequently acquire different meanings within in a relatively short period of time, with certain constitutional judicial bodies delivering contradictory and inadequately reasoned judicial decisions on those subjects. Basically, in certain jurisdictions, the constitutional norm is everywhere but nowhere: in the text, in the minds of legal operators, in the thinking of law-makers, or in the writing of judges, even acquiring differing/divergent meanings in identical or parallel situations.

This sort of constitutional fluidity has several causes, some of them derived from the irradiation of "liquid modernity", as sketched above: (i) the expansion of supranationality and the deterritorialization of power, coupled with a multiplier effect of real or supposed new fundamental rights guaranteed by international jurisdictions, generate new exogenetic decision-making criteria that drive constitutional reinterpretations not always reflecting national realities; (ii) the loss or deformation of legal methodology in the process of interpretation of constitutional norms by the courts; (iii) the fading of normative prominence of the legislative power as a popular legitimized institution to make public policy choices, in favor of constitutional justice "law making" as an autonomous function of the judiciary, self-invested with the authority to fill power gaps, to arbitrate institutional power-plays, to correct and even replace constitutional and ordinary legislators.

Each of these causes of constitutional liquefaction may be examined in more detail.

Supranationality, notably within the European Union, raises unresolved problems in the field of regulatory certainty. In particular, we are constantly confronted with the overall question of the supremacy of European law over the member state constitutions, as supported by the Court of Justice of the European Union. This relationship is at times denied or relativized by several constitutional courts, notably the German Federal Constitutional Court of Karlsruhe, which uphold the supremacy of the normative fundamental structure of the national constitution. Resistance to the supposed supra-constitutional role of European law has prompted doctrinal currents such as the "Multi-Level Constitution"[3] approach in order to overrule dissent.

Some authors who support the supranational trend, identified with the so-called "constitutionalism of the social sciences", sustain/ a need to replace an "old" constitutional theory, erected on the allegedly eroded bases of the sovereign state (the nation state), by a new constitutional theory, in line with a postmodern state model, at once interdependent and inserted into the orbit of a European and even global constitutionalism.[4] The Constitution would become normatively malleable, made of composed principles, served by a low intensity system of constitutional control, and porous to the influence of international law. Such a Constitution would be opening its interpretation to the "normative environment" of the internal and external political and financial reality that would accommodate norms to the realities of the market.

The meaning of positive constitutional norms would thus assume various forms and qualities, based on a sort of jurisdictional "interpretivism", conditioned by genetic factors external to the Constitution and to the state itself. Here, certain scholars argue that the Constitution, despite its hierarchical superiority, should be interpreted in accordance with international law and even with the soft law of international market rules.

At the same time, there are symptoms which signal the fading of the legal methodology in the interpretation of constitutional norms, resulting in a lack of objectivity and perceptiveness. This is a slippery phenomenon that derives from a number of factors, such as the kaleidoscopic multiplication of disparate interpretative theories[5]; the topical temptations of an impatient interpreter with an eagerness to bend the norm to the fact; the use and abuse of balancing, a technique that raises uncertainty in resolving cases that at times are straightforward; and the use of manipulative decisions of all kinds. The excessive weight that supra-positivistic and moralist jurisprudence confers on legal principles, the ease with which rules are dissolved into principles of neutral and diffuse object, the agility with which jurisprudence changes without sound reasoning, and the "hocus pocus" brand of normativity given to legal formulas created by certain constitutional courts, all combine to create a picture of anomie and insecurity regarding the outcome of judicial proceedings.

Certain scholars tend to speak of an era of weakening of legislative power to the benefit of constitutional courts, which thereby become the masters rather than servants of the Constitution. These masters try to combine the functions of "vigilante"

[3]On "multilevel constitutionalism", see Perez Luño (2011), p. 86 ff; Häberle (1993, 2000a), p. 120 ff; McCormick (1993), p. 1 ff; Maduro (2003), p. 76; Kumm (2009, 2012); Camerlengo (2007).

[4]See Kumm (2012), p. 263 ff.; Tuebner (2016), pp. 51, 68 ff; Medeiros (2015), pp. 20 ff., 32 ff.

[5]Canosa Usera (1988), p. 135, although defending the plurality of interpretive methods and the specificity of constitutional interpretation attentive to the political and axiological openness of norms, admits that *"the amalgam of data and instruments constitutes interpretation as an almost chaotic reality" that would recall a "pharmaceutical product"*.

with authoritative interpreter, giving the ultimate word on the meaning of norms, with the self-invested status of a broker, arbiter and even supplementary legislator.

By virtue of the at times contradictory appeals of a dissatisfied and atomized society, certain constitutional courts rule on cases concerning subjects which should be more properly integrated in the hemisphere of politics and morality. On the other hand, due to excessive exposure to political and partisan criteria in the appointment of judges, constitutional justice organs tend to politicize the administration of justice in their rulings. As a result of all this, such courts in some jurisdictions abandon the role of Kelsen's negative legislator and the status of *the least dangerous branch*, to a disquieting role as at the head of a moderating function, identical to dualist monarchs of the nineteenth century.

When constitutional courts opt to appeal to "values" discovered behind the underlying principles, often shaped by the preconceptions of the judges themselves or the noise of the street, the Pandora's box of the so called "tyranny of values" anticipated by Schmitt (1961), p. 65 ff. is opened, releasing a tendency towards the contamination of judgments by politics and by the dominant morality of the Day, which in turn generates a concerning degree of legal insecurity. As a body of power, constitutional justice is subject to the principle of the separation of powers, under which the exercise of its function can't overstep the constitutional limits inherent in an authority of control to became an institute of political command.

The way in which some constitutional courts treat the meaning of constitutional and ordinary norms, observing neither literal, systematic nor historical limits, contributes to a gradual loss of constitutional normativity, certainty and respect for the will of democratically elected majorities. The concept of constitutional justice as a counter-majoritarian body is a dangerous absurdity. Constitutional courts are required to be independent and impartial in the application of constitutional law to the litigation submitted to them by those who have *locus standi* for this purpose, be they majorities or minorities, government or opposition, individuals or public institutions. Their role is as much the defence of majorities as of minorities, all depending on the relation of meaning that they attribute to the norms, through an interpretative method that must be juridical, since it is expressed by a court. The constitutional courts cannot be converted either into a second or third parliamentary chamber, nor into a sovereign moderator, nor into a political veto-player legitimized by a form of "minority principle, that empowers all sorts of oppositions to challenge the law adopted by the majority".

All the problems that arise regarding the "liquidity" of constitutional norms, as noted in the previous section, are inseparable from the transformations experienced by these norms, as a result of the activity of interpretation they occasionally experience at the hands of constitutional justice.

This groundbreaking "transformism" connects the notion of "judicial activism" introduced in 1947 by Arthur Schlesinger Jr., who used it to criticize a particular US Supreme Court ruling.[6] For critics, "activism" would be based on scenarios where

[6]See Green (2009), p. 1195.

judges, rather than following and applying the rule of law, would follow norms built by themselves, according to their own preconceptions and unsupported in the Constitution or the law.[7] In such cases, a phenomenon emerges of usurpation of the functions of the legislative and executive bodies by the court, albeit partial in nature and exhibiting diverse degrees of intensity.[8]

The definition of judicial activism that is evoked here follows with some twists one of the most solidly methodologically sound works on the subject in the Portuguese language world.[9] Activism *consists of a deviation in the exercise of the jurisdictional function, exceeding the constitutional limits of the principle of the separation of powers and which is characterized by a deliberate incursion of decisions of the courts in the core of the substantial functions constitutionally committed to the legislative and executive powers.*

As already noted, judicial activism assumes varying degrees and forms, but the dimension that fundamentally concerns this paper lies in the incursion, by the bodies of constitutional justice into the substantive field of the constitutional legislator.

As higher law, itself the product of an unconditioned sovereign act, and legitimized by a free decision attributed to the will of the people (de Morais 2018, p. 196), modification of the Constitution requires a qualified deliberation and thus, a more intense democratic decision than that involved in the production of ordinary legislative acts. By definition, there needs to be a formal act of constitutional amendment. Constitutional amendment procedures presuppose the adoption of normative modifications, deletions and additions by a qualified majority in a representative assembly, all in compliance with a set of formal, substantive and, in some cases, temporal limits enshrined in the constitution. Constitutional rigidity contrasts with the common procedures required in ordinary legal acts, with the purpose that the consensus of regime subsists as time goes by and is not object of contingent or accidental modifications.

Changes in the contents of constitutional norms made under the pretext of an interpretative activity, ignoring the amendment procedure established by the Constitution itself, may constitute either a misuse of power (deviation of the end of the interpretative function) or an usurpation of powers (incursion of a power at the heart of a state function committed to other powers).

This raises the problem of *informal changes* in the Constitution (de Morais 2016, p. 65), as norms of politically innovative content generated and gradually consolidated in time by political and judicial powers, and which operate derogations on constitutional rules, stoppage of their effectiveness, transformation of the meaning of their political program or "ex novo" additions to the constitutional order, without any visible grounding on text that subsists untouchable.

---

[7]See Alexander (2015), p. 16.

[8]Idem.

[9]See Ramos (2010), p. 116 ff.

Informal constitutional changes can have varied sources, of which the following are the most significant: (i) *sources of spontaneous formation*: this is the case of custom (*praeter* and *contra legem*); practices and constitutional conventions that modify the functioning of the political system by creating informal, binding or soft law rules; as well as the misuse of principles and rules, which generates their progressive nominalization or normative expiration; (ii) *legislative and conventional sources*, generated by the infra-constitutional will of political institutions that informally dislodge or derogate the contents of constitutional norms, without relevant opposition or sanction: this is the case of legislative and administrative decisions *contra constitutionem*; European Union law which is contrary to written constitutional rules; and the political impact of cosmopolitan "trans-constitutionalism" embodied in treaties; (iii) *jurisprudential sources* of interpretative and integrative basis that create innovative constitutional norms and involve decisions of the Court of Justice of the European Union; the so-called additive judgments of constitutional amendment; and an impalpable constructive activity based on jurisprudential formulas extracted from principles or values and expressed in the hermeneutical function of the constitutional courts (de Morais 2018, p. 234; Carducci 2009, p. 1911 ff.).

The weight of constitutional justice in the phenomenon of informal mutation of the constitution is considerable, not only because, aside from the normative transformations it itself generates under the pretext of its interpretative function, it has also the power to invalidate informal changes generated by the other constituted powers through its activity of judicial review. In fact no possible informal mutations can be effected against the will of constitutional justice.

The liquefaction of constitutional norms is accordingly one of the effects of the substantive changes effected by the constitutional court, since the content of constitutional norms is transformed with a jurisdictional "stroke of the pen" and not through due observance of the constitutional process, converting the guardian of the Basic Law into a substantive legislator. It has been remarked that a Constitution is fundamentally a prescriptive rule invested with a position of supremacy, strength and solemnity that must be internalized and accepted by institutions and citizens. However, it must be asked whether a strong concept of the Constitution legitimized by the constituent power can be compatible with a decisionist act of a constitutional court which awards itself/invest itself with the competence to replace the "we the people" rule-making standard by a form of "constitutional production" rule-making dictated by "we the judges"[10]?

Laband during the nineteenth century noted the existence of these tacit changes, and identified some of their modalities, pointing out that they represented a "*contradiction between the constitutional situation and constitutional law*" and established a conceptual differentiation between reform and constitutional informal change.[11] Jellinek, however, outlined an attempt to categorize mutations, with severe

[10]See La Torre (2015), p. 5.

[11]On Laband's differentiation, see Hesse (2009), pp. 151–152.

restrictions on their admissibility. At the same time he pointed out the difficulty, which still persists, in fixing legal limits to these silent/unexpressed/tacit transformations, which are characterized by being a "fait accompli" "*against which any opposition may be a vain attempt*".[12] Lin (1998), a Chinese jurist and disciple of Smend, has carried out a re-elaboration of the types of mutations during the Weimar Constitution. Accordingly, the Constitution could not remain in a static position *vis-à-vis* a state and a society in flux, with informal changes resulting naturally from an imperative adjustment of constitutional norms to changing reality. The "*raison d'être*" of mutations would thus lie in the political necessity and vitality of an evolving state.

In the United States, informal changes were expressed in the nineteenth century through the notion of the "living constitution" created by political practice and jurisprudence. The issue gained special prominence with the McCulloch v. Maryland case (1819), and Marshall defended a certain constitutional constructivism, relying on the implicit powers clause, which met with little resistance.[13] It should be noted, however, that in the Anglo-Saxon world, informal changes to the Constitution are bound up with customary law and common law statutory interpretation in a long-standing process that leads Tribe (2008, p. 22) to assume that, alongside a visible textual constitution, there is an invisible constitutional normativity that challenges the linearity of the fundamental law as the finished product of a constituent decision.

During the twentieth century, there were cycles in which the U.S. Supreme Court sustained a dynamic ideology of interpretation rooted in constructivism, "jurisprudence of values" and realism itself, inaugurating activist periods that paved the way for further legislative reform processes. During the Earl Warren Presidency (1953–1969), the U.S. Supreme Court convened the 14th Amendment (equality), based on which Brown v. Board of Education adjudicated the unconstitutionality of segregation in schools ("separate but equal"). In the case of Griswold vs. Connecticut, the Court upheld the right to privacy and reinterpreted the 1st Amendment (freedom of expression) so as to consider pornography legal, insofar as the material was not reduced to something unconditionally worthless (Memmoirs vs Massachussets). Under the Earl Burger Presidency (1969–1986), the Court went significantly further and supported the validity of affirmative racial actions, with university quotas for blacks (University of California vs. Bakke). Based on "privacy" and the substantive due process clause (a principle of diffuse object), the right of women to abortion was accepted (Roe vs. Wade). The resulting set of political criteria subsequently influenced other jurisdictions.

However, the realities described in terms of constitutional changes do not detract from the contemporary liquefaction of constitutional norms derived from informal changes seen in Europe and South America particularly, for two fundamental reasons.

---

[12]On Jellinek's construction, see Hesse (2009), pp. 154–155.

[13]See de Morais (2018), p. 698 ff.

First, the object of this analysis is based on informal changes from a jurisprudential source, so that the transformations generated in nineteenth century Germany, at a time when there was no constitutional justice outside the United States, not only had scarce fundamental impact, but they also lie outside of the scope of this analysis. Second, the U.S. jurisprudential system has long lived with the logic of law-creating judges passing judgments with a degree of innovative content. This is a different reality from the European civil law legal systems, where positive law is given greater weight. Within civil law systems the role of the courts was always limited in this respect and the constitutional court was born in the twentieth century out of the paradigm of Kelsen's negative legislator.

What is most interesting to note, particularly in Europe and in the greatest power of South America, Brazil, is the way in which the negative legislator has been taken over by an increasingly creative normative jurisdiction that has not hesitated, with more or less discretion, in effecting transformations in the content of constitutional norms.

It should be pointed out, however, that not all jurisdictional creativity results in political innovation, that not all the evolutionary interpretation of the courts involves constitutional change, and also that not all constitutional informal changes violate the separation of powers principle and as such are legally illegitimate. The normativity of a constitution can never be reduced to its text alone, since any constitution that is positively decided is never a finished construction.

In addition to formal amendments through textual changes, constitutions also suffer informal and diffuse changes that weaken, add or modify its normative meaning, without the corresponding precepts undergoing any transformation in the respective text. In a certain metaphorical way, as alluded to by Wheare (1966): "*constitutions are not made: they grow*". In theory, this sort of enlargement can result from formal changes. In certain cases, however, informal mutations stem from a jurisdictional source, and this sort of phenomena deserves additional attention in these lines.

3 Jurisdictional Interpretation as Pretext and Path Towards the Permanent Exercise of a "Diffuse Constituent Power"

There are interpretative operations of an evolutionary nature which, in essence, respecting the content of a constitutional provision, modify the meaning previously given to them, insofar as they adjust the object and scope of those rules to variations that occur in the present moment in the universe of values, facts and economic and political changes.

Contrary to the situation described, but intersecting with it, some informal changes in the Constitution take place when constitutional jurisdictions, with or without connection with positive constitutional law, invoke their interpretative powers to produce material norms contained in judgments, that is, innovative criteria of decision-making policy inserted in judicial rulings. This phenomenon cannot be reduced to a question of simple normative creativity by extending or adjusting the law to new realities safeguarding the text and the basic program of the precept, but rather a political-normative innovation that transforms the content of the norm, resulting from a free or discretionary choice made by the Court between political options attached to the legislative activity.

Basically, those judgments segregate "de facto" primary material norms of constitutional status that have not been decided by anyone to whom the Constitution confers legal and political legitimacy for this purpose. As Schmitt warned (1983), p. 79, a law is not the same as a judgement and vice versa. From the moment the judge models the Constitution in an innovative way, he will remove the ideas of justice, impartiality and independence from the activity he is developing.

For various illustrious exponents of the *morally reflexive constitutionalism* (a sort of secular supra-positivism or "jus-naturalism without natural law"), who acted as constitutional judges, the informal changes in the Constitution are no more than expressions of interpretative activity, not keeping a true autonomy in relation this same function.[14] It is an intelligent and sagaciously understanding that was adopted perhaps less from deep conviction on its dogmatic accuracy and more as a pragmatic strategy of decision, since it is a source of a diffuse legitimation narrative for normative changes produced by some activist Constitutional Courts. The modern architect of this thesis which merges interpretation and informal changes of the Constitution is the German constitutionalist Peter Häberle, whose hermeneutic prescriptions lie for Constitutional Theory as George Soros does for politics.

Häberle is, in our days, the great somber reference of constitutional liquidity processed through a viscous interpretation "model", whose objective is to dehydrate the objective normativity of constitutional precepts. For the author, a Constitution would be a permanent development project in a pluralistic society, open to external influence, cultural changes and utopia itself, so that its norms would not be shaped by eternal truths but by provisional truths (2000a, b, pp. 85 ff., 105). Legal norms can only be interpreted norms and interpretation implies the placement of the same norm in the time and in the public reality, thereby conferring a provisional nature to the validity of the solutions of the interpretive activity. The interpretative role of Constitutional Court should be relativized since it would work in an "open society of interpreters" that would refuse a closed cast of interpreters of the Fundamental Law (2002, p. 13). The open society of interpreters of the Constitution would be participant in the process of trial and error, in the "*discovery and obtaining of the law*", registering a tendency for the "*overestimation of the meaning of the text*".[15]

---

[14]See Mendes (2016), p. 255; Ribeiro (2014), p. 606 ff.

[15]Häberle (2002), p. 43.

At the methodological level, Häberle proposes the reasoning path of "*possible alternatives" and* offers the comparative route as a new element of the interpretative process (which constitutes the great escape for "constitutional cosmopolitanism" and for the motorized circulation of jurisprudence sedimented around an European "ius comunne" of federal bias). For the author[16] the "thought of the possible" is the thought of alternatives. It should be open *"for third or fourth odds as well as for compromises"*, and for him the Science of Constitutional Law should not renounce the fantasy and the creative force of interpreters. This thought would pave the way for today's reality to correct that of yesterday, adapting the norm to the "fait divers" of the moment, even if the new is not necessarily better.

As a concrete effect of this line of thought on the issue at hand, Häberle (1978): denies any dogmatic autonomy to the phenomenon of informal changes of the Constitution, stating that there is only constitutional interpretation and that "mutation is a problem of interpretation".[17] Such an understanding has relevant consequences, insofar as the author defends with his theory of probabilities, a dialogical interpretation with topical bias and a way of reasoning that is inherently provisional, allowing constitutional norms to change color, like chameleons. For the constitutionalist-philosopher the validity of interpretive solutions, always being provisional. This supposed hermeneutical discourse, now with little weight in Germany, but with great prominence in very activist jurisdictions such as the Court of Justice of the European Union and the Brazilian Supreme Court, has been the subject of well-founded objections.

Four points of this line of thought must be critically appraised.

In first place, the understanding that any legal norm is an interpreted norm violates the principle of separation of powers if it coincides with the understanding of Müller (1993), p. 224 ff, according to whom, to interpret is to produce the norm and that before the operation of interpretation there is no norm but a text. But it is not so. A constitutional rule is not a mere text or sheet of paper (in the line of Lassalle (2013), p. 102), but a legal command based in a political criterion of decision, adopted by the constitutional legislator who aims to order the State and the society. It involves not only a drafting process, but also a political approval of a binding standard or prescription that the legislator introduces with constitutive effectiveness and democratic legitimacy.

The same legislator cannot be reduced to a coroner, since he was democratically legitimated to act as a decision-maker, to produce innovative law invested in hierarchical supremacy on the basis of a political program or a consensual articulation between various programs. On the other hand, the courts are bodies that perform a secondary, impartial and passive state function and, as such, they do not have a positive legal and democratic legitimacy to produce primary law competing or derogating the current Constitution. The interpretation of norms, as an instrumental activity of judicial review (control of constitutionality), is a legal task and must, by

[16]Häberle (1980), p. 3 ff.

[17]Häberle (1978), p. 88 ff.

means of a legal method, reveal the meaning of the constitutional commands decided by constitutional legislator or, even, concretize it in its adjustment to a given fact, but not transform or twist what was objectively decided upon in it.

Secondly, the "open society of interpreters" is a commonplace whose semantic hyperbolization ends up decreasing the authority of the Constitutional Court and precariously emphasizing the unity of interpretation, extending the number of interpretive agents "ad infinitum" and allowing changes in the content of the precepts that are unstable and fortuitous, floating to the taste of new fashions, moral bias and dispersed realities. The fact is that the plurality of interpreters is a long-standing fact since all procedural subjects assert their points of view in the contradictory mechanics inherent to a constitutional process (or outside it, in the spheres of scholarship and public opinion). But the fact is that the last word on the authoritative interpretation proceeds from Constitutional Justice, unless its interpretation is overruled by the legislative power of constitutional amendment, the last seat of an authentic interpretation.

The author seeks to sketch, on the basis of a constitutional theory of "murky waters", two objectively distinct realities: the activity of constitutional control and constitutional interpretation. The interpretation of the Constitution is a legal process anchored in a method whose objective is to understand, reveal and establish the meaning of the normative dispositions that integrate it. It is an indispensable but instrumental activity to the function of control of constitutionality in a judicial review process. However, an activity of control consists on determining whether a certain norm is consistent or not with a given constitutional parameter. Interpretation, as a tool of control, extracts the correct meaning from the content of the two norms in tension and then focuses on the norm object of review, accordingly issuing a judgment of conformity or nonconformity with the Constitution. The construction of Häberle inverts this position: it converts the main activity of Constitutional Justices into an interpretative function, and places it in competition with a number of other entities. This "mélange" of review and interpretation moves the activity of normative command from the legislator to a network cloud of interpreters mediated by the Court, which is converted into a floppy Phytoness,[18] thereby reducing the scope of separation of powers.

Interpretation, to assume a minimum of scientific credit, must conform itself to a framework and must follow a legally-based method, even if there is no single method for it and even if it can assume some complementary or concrete normative creativity. As for the "consensus" obtained in this pluralist society of interpreters, interpretation does not amount to an act of "social dialogue" in which the meaning given to the norm, even without any fidelity to its text, results from an utilitarian compromise between the main legal and political operators, before whom the Constitutional Court is reduced, as the case may be, to a notary or a cash register of external impulses.

Third, at the methodical level, floating interpretations around "possible alternatives" conceived by the judge on the basis of exogenous factors (such as social

[18]Priestess in Delphi who acted as an oracle, predicting the future.

fashions, topical exercises, street noise, foreign jurisprudence, the public opinion, and the politician-philosophical convictions of the magistrate) tend to generate legal uncertainty, loss of the normativity of the Constitution, and erratic judicial decisionism. Far from revealing the meaning of constitutional law, the judicial decision-maker zigzags between probabilities, many of which have no textual basis, logic, or consistency with the legislative will. In reality, when the Court follows this method, it interprets nothing: it rather amends the Constitution without an enabling credential to do so.

Still at the methodical level, Häberle tried to create a fifth element of interpretation in addition to the literal, logical-systematic, historical and teleological ones: it would be the comparison standard, which would serve as a way of promoting constitutional cosmopolitanism. This proposal generates the hypertrophy of a mere auxiliary tool of interpretation, incapable of functioning as the fifth autonomous element of an interpretive program. In the first place, as Perelman and Olbrechts Tyteca (1999), p. 221 ff. argues, comparison is a "point of view" or a complementary resource that reinforces an argument under construction and not an interpretive stage or canon by itself. It can be a component of the historical element whose composite morphology also includes the jurisdictional precedent, *occasio legis*, and genetic interpretation linked to the intention of the legislator. And this integration in the historical element is justified by the fact that it involves the study of past or present legal regimes as well as pre-existing jurisprudential and doctrinal guidelines which are useful the actual interpretive operation and that, due to the similarity of situations, can compete from an argumentative point of view.

The truth is that the comparative "element" is scarcely visited by the most powerful constitutional courts in the world—the Supreme Court of the United States and the German Federal Constitutional Court—, which are quite self-referential and, with few exceptions, follow the quote that foreign scholarship or jurisprudence "must be known but not quoted". The concrete use of comparison, in order not to turn it into an odd argument of authority or a dazzled manifestation of legal provincialism, implies that: (i) comparisons must be made between similar legal orders and within the same constitutional family; (ii) they must concern rules which are equal or have a relevant identity between themselves and which are applicable in very analogous political and socio-cultural environments; (iii) the problematic situations to be clarified or fulfilled must be alike; (iv) and the guidelines convened must remain actual and be practiced in the legal order that prescribes them.

If comparison is used in a cherry-picking logic of stray orientations, to justify the removal of a solution derived from a solid interpretive course in favor of a foreign precedent, the use of comparison compromises the primacy of the Constitution and the effectiveness of its standards. Worse, it may lead to the capture or colonization of constitutional regulation by external normative sources with the "liquefaction of the sovereign nature of the constitutional order" (de Morais 2018, p. 648).

Finally, normative activism and constitutional informal change do not technically relate to the interpretative activity. When one invokes the interpretation or integration of gaps to directly address an absolute unconstitutional omission, with the partial fabrication of a new norm by a court of law, on the basis of a political choice judgment of the best option from among a plurality of not unconstitutional solutions, that operation goes beyond the limits of interpretation and integration. This was the case in Brazil with an injunction regarding the right to strike by public servants, who, due to a legal omission, applied to them the legal regime of strike for private sector workers, but with normative amendments created by the Brazilian Federal Supreme Court itself.

When, in Germany, the application of constitutional rules to new and relevant legal developments which are not set out in the text nor represented in the legal community—as in the case of the Federal Constitutional Court's Lüth judgement (BverfGE, 7, 198)[19] in which it was decided that fundamental rights should not only bind public powers, as the Constitution expressly provides for, but also private parties—, the Constitution is being changed and not merely technically interpreted anymore.

In both situations, the first involving some sort of capture of ordinary legislative powers and the second an informal constitutional change with an interpretative disguise, the constitutional norms are not interpreted, but rather amended *ex novo* by the Court.

Constitutional Courts were created to defend the Constitution and not to change it. When constitutional justice materially produces primary constitutional norms, it bypasses both the consensus required by the Constitution from other powers and the cumbersome procedures that the Constitution itself establishes for amending the "rules of the game" on institutional relations. It is a matter of concern when de Court does so in the context of an existential aura of absolutist sovereignty, invoking the last word on the authentic interpretation of the Constitution. This situation goes to the point of the Court being able to challenge the possible overruling of his decisions by the legislator through constitutional amendment, with the informal warning by some judges that the amendments themselves will be considered unconstitutional by offense of substantial limits of amendment that the same Court converts in elastic standards.[20]

[19]Böckenforde (2000), p. 192 ff.

[20]In response to uncommon statements of unconstitutionality of constitutional amendments made by the Brazilian Federal Supreme Court, based on the violation of substantial limits for constitutional amendment, a constitutional amendment was drafted, PEC 33, which was presented in the Congress in order to limit the competencies of the Supreme Court. According to this proposal, the Federal Supreme Court would need to rule on the invalidation of any amendment by a qualified majority and, in case of opposition from the Congress to that ruling, the matter would have to be decided by the people in popular consultation. Some Federal Supreme Court Justices warned, in public statements, that if passed, PEC 33 would be deemed unconstitutional for violation of the substantial limit of separation of powers. PEC 33 was not yet adopted. But if such a hypothesis occurs, the Supreme would have self-government over all its legal status, assuming itself as an unlimited power and not as an body subject to the same checks and balances other powers are bound to.

The stronger and more politicized the Constitutional Courts have become, generating constitutional mutations, the weaker and the more liquid have become the constitutional norms whose content is plasticized and placed at the mercy of their political discretion. The political result of this empowerment may be the confrontation between sovereign institutions (as in the crisis between the U.S. Supreme Court and Roosevelt and the recent crises in Poland and Hungary) or the risk of exercising some sort of "diffuse constituent power" (Burdeau 1969, p. 246 ff.) that can create a constitutional breakdown. The notion of "diffuse constituent power" must be relativized, since the original, unconditional, foundational, legally unlimited and popular legitimized act, which marks the nature of classic constituent power, is absent from the informal change of jurisprudential source, which is a reality segregated by a constituted power and devoid of popular legitimation.

Nevertheless, extreme forms of informal change contained in judgments that derogate or transform the identitary pillars of a Constitution (national independence, civil and political rights, as well as the political regime and the system of government) without reaction of other institutions in due time can materially give rise to a new Constitution born out of the envelope of a dying one, whose ethos is slowly extinguished. Here, the constituent power as a force of nature capable of assuming various forms would discreetly render its diffuse appearance through an informal change of jurisprudential source.

This hypothesis is not pure fiction if we look at the political context that surrounds the European Union's expansive and integrative dynamics. If constitutional courts just surrender to the guidance of the Court of Justice of the European Union in favor of an implicit clause of supremacy of all European law over all domestic law, including the constitutions, there may be a constitutional mutation "ad libitum" of jurisprudential source that distorts the sovereignty of the states in favor of the erection of a European Federation. To that end, it would suffice that ambiguous reforms in the treaties on finance, judicial organization, security, foreign affairs and defense policy would acquire a federalizing interpretation granted by the Court of Justice of the Union and that the same interpretation would be accepted without controversy by the constitutional courts of the Member States, even if it collided with the structural principles of the respective constitutions and their substantial limits of amendment.

It is clear that these sorts of problematics accentuate critical or extreme scenarios, although the issue of informal changes is, normally, evolving in a politically less controversial and less dramatic sphere. They usually float in the realm of the fine lines of separation between the limited normative creativity inherent to the interpretative activity and the political innovation related to informal change. And it is clear that there are, also, areas of penumbra between the material norms derived from evolutionary interpretation and the jurisprudential realization of undetermined principles and concepts.

4 The Normative Judgments and the Assumptions of Invalidity of Constitutional Changes

4.1 The Creative Interpretations of Ordinary Laws

It has been observed that the definition and identification of a constitutional informal change performed by an interpretative path is not an easy operation from a dogmatic point of view.

There are interpretative essays that evolve tangentially in the borders of constitutional mutation, but do not constitute, technically, genuine tacit changes of the Constitution, because they flow from the constitutional norms with a minimal respect for the text, the structure of the norm and its political purpose. Böckenförde (2000, p. 185), in a selective-negative approach, considered several borderline interpretative cases that do not fit into the concept of informal change.

Among some examples of interpretation of a limited normative creative dimension, we can cite the following:

- (i) The need to update the meaning and scope of a constitutional norm in the light of new contemporary realities, in order to avoid unnecessary gaps and to regulate new realities of a similar nature that the constituent did not contemplate, leads the interpreter to relativize the literal and historical elements in its genetic dimension, in favor of the teleological element, so that the norm can embrace new situations collected from the "normative environment" without neglecting the old ones[21]; (ii) The need to adjust a constitutional rule to changes in the so-called "regulatory environment", when, for example, the protection afforded to the fundamental rights of a category of persons may no longer be justified due to changes in their social and occupational status[22]; (iii) The necessity to perform a legally creative interpretation of the principles, standards, and indeterminate legal terms

---

[21]This is the classic case of "Free Speech" foreseen in the first amendment of the US Constitution that in the original context referred only to the oral expression, but as time passed, included many other realities such as writing, gestural, images, pamphlets and communication in the cyberspace. A purely literal interpretation of the formula would leave many contemporary forms of freedom in communication without constitutional protection (Tribe 2008, p. 25).

[22]In Portugal, we had the case of the value of the pension attributed to the widows' when their husbands died in work-related accidents, value which was higher than that of widowers under the analogous circumstances. This difference in the value of pensions in 1976 was not originally unconstitutional due to women's financial dependence on male spouses, in view of the lower female access to the labor market. They constituted, therefore, a materially well-founded positive discrimination. Over time, women began to access the labor market on a regular basis, and the remuneration status between men and women was overall equalized. Consequently, the difference in the amount of pensions became unjustified because it violated the principle of equality and was found to be unconstitutional (Ac. 449/87 of Constitutional Court). The decision formed a mix of judgment based on a sliding unconstitutionality and an additive ruling, tending to provide, with the addition of a normative criterion, the equalization for both sexes of the subsidy by the greater value (the one that was attributed to widows).

contained in the Constitution, which awards the Court the possibility of setting normative secondary parameters which result from the densification of those principles and standards, legitimized by an implicit delegation of the legislator in Constitutional Justice (because, by lack of consensus or other reason, the legislator chose not to clarify those parameters, preferring to opt for indeterminate norms prone to judicial interpretation and concretization[23]); (iv) The requirement that legislative acts with alternative meanings should be decrypted by Constitutional Court in order to assess if those alternative ideal normative significations are in conformity with the Constitution or not[24]; (v) The corrective need to judge and repair violations of the principle of equality by means of interpretative judgments with additive effects, when, for example, a law by its silence discriminated, without grounds, a particular category of persons, by not granting them an equal benefit granted to other category of persons who were addressed by the same law and placed in an equal or identical position, situation that generates a relative type of omission that will imply that in the future, the rule should be read in order to cover that forgotten category, under penalty of invalidity[25]; (vi) The need to integrate technical gaps found in the Constitution by analogy.

In most of the described situations, the interpretative judgement exhibits a normative content of limited innovative range, since the interpreted constitutional norm does not allow the Court to meddle in fundamental political choices and daring judgments of political optimization. When it enlarges or reduces the object or the scope of the legal standard, it necessarily does so following the political program of

[23]In Germany (BVerfGE 63, 356, 360) and in Portugal (Ac. n. 188/2009 of the Portuguese Constitutional Court), constitutional jurisprudence has extracted from the principle of democratic rule of law the subjective dimension of the principle of legal certainty, which has been designated as the principle of the protection of trust, converted in a parameter of constitutionality. Afterward, the Court began to densify criteria or tests of normative nature in order to gauge its compliance. The same was true with the principle of proportionality, which the constitutional justice concretized, identifying the governing criteria of its compliance by the legislator, as is the case of adequacy, necessity, and proportionality *stricto sensu* (Ac. n. 632/2008 of the Portuguese Constitutional Court). Also in Portugal, the provisions of Article 32(1) of the Constitution concerning the "principle of the universality of the defendant's guarantees of defense" have been densified with some creativity by the Constitutional Court (Acs. n. 340/90 and n. 173/92 of the Portuguese Constitutional Court).

[24]The German Federal Constitutional Court's interpretation in accordance with the Constitution creates a binding effect for the courts and the public administration regarding the motivation of the judgment. This interpretation therefore assumes a normative effect that becomes problematic when a norm can be interpreted through more than one meaning according to the Constitution. After an oscillating jurisprudence, the German Federal Constitutional Court (BVerfGE 40,88 [93]) admitted that before a plurality of meanings of a norm, some of which would be constitutional and others unconstitutional, the binding effect would only cover those which were contrary to the Constitution (Simon 2001, p. 842).

[25]See Ac. n. 103/87 of the Portuguese Constitutional Court, which declared the unconstitutionality of a rule of the National Defense Act insofar as it restricted the right of military personnel to complain to the Ombudsman, creating an unequal situation with other citizens. The standard was read *ad futurum* as allowing the full right of complaint to the Ombudsman.

the same norm and its systematics. And when it is forced to create denser normative criteria intended to give effect to an undetermined principle or standard lacking specificity, the Court enacts substantive sub-constitutional norms, which are, however, within.

But, just as Aristotelian political regimes could suffer different sorts of degradation (monarchies in tyranny, aristocracy in oligarchy, and "politeia" in demagoguery), the interpretative rulings of Constitutional Justice can also degenerate into activist manifestations that intrude into the chamber of the legislator or even in the competence of ordinary courts. Without excessively dwelling on the phenomenon, there are rulings *which deal not with constitutional norms but with ordinary laws*, and therefore constitute an unauthorized passage from a creative interpretation to a materially legislative activity. We can foresee some examples (i) Under the pretext of updating a legal formula, the Court replaces one rule for another of its own creation which, because it implies political and axiological choices, should have been a task performed by the legislator[26]; (ii) The Constitutional Court eliminates norms and replaces them by new judicially created provisions, based on principles of indeterminate or fuzzy object or on foreign legislative models, materializing political and technical choices that go beyond the jurisdiction of the court because they are in the heart of legislative function[27]; (iii) Also under the pretext of filling in a relative omission violating the principle of equality, the Constitutional Court constructs a rule to fill this omission, being certain that the void could be filled by other non-constitutional normative solutions whose selection would imply a political choice that does not compete to the same Court.[28]

[26]See *Sentenza* n. 409/1989 in which the Italian Constitutional Court, in light of the principle of separation of Church and the State, eliminated a formula of oath of office holders invoking God to replace it with another a formula invoking the values of the Republic.

[27]The Brazilian Federal Supreme Court, in a monocratic decision of judgment of the Habeas Corpus 124,306, decriminalized abortion by request, based on the autonomy of decision the woman, on her sexual and reproductive rights, on her psychic and physical integrity, on the principle of equality (as men would not get pregnant). It ruled also that this decriminalization would operate during the first 3 months of pregnancy, because "no democratic and developed country in the world" treats the termination of pregnancy during the first trimester as a crime. The court amended the law in this case, not only by decriminalizing abortion but also by setting specific periods of closure for such decriminalization, based on some kind of "legal tourism" conducted among a mix of foreign systems.

[28]As examples, one can invoke some of the very controversial (and resisted) *Sentenze* n. 190, 1970 and 7 of 1971 of the Italian Constitutional Court, whose additive nature with general obligatory force was not respected in its normative component by common courts, when it determined the necessity of the presence of the defendant in the interrogation of a suspect.

4.2 The Normative Rulings of Constitutional Change

Within the normative decisions described in the previous heading, there is a deviation from the interpretative function because, instead of revealing the meaning of norms of ordinary legislative law or proceeding to its densification, those rulings constitutively transformed the same law, embodying the role of legislator and seizing it.

The fact is that the same type of functional usurpation of power assumes greater seriousness when it involves the *ex novo* creation, not of legal rules of ordinary law, but of materially constitutional norms, fostering the phenomenon of informal changes in the Basic Law. So, when constitutional amendment rulings with additive effects make their appearance, the Constitutional Court subrogates itself to the Parliament in the role of reviser of the Constitution. It is worth paying attention to some emblematic cases where the political intensity of the informal production of constitutional rules by Courts can show some variations. Following a criteria of increasing intensity of political innovation we can highlight five different situations.

In the *first case,* the Constitutional Court extends the application of positive constitutional norms to new situations not explicitly encompassed in the norms text based on systematic logic. It involves a limited scope of innovation which does not contrast with constitutional positive materiality. This is the example of the *Lüth* case in Germany (BverfGE, 7, 198), which recognized not only the vertical effect of fundamental rights (*vis-à-vis* the State) but also its horizontal effect (within private relations).[29]

[29]See Böckenförde (2000), p. 191 ff. Article 1(3) of the German Constitution states that "*The fundamental rights, which are described below, constitute directly applicable rights and bind the legislative, executive and judicial branches.*" The norm was originally understood as a command to public authorities but not a binding link between private parties. The Court held that fundamental rights were binding on civil law and that freedom of expression could be limited by general laws, pursuant to Article 5(2) of the Constitution (in this case, there was the possibility of Article 826 of the Civil Code to allow accountability for manifestations of freedom of expression with an immoral character that would cause harm to others), and should be evaluated in accordance with the Constitution itself. *In casu,* it considered that the call for a boycott of a film made by an ex-Nazi filmmaker would not necessarily be an immoral act and could be justified in light of the balancing of the interests involved. If the general laws that govern Private Law place limits on a fundamental right as relevant as the freedom of expression, they need to be interpreted in light of the axiological meaning of this fundamental right in those points where they manifest their limiting effects of fundamental rights. The court held that the reasons for the boycott call were intended to avoid the idea that there would be a return to national-socialist filmmaking and that it was not an immoral conduct. And it recognized that the fundamental right to free expression of thought also applies to private relations in the case where it conflicts with private interests.

The mutation generated did not confront the text of the Constitution since, by extensive means, it considered that private relations are not immune to the application of the rights of freedom, since the general civil laws that regulate or limit these rights are subject to them. And that this subjection requires balancing judgments about conflicting rights and interests among the individuals covered by the same law.

Despite the great impact of this decision, including across borders, and the critical reactions in private law scholars, it is not possible to state that the informal change generated has involved a high intensity in terms of political cleavage with the Constitution. The normative content of case-law rule has departed from the positive and democratically determined constitutional norm and the normative innovation (in this case the horizontal effectiveness of freedom of speech) did not exceed a function of evolutionary development of the law previously enshrined in the Constitution.

In the *second situation*, under the pretext of filling a legal gap, the Italian Constitutional Court created a new system of validity/efficacy control of rules which the Constitution does not explicitly provide for, and which could incorporate, in alternative, a different sort of system.

The Constitutional Court's innovative ruling (which created a diffuse judicial review of ordinary Italian laws contrary to European Union law) has filled a legal gap related to the control of compliance of ordinary acts of the State and regions with European Union law and its legal effects. The Italian Constitutional Court took an ambiguous wording of article 11 of the Constitution which consents, on par with other states, limitations to its sovereignty regarded as indispensable for a legal order that ensures peace and justice among nations.[30] In its ruling, the Court expressed the understanding that common courts may not apply ordinary laws contrary to obligations stemming from European Union law which is invested in a supremacy, indirectly recognized by the mentioned article 11 of the Constitution, when it accepts limitations to sovereignty. The case-law oscillated between conferring upon the courts the power to pass a judgment of unconstitutionality of national laws from article 11, in conjunction with the European Union treaties, or a judgment of "irrelevance" of the same national law.[31] In both situations the result would be the same: the disengagement and ineffectiveness of national law. From *sentenza* n. 170/1984 onwards, the question came to be understood not so much as a judgment of unconstitutionality as one of irrelevance.

Constitutional jurisprudence has thus created a material rule of constitutional nature that does not contradict the positive Constitution, but rather fills in a normative gap in it about the jurisdictional guarantee of the supremacy of European Union law over national ordinary norms, giving to the ordinary courts the possibility of solving normative antinomies that arise in the facts submitted to its judgment.

In the *third situation*, consideration should be given to the addition of an entirely new materially constitutional rule to the constitutional text, which derives neither from the text, nor from an analogy or extensive interpretation nor still from a concretization of a standard or principle.

[30]See Spadaro (1998), p. 112 ff.

[31]The Court nevertheless does not exclude to review the constitutionality of regional laws which violate European Union law, in light of article 11 of the Constitution.

In the Portuguese case of Ac. n. 353/2012, the Constitutional Court conceived a rule of self-authorization to safeguard the future effects of a previously declared unconstitutional norm. This judicial ruling was built up from a constitutional norm, article 282(4) of the Portuguese Constitution, which, for reasons of legal certainty, equity and qualified public interest, allows the Court to safeguard the already produced effects of the norm declared unconstitutional. The judgment did not concretize or clarify the rule it conceived inside article 282, whose textual and logic statement does not safeguard the future effects of a previously declared invalid law, but created, instead, another rule which points to that odd solution. To start with, it did not make an extensive interpretation from 282(4) because the constitutional *travaux préparatoires* made it clear that the constituent did not accept this sort solution, making a very restrictive use of manipulative rulings. In addition, it replaced the constitutional legislator who, if there was the desire to opt for this solution, could have copied the exceptional Brazilian or Austrian legal regimes that admit this possibility. Finally, if it were to resolve the real problem under consideration regarding the constitutional order (the need to ensure that the unconstitutional state budget would expire only by the end of the year for financial reasons and legal certainty), it would not be obliged to add a new rule, but could have instead used the traditional procedure, which had already been called before in Portugal and in Italy, that consisted in declaring publically the law unconstitutional and retain the publication of the ruling until a certain date (in this case, the end of economic year).

In *the fourth situation,* it is important to consider the extraction of politically innovative rules built by the judge from the principles with a diffuse object, which invalidate ordinary positive laws that had never contradicted the original meaning of the Constitution. Ely (1987), p. 87 ff strongly criticized the "judicial paternalism" inherent in the *Rode v. Wade* case, which validated abortion, considering that the Supreme Court was addressing moral conflicts through the innovative densification of values or principles without a definite purpose. Regarding the validation of abortion using privacy standard and the undetermined material dimension of the due process of law, the Court replaced the legislator by creating a rule based on a moral and political choice.

Even if there is public pressure from a minority or majority for a legislative change in order to resolve a morally and criminally controversial issue such as abortion and the right to protect intra-uterine life, it would be for the legislator, be it constitutional or ordinary, based on a democratic popular mandate, to decide on this matter and not a judge lacking that mandate and therefore missing any qualified constitutional credential. With that jurisprudential norm, the Court arrogated itself greater powers than the constituent and the ordinary legislators to predict the future and "*to contradict the political majority of today with the values of the majority of tomorrow*" (Ely 1987, pp. 4, 11 ff., and 61 ff.).

In the *fifth and final situation*, is important to point to the misuse or distortion of dogmatic elements, canons, and interpretative techniques in order for the Court to extract a substantial political rule that is built by case-law as an instrument to solve a problematic situation (as in the case of derogating positive constitutional rules through other rules that have its origin in judicial creation and are erected from a jetty of blurred principles[32]).

Is it relevant to verify and differentiate the five cases exposed, whose common denominator was a constitutional informal change extracted from a jurisprudential source. The norms created by informal mutation in the first and second cases resulted from an evolutionary interpretative process whose innovation departed from the text without confronting it, without contradicting the political program of the Constitution, without involving deep political choices. It is essentially an evolution from the constitutional positive norms,[33] concretizing, updating, and reconstructing constitutional principles in order to adjust them to new situations which should be regulated. This means that the jurisprudential rule at stake introduced a constitutive change which assumed an *endogenetic* nature and a moderate range of innovation that does not conflict with the Constitution, reason why it may be described as a "pure" constitutional informal change.[34]

In the three other situations, the rulings created jurisprudential norms that interfered in the material reservation of the Constitution, producing political choices centered on juridical and philosophical preconceptions or on criteria of opportunity that confronted the constitutional text and replaced the legislator in the exercise of its competences. These can be described as "impure" mutations since they have transposed the constitutional normative reservation, broken the "telos" of their rigidity, twisted the limits and techniques of the interpretive function, affected the structure of original norms and made political choices incompatible with the passivity and impartiality of a jurisdiction.

4.3 Episodic Changes and Constitutional Informal Changes

It is important to take into account the definition of constitutional informal change given above (Sect. 2), which emphasized the existence of innovative material standards "*generated and gradually consolidated in time*".

Considering the "time" factor as a constitutive presupposition of a constitutional mutation is a controversial issue. Some authors do not elaborate on the question and others exclude that the mutation requires a more or less long period of time. The question is pertinent but complex. If a judicial norm that produces an innovation in

[32]In Brazil, this is the case of ADI n. 4.277 and ADPF n. 132 / RJ, which recognized stable same-sex unions based on a conjunction of principles (the right to happiness and the principle of equality), thereby derogating article 226 § 3 of the Brazilian Constitution, which only recognizes stable unions between a man and a woman.

[33]See Böckenförde (2000), p. 193.

[34]On this classification, see Carducci (2010).

Constitution contents turns out to be an episodic, isolated act which the Constitutional Jurisdiction does not repeat in the future, has it created a constitutional change or informal mutation? If an innovative sense is given to a norm of the Constitution and that same meaning is subsequently contradicted by another one, and followed by contradictory rulings that opt for one or the other, can one speak of an informal change? If a jurisprudential rule creates a new meaning for a constitutional norm, mindful of the supposed disuse of a contrary constitutional rule, but this disuse does not really occur, will it be a constitutional informal change?

In fact, temporal consolidation distinguishes informal change from a mere case-law ruling that collides with the Constitution, and can be named as an episodic breach of the same Constitution or a singular constitutional derogative ruling. The consolidation of the judicial innovative norm does not involve, necessarily, the course of a long time, but only of a due time indispensable to know if the established rule of jurisprudence has been spontaneously accepted, stabilized, and has the conditions to be followed in the future.

For example, the decision of Ac. 353/2012 of the Portuguese Constitutional Court, which *in casu* confronted and enlarged the object of article 282(4) of the Portuguese constitution (supra Sect. 4.2), allowing the postponement for the future of the effects of the judgement of unconstitutionality, has received a hostile reaction from the legal community and was not seconded until 2019 by other similar decisions. It was a fortuitous constitutional breach of the constitutional program, but not an informal constitutional change, since it does not seem to have sequential perspectives. The *Roe v. Wade* case, differently, by virtue of the precedent established and the absence of significant contrary reactions in the judiciary and in Congress, generated a constitutional informal change, since it was consolidated and has been serving as a parameter for other judicial decisions. The same will be said of the decision on same-sex unions in Brazil, since it has not been challenged by the political and judicial institutions and, most importantly, the majority of the society accepts the solution, regardless of the unconstitutional way in which it was constructed and justified.

In short, for an informal constitutional change to be formed, a minimum period of time must elapse so as to allow its consolidation. The main factors that will cause or reveal its consolidation will be lack of opposition to it, the force of precedent, the absence of jurisprudential contradiction, and/or to the fact that there are institutions willing to accept or conform themselves with it to apply or abide by the meaning of the jurisprudential norm created.

This consolidation involves a spontaneous and even existential component, depending on one of two factors. On the one hand, it might depends on the occurrence of a "normative situation" in which institutions and legal and political operators intuit that the jurisprudential change is difficult to reverse, tending to be complied with in the future. On the other hand, the institutions might intuit, differently, that the normative ruling rather dissipates into a topical expedient to solve an exceptional problem which, in the light of criticism or resistance in the legal and political community, will not be repeated.

In any case, changes that have temporarily solidified over a long period, with a broad acceptance or tacit acceptance in scholarship and jurisprudence, become part of a "constitutional *acquis*". As such, even if they were born in a state of potential invalidity, their unconstitutionality can be excused by the factual force of the respective consolidation. In this specific point those sort of mutations have something in common with the existential nature of constituent power.

4.4 Grounds for the Invalidity of Impure Informal Constitutional Changes

We have explored, by means of some examples, assumptions about the invalidity of several types of constitutional change of jurisprudential origin (supra Sect. 4.2).

We may, without intending to present an exhaustive list of all the illustrative hypotheses of the invalidity described, align some criteria for the repeal constitutional informal changes that degenerate on impure or invalid mutations.

i) *The amendment, through a normative court ruling, of explicit competences constitutionally attributed to a constitutional institution to assign them to another institution.*

This would be hypothetically the case of the "constitutional mutation" invoked in the vote of some Justices of the Brazilian Federal Supreme Court (Complaint No. 4,335-A/AC). If that position would have prevailed, it would imply that, by judicial decision, the explicit powers of the Brazilian Senate as regards the possibility of suspending, with *erga omnes* binding force, rules deemed unconstitutional by that same court in concrete judicial review cases,[35] would be removed and transferred to the Federal Supreme Court, without the norms conferring those powers to the Senate having unequivocally fallen into disuse. This solution did not happen, as no mutation based on disuse occurred: the Senate, in the framework of a constitutional tradition prior to the 1988 Constitution, continues to occasionally suspend laws deemed unconstitutional under concrete control.

ii) *The repeal of constitutional rules followed by their replacement by other norms discretionally created by the judge, based on topical exercises or on appeal to values or principles with a diffuse and not densified object.*

There are many situations of this nature, some of which have already been treated as: (i) The Habeas Corpus decision 124.306 of the Brazilian Federal Supreme Court, that decriminalized abortion at the will of the woman during the first 3 months of pregnancy, violating caput of article 5 of the Constitution and abrogating and modifying, for that case, the relevant Criminal Code provisions; (ii) The decision of Habeas Corpus n. 126.292, within the framework of a change of interpretation of

[35]Which have *inter partes* effects.

the Brazilian Federal Supreme Court, that allowed the arrest after trial in second instance in a process that awaits appeal, despite the fact that article 5(LVI) of the Brazilian Constitution stipulates that "*no one shall be held guilty until a final judgement of conviction has passed*", and *res iudicata* requires the exhaustion of all appeals; (iii) *Sentenza* n. 16 of 1978, which established new limits in Italy for the admissibility of referenda, and *Sentenze* n. 29 of 1979 and 15 of 1982, which introduced into Italian law the new institute of "suspension of constitutional guarantees".

iii) *The erroneous or deformed use of elements, techniques, or canons of constitutional interpretation or integration in order to force the artificial extraction of a judicially constructed rule to regulate and compose a problematic situation.*

Several cases have already been mentioned, such as those involving the revocation of positive rules through *norms of judicial creation imaginatively erected from a jetty of principles*[36]; *the use of interpretation in conformity with the Constitution over non-polysemic legal rules*[37]; *the convening of manipulated analogy as pretext to fill a false gap*[38]; and the *call for extensive or restrictive interpretations outside their consolidated assumptions*.[39]

[36]The already named case of ADI n° 4.277 and ADPF n° 132 / RJ, in Brazil, which allowed same-sex unions based on the conjunction of a complex of principles (from the right to happiness to the principle of equality).

[37]About the same question expressed in the previous note, the reasoning of the Brazilian Federal Supreme Court rapporteur who judged ADI n° 4.277 and ADPF n° 132 / RJ, wrongly invoked an interpretation in conformity with the Constitution based on a norm which was not polysemic (but instead could only consent an indivisible interpretation (article 1.732 of the Brazilian Civil Code, articulated with article 226, § 3 of the Constitution—see Mendes 2016, p. 221 ff.).

[38]See Ac n°.786/96, of the Portuguese Constitutional Court. Article 282(3) of the Constitution protects *res judicata* from the repressive *ex tunc* effects of a decision on unconstitutionality of the norm applied in those cases. The Court, however, included in the same protective provision another institute, the administrative figure of "decided administrative case" (administrative acts based on an unconstitutional rule but consolidated, because they were not syndicated in administrative courts during the period that the law establishes for their annulment). This assimilation of "decided administrative case" to *res judicata* is absurd, not only because it is not possible to resort to the analogy when two institutions have a very different nature, but also because article 282(3) of the Constitution is an exceptional rule, and analogic constructions are not allowed to depart from those sort of norms.

[39]See Ac. n. 121/2010 of the Portuguese Constitutional Court, which ruled that same-sex marriage is in conformity with the Constitution. The ruling was based on a restrictive interpretation of article 16(1) of the Universal Declaration of Human Rights, a document of constitutional qualified value in Portuguese order, pursuant to Article 16(2) of the Constitution, which requires that the rights, freedoms and guarantees must be interpreted and integrated in accordance with that Declaration. Since Article 16 (1) of the Declaration proclaims the right of men and women to marry, which would forbid same-sex marriage, the Constitutional Court considered that the same norm should be interpreted only in a more favorable sense to fundamental rights and not in a restrictive sense. In consequence, the law consenting same-sex marriage would not violate that provision. Such an amputation of the scope of a rule which the Court describes as 'quasi-supra constitutional' (would result, in the opinion of the former President of the Court, from a restrictive sort of interpretation.

iv) *The production of a politically innovative norm that is added to the Constitution's binding environment build up on principles deprived of a defined object or produced in a purely decision-making way, without any basis in the precepts and in the constitutional program.*

In the first case, in the United States, the case of *Roe v. Wade*, already mentioned (supra Sect. 4.2). In the second situation, we can point to the aforementioned Ac. n. 353/2012 of the Portuguese Constitutional Court, in which it could not have created a material rule that allows to the sane jurisdiction to safeguard the future effectiveness of a legal norm previously declared unconstitutional (supra Sect. 4.2).

5 The Legal Non-existence of Acts Which Result from "Impure" Informal Changes and the Revaluation of Hermeneutics as Central Issues of Constitutional Politics

Interpretation and informal changes of the Constitution orchestrated by case-law are distinct figures, despite the fact that informal changes progress under the guise of interpretation or integration. Those changes operate with a semantic legitimation of a *fait accompli* created by a Constitutional Court that, instead of revealing the meaning of a constitutional provision, transforms the content of that provision, ignoring the legislative due process established by the Basic Law.

The most problematic issue occurs with unconstitutional or impure mutations already listed in some of its assumptions (supra, Sect. 4.4). The problematic character of unconstitutional mutations in the Basic Law arises from the fact that they are figuratively sealed by an aura of jurisdictional sacredness and a claim of a last word ("*le dernier mot*") dictated by a Constitutional Court on the validity of norm applied or not applied on a litigation. That supposed sacredness creates in civil and political society the idea that harsh criticism, forceful opposition, or even no compliance on the part of Legislative, Executive or common courts to a ruling from a Constitutional Court, even abusive and invasive in its innovative content, generates an anathema of disobedience to the judiciary, breach of legality and, even, threat to the rule of law.

The fact is that some Constitutional Courts are, sometimes, losing its political distanced status and, even, impartiality in an a very ideological word environment in twenty-first century.

For example, in the United States of America, the fight for the appointment of judges to the Supreme Court in the last 3 years has assumed a pitched battle bias

---

However the Constitutional Court decoupled restrictive interpretation from its dogmatic foundations: there was no contradiction in the law; no exceedance by the principle of the end for which it was created; and the inexistence of an incorrect verbal content that needs correction. None of these due conditions were present to support the restrictive interpretation.

between the two major parties, to the point of deplorable public turmoil in the Senate and dispersed vocal accusations about the capture of the Supreme Court by this or that ideology. In Poland and Hungary, the attempt by progressive parties to try to turn constitutional courts into a third counter-majoritarian chamber against conservative governments appointed in fresh elections led to unprecedented confrontations between the constitutional courts and other institutions that culminated in the capture or neutralization of such courts by the dominant majorities in Parliament. And in Brazil, besides some vague threats of impeachment of judges that rule activist decisions, there is small talk about an amendment that would limit the power of the Brazilian Federal Supreme Court to invalidate constitutional amendments or, even a court packing law in case the court assumed itself as a "Jupiterian" force of opposition.

The conflicts between the Legislature and Constitutional Justice, even in a limited number of Western states, seems to be deeply detrimental to the democratic rule of law, inasmuch as it compromises the impartiality of the Courts and exposes them to risks of capture or devitalization of the former after a tough conflict. Hence, with respect for the independence of constitutional justice and the separation of powers, the decision to approve normative provisions is within the province of the legislator, at the constitutional and ordinary level. It is therefore up to the legislator to create solutions that might preclude those potential future conflicts with the courts, and among those measures, it should be considered in the first place the adoption of remedies against invalid constitutional changes from jurisprudential source.

Without attempting to address the subject of the designation of constitutional justices, which is relevant but involves a broader discussion on the containment of activism and on the reduction of partisan bias in the composition of Constitutional Justice bodies, it would be important to address three forms of containment of impure informal changes: (i) the penalty of legal non-existence for qualified usurpation of powers; (ii) the introduction of methodical binding criteria of interpretation in the laws that Constitutional Courts should consider and apply; (iii) and the requirement of qualified majorities in those Courts to adopt manipulative interpretative decisions and to the use of balancing as an exclusive basis of a judgment of unconstitutionality.

In Portuguese scolarship, legal non-existence consists in the total unfitness of an apparent act to produce the legal effects that correspond to a typical legal act, when it lacks the most elementary requirements of constitutional identification.

Apart from all the situations of non-existence foreseen in the Portuguese Constitution[40] and those with which they have an analogy,[41] scholars have identified the

[40]Cases of lack of enactment of laws and signature of regulatory decrees and international agreements by the President of the Republic (article 137); lack of ministerial counter-signature on certain acts of the President (Article 140 (2)); decree of parliamentary dissolution during the state of emergency and during a 6 month period after election of Parliament (article 172(2) of the Portuguese Constitution).

[41]Like the publication of treaties without the President's ratification and the amendment of the Constitution during the states of emergency.

following other cases of legal non-existence: (i) the absence of regular legislative will in the genesis of a public act (the body which created the act is not yet officially working or the existence of fraud or coercion over the head of the body); (ii) serious deformity in its typical form (lack of approval, disrespect for qualified majorities, total absence of form); (iii) and the guarantee of the core of the separation of powers (serious usurpation of powers), in such a way that it irreparably affects the imputation link of the same act to a competent body.

In what the constitutional amendment procedures are concerned, constitutional scholars consider that violations of the constitutional norms related to the initiative of the amendment (which is exclusive of members of Parliament), to the exclusive competence of the Parliament to approved it or to the majority of approval of the amendment law (qualified majority) generate the non-existence of the amendment law because it no longer has the minimum qualification requirements to be identified as such type of law.[42] As such, the President of the Republic, despite not being able to veto constitutional amendment laws, can return back to the Parliament that bill as an act that he qualifies not as an amendment law, but as an apparent law of that sort, wounded with non-existence. The same would be true if an absolutely incompetent organ (the Government) would approve a law that has the purpose of changing the Constitution.

Some dogmatic features of the non-existent amendment law consist of its total legal unfeasibility, the no compliance with a *res judicata* that applies this appearance of norm, and the total inapplicability of the act in, to, or by sovereign bodies, as courts, or the public administration. This means that any public body has a duty not to apply the rule and to declare its non-existence. The Constitutional Court has the power to do so, but it does not have the monopoly of that decision; hence, the President of the Republic may refuse to promulgate a non-existent amendment law, according to the judgment he can made about the lack of formal or organic requirements imposed by the Constitution.[43] If this radical sanction is applicable to unconstitutional amendment laws, even when approved by the only competent body for such, the Parliament, it should be applicable *a fortiori* to normative components of Constitutional Court rulings that create constitutional parameters built on politically innovative criteria that derogate, modify the content, or devitalize the force of positive constitutional norms that have not expired.

And to the extent that these "constitutional amendment judgments" come from a Constitutional Court, an incompetent body to decide constitutional amendments, those decisions that transform the Constitution incur in usurpation of powers which determine the legal non-existence of the act.[44] As so, it must be understood that the Parliament, the Government, and the ordinary courts have the prerogative to declare

[42]de Sousa (1988), p. 286 ff; Canotilho and Moreira (2014), p. 1003; Miranda (2013), p. 215; de Morais (2006), p. 204 ff.

[43]See Miranda (2013), p. 217.

[44]See Miranda (2013), p. 106.

the non-existence of the normative component of the ruling and refuse its application.

The question of the method of constitutional interpretation was considered one of the most important challenges posed to the Theory of the State and to the Theory of the Constitution.[45] The option of Constitutional Justice for hermeneutics based on one of the existing legal methods or, instead, for topical approaches, evolutionary interpretations of moralistic clipping, or discretionary considerations have innumerable consequences. The fact that the rule of law requires that juridical science masters a legal order and being the method something inseparable to any scientific reasoning, it will be inadmissible that the Constitution, like any law, could be interpreted and integrated in the shadows of a legal method. If Civil Codes provide for norms on the methods of interpretation and various types of hermeneutic criteria in ordinary laws, it would be surprising if Constitutional Courts would not be governed by norms of similar content when they interpret the principles and rules of the Constitution, even *a fortiori*, given the fact that the Constitution is a law invested in a position of supremacy.

Without necessarily going so far as to introduce rules on normative interpretation in the Constitution itself, as did the Republic of Ecuador,[46] it seems perfectly reasonable to add a set of juridical criteria or standards for constitutional interpretation in the laws that rule the organization and procedures of Constitutional Courts. These criteria, departing from an hermeneutics based in the Theory of Constitution[47] that evolves the structural elements of a specific Basic Law, would presuppose the combined observance of the classic stages of the interpretative program, the use of logics, balancing guides between colliding principles, the limits of evolutionary interpretation, the ways of achieving indeterminate principles and concepts, and the integration of constitutional gaps. In Portugal and Spain, the reinforced status of these laws, qualified as organic laws, give additional weight to their normativity, and would justify a special sort of complaint or appeal to the Chief Justice in case of gross non-observance of such criteria.

Finally, certain manipulative decisions, such as additive judgments or interpretative decisions in conformity with the Constitution, as well as balanced rulings when they operate as the sole argument of unconstitutionality, although justifiable in several situations in which there is an unconstitutional evidence, may in other cases slip into judicial decisionism. Although in most cases these situations concern issues of invalidity of ordinary law acts, in others the rulings can generate informal constitutional changes (as in the case of interpretation in conformity with the Constitution, added to a binding *erga omnes* effect).

---

[45]See Rubio Llorente (1993), p. 606.

[46]Cfr article 427. of the Constitution of Ecuador: *"The constitutional norms will be interpreted by the literal wording that best suits the Constitution in its entirety. In case of doubt, they will be interpreted in the most favorable way that assures the full validity of the rights and that best respects the will of the constituent, and in accordance with the general principles of constitutional interpretation"*.

[47]See Böckenförde (2006), p. 102.

Hence it is considered that intermediate rulings of a manipulative nature, given the constitutive effects that they produce in the legal order, must have conditioned their delivery to judgments of evidence. This evidence can only be measured by a broad consensus, which requires its adoption by a qualified majority of judges, such as a two-thirds majority of the bodie's plenary.

To defend that constitutional informal changes or mutations do not exist and that they constitute a normal creative manifestation of Constitutional Justice, under its interpretive powers, as Häberle sustains, is equivalent to that popular maxim according to which one of the best arts of the devil is to make believe that it does not exist.

Limiting the power of the more "Jupiterian" Constitutional Courts in their self-proclaimed role of tacit and supplementary constitutional legislator is an imperative of the principle of separation of powers that binds all sovereign institutions, including the Constitutional Court itself. This limitation seeks to preserve that jurisdiction as the "least dangerous branch" and to reverse the dangers of constitutional liquefaction, in order to give back to the Basic Law its necessary objectivity and indispensable legal force.

References

Alexander, L. (2015). Judicial activism: Clearing the air and the head. In L. P. Coutinho, M. La Torre, & S. Smith (Eds.), *Judicial activism* (p. 16 ff). Heidelberg: Springer.

Bauman, Z. (2001). *Modernidade Líquida*. Portuguese translation by Plínio Dentzien. Rio de Janeiro: Jorge Zahar Editor.

Böckenförde, E.-W. (2000). *Estudios Sobre el Estado de Derecho y la Democracia*. Spanish translation by Agapito Serrano. Madrid: Editorial Trotta.

Böckenförde, E.-W. (2006). Stato Costituzione, Democrazie. In M. Nicoletti & O. Brino (Eds.), *Teorie de Interpretazione e Diritti Fondamentali*. Italian translation org. (p. 102 ff). Milano: Giuffrè.

Burdeau, G. (1956). Une survivance. La Notion de Constitution. In AAVV (Ed.), *L'Évolution du Droit Public - Etudes offerts à Achille Mestre* (p. 1956). Paris: Sirey.

Burdeau, G. (1969). *Traité de Science Politique. IV*. Paris: LGDJ.

Camerlengo, Q. (2007). *Contributo ad una Teoria del Diritto Costituzionale Cosmopolitico*. Milano: Giuffre.

Canosa Usera, R. (1988). *Interpretación Constitucional y Formula Política*. Madrid: Centro de Estudios Constitucionales.

Canotilho, G., & Moreira, V. (2014). *Constituição da República Portuguesa Anotada, I*. Almedina: Coimbra.

Carducci, M. (2009). Dualismo e Monismo nela Osservazione dei Mutamenti Costituzionale Informali. *Diritto Pubblico Comparato ed Europeo, IV*, 1911 ff.

Carducci, M. (2010). Sobre a Distinção entre Mutações Constitucionais Puras e Impuras. *Revista Brasileira de Direito Constitucional, 4/15*, 199 e seg.

de Morais, C. B. (2006). *Justiça Constitucional. I*. Coimbra: Coimbra Editora.

de Morais, C. B. (2016). As Mutações Constitucionais de Fonte Jurisprudencial: a fronteira crítica entre a interpretação e a mutação. In C. B. Morais & G. Mendes (Eds.), *Mutações Constitucionais*. São Paulo: Saraiva.

de Morais, C. B. (2018). *Curso de Direito Constitucional, II*. Almedina: Coimbra.

de Sousa, M. R. (1988). *O Valor Jurídico do Acto Inconstitucional*. Lisboa: Imprenta.
Ely, J. H. (1987). *Democracy and distrust*. Cambridge: Harvard University Press.
Green, C. (2009). An intellectual history of judicial activism. *Emory Law Journal, 58*, 1195 ff.
Häberle, P. (1978). *Verfassung als Öffentlicher Prozess - Materialen zu einer Verfassungstheorie der Offenen Gesellsshaft*. Berlin: Duncker & Humblot.
Häberle, P. (1980). *Die Verfassung des Pluralismus* (p. 3 ff). Königstein: Athenäum Verlag.
Häberle, P. (1993). Derecho Constitucional Común Europeo. Spanish tranlation by Emilio Mikunda Franco. *Revista de Estudios Políticos, 79*, 11 ff.
Häberle, P. (2000a). *Pluralismo y Constitución: Estudios de Teoria Constitucional en la Sociedad Abierta*. Spanish tranlation by Emilio Mukunda. Madrid: Tecnos.
Häberle, P. (2000b). *Diritto e Veritá*. Italian translation by Fabio Fiore. Torino: Einaudi.
Häberle, P. (2002). *Hermenêutica Constitucional: a sociedade aberta dos intérpretes da constituição – contribuição para a interpretação pluralista e procedimental da Constituição*. Portuguese translation by Gilmar Ferreira Mendes. Porto Alegre: Sergio Antonio Fabris Editor.
Hesse, K. (2009). Limites da Mutação Constitucional. In *Temas Fundamentais de Direito Constitucional*. Portuguese translation by Gilmar Ferreira Mendes et al. (p. 151 ff). São Paulo: Saraiva.
Kriele, M. (2009). *Introdução à Teoria do Estado*. Portuguese translation by Urbano Carvelli. Porto Alegre: Sergio Antonio Fabris Editor.
Kumm, M. (2009). The Cosmopolitan turn in constitutionalism. In J. Dunoff & J. Trachtman (Eds.), *Ruling the World?* (p. 258 ff). Cambridge: Cambridge University Press.
Kumm, M. (2012). Global constitutionalism: Human rights, democracy and the rule of law. In A. Wiener, A. Lang, J. Tully, & M. P. Maduro (Eds.), *Global constitutionalism* (Vol. I(1), p. 1 ss). Cambridge: Cambridge University Press.
La Torre, M. (2015). Between nightmare and noble dream: Judicial ativism and legal theory. In L. P. Coutinho, M. La Torre, & S. Smith (Eds.), *Judicial activism* (p. 5 ff). Heidelberg: Springer.
Lassalle, F. (2013). *O Que é Uma Constituição?*. Portuguese translation by Inês Espada Vieira. Lisboa: Vega.
Lin, H. D. (1998). *Mutación de la Constitución*. Translation by Christian Förster. Vitoria Gasteiz: Instituto Vasco de Administración Pública.
Maduro, M. P. (2003). Europe and the Constitution: What if this is as good as it gets. In M. Ward, J. Weser, & M. Wind (Eds.), *European constitutionalism beyond the state* (p. 76 ff). Cambridge: Cambridge University Press.
McCormick, N. (1993). Beyond the sovereign state. *Modern Law Review, 56*, 1 ff.
Medeiros, R. (2015). *A Constituição Portuguesa num Contexto Global*. Lisboa: UCP.
Mendes, G. F. (2016). Limite entre a Interpretação e Mutação: análise sobre a ótica da jurisdição constitucional brasileira. In C. B. Morais & G. Mendes (Eds.), *Mutações Constitucionais*. São Paulo: Saraiva.
Miranda, J. (2013). *Manual de Direito Constitucional. II*. Coimbra: Coimbra Editora.
Müller, F. (1993). *Discours de La Méthode Juridique*. French translation by Olivier Jouanjan. Paris: Presses Universitaires de France.
Perelman, C., & Olbrechts Tyteca, L. (1999). *Tratado da Argumentação- A nova Retórica*. Portuguese translation by Maria Ermentina Galvão. São Paulo: Martins Fontes.
Perez Luño, A. (2011). *El Desbordamiento de las Fuentes del Derecho*. Madrid: La Ley.
Ramos, E. D. S. (2010). *Ativismo Judicial*. São Paulo: Saraiva.
Ribeiro, J. S. (2014). Mutações Constitucionais: um conceito vazio? In AAVV (Ed.), *Estudos Homenagem Artur Maurício*. Coimbra: Coimbra Editora.
Rubio Llorente, F. (1993). La Forma del Poder. In *Estudios sobre la Constitución* (p. 606 ff). Madrid: Centro de Estudios Constitucionales.
Schmitt, C. (1961). La tirania de los valores. Spanish translation by Anima Schmitt de Otero. *Revista de Estudios Politicos, 115*, 65 ff.
Schmitt, C. (1983). *La Defensa de La Constitución*. Spanish translation by Manuel Sanchez Sarto. Madrid: Editorial Labor.
Simon. (2001). In Benda, Maihofer, Vogel, Hesse, Heyde, & trad Antonio Lopez Pina (Eds) *Handbook of Constitutional Law (Manual de Derecho Constitucional*) (p. 842). Madrid: IEP.

Spadaro, A. R.-A. (1998). *Lineamenti di Diritto Costituzionale*. Torino: Einaudi.
Tribe, L. (2008). *The invisible constitution*. Oxford: Oxford University Press.
Tuebner, G. (2016). *Fragmentos Constitucionais: Constitucionalismo Social na Globalização*. Portuguese translation by Pedro Ribeiro e Ricardo Campos. São Paulo: Saraiva.
Wheare, K. C. (1966). *Modern constitutions*. London: Oxford University Press.

Carlos Blanco de Morais is Full Professor at the University of Lisbon's School of Law. Coordinator of CIDP—Lisbon Centre of Research in Public Law. His works include *As Leis Reforçadas* (Coimbra Editora, 1998), *Justiça Constitucional (Coimbra Editora, several editions), Curso de Direito Constitucional (Almedina, several editions), and, as co-editor, Perspectivas da Reforma da Justiça Constitucional em Portugal e no Brasil (Almedina, 2017).*

Part IV
The Problem of European "Constitutional Law"

A Functional Alternative to Political Right: Social Contract Without a People

Massimo La Torre

Contents

Abstract Ordoliberalism is a German doctrine of law and political economy that has been influential in the self-definition of German economic and political system after the second world war. Though a product of the Weimar Republic crisis, ordoliberalism could be developed as a school and be displaying its practical impact only once a new democratic Germany had to be rebuilt from the ruins left by the totalitarian State. It was moreover instrumental in projecting and shaping the European community as a free market area, somehow disembedded from welfare nation-States. The basic functionalist legitimacy it offered to political authority indeed proved very powerful in the case of supranational institutional engineering. However, for several years such school of thought remained ignored in the narratives offered of European integration and its ideological motives. This article tries to reintegrate ordoliberalism in the narrative of European Union evolution especially by showing the centrality of such school of thought within the predicament of a polity under conditions of severe social (and national) pluralism. The article is also meant as a first attempt of a more general thesis: That ordoliberalism offers a foundational model, indeed a political theory, for a political right without politics, or, said differently, for a social contract without people.

M. La Torre (✉)
"Magna Graecia" University of Catanzaro, Catanzaro, Italy
e-mail: mlatorre@unicz.it

© Springer Nature Switzerland AG 2020

M. Nogueira de Brito, L. Pereira Coutinho (eds.), *The Political Dimension of Constitutional Law*, https://doi.org/10.1007/978-3-030-38459-3_8

1 The Burden of Our Time

Michel Foucault's analysis of neoliberalism[1] is well known. A pathbreaking analysis, retold and re-elaborated in several works and research on "the burden of our time", to use a phrase by Hannah Arendt, which is actually the British title of her *Origins of Totalitarianism.*[2] "The burden of our time" is no longer the totalitarian State—Orwell's *1984*—but the commodification and marketization of our entire social life, and the intrusion of market logic into every, even the remotest, corner of the public sphere. This intrusion we experience happening in Europe more and more under the banner of European integration. The European Union's democratic deficit has mutated in a deeper sort of flaw, a big social deficit, a stubborn negligence of all that has to do with social needs and rights, with social equality and solidarity, with "society"—whose existence has indeed been authoritatively put in question.

What we are confronted with in the European Union in particular after the economic and fiscal crises of 2008 and 2010 seems to be an institutional machinery taking decisions about the Member States' society, especially on those members States that have been asking for financial assistance, without any consideration of their societal interests, and of their constitutional character as Welfare States. We had an anticipation, though milder, of this approach, Foucault would say of this style of governance, or "governmentality", in a few decisions of the European Court of Justice, when for instance environmental protection was doomed to be weighed against market's freedoms (in particular free movement of goods) and thus declared less relevant than those fundamental positions (Case 28/09), or when industrial action by Unions was stamped as deserving a lower legal protection than economic competition (Case 438/05).

We are also confronted with a cunning discussion about the possible constitutional character of the European Union/European Community and its Treaty. We know this has already been claimed and proclaimed by the European Court of Justice in a series of decisions many years ago (starting with Case 294/83). And even if it were not so publicly announced, the fact that such court could affirm a doctrine according to which the European Community Treaty provisions, or at least some of them, prevail over the member State constitutions and their holiest grail, fundamental rights (Case 11/70), is a clear mark of the constitutional character lavishly offered to the Treaty by those generous judges.[3] But here the question remains of what we do mean by all this talk of constitution and constitutionalization. If we mean that some of the European Community/European Union Treaties claim to be the highest rules applicable within certain fields, we should be aware that this indeed is the case. But, on the other hand, it is just this recognition that opens the gate to the real constitutional *problématique*.

[1]Foucault (2004).
[2]Arendt (1951).
[3]Grimm (2016), chapter I.

How, we should ask, is it possible that the substantively powerful and ambitious constitutions of member States grounded in strong democracies could be put under pressure by such a tiny group of judges who base their decisions on controversial legal doctrines? How could we accept that what is basically a bundle of economic rights, not originally drafted as such, the so-called four freedoms, producing the European common market and, after a significant doctrinal shift, a single market, had to be getting the upper hand over such sacred rights as political and social rights? The narrative offered to justify this turn has been an evolutionary one, a sort of "whig" history. Following an optimistic and somehow messianic view,[4] the nationalist strictures of Member States' law have been considered as progressively overcome by the cosmopolitan statesmanship of brave Luxemburg judges, supported by similarly wise and courageous European commissioners and astute European law scholars. National sovereignty, this terrible beast that brought about two world wars, has been slowly tamed by the judicial production of a novel legal order, beginning with *Van Gend en Loos*, case 26/62 (where however such novelty was still ascribed to international law) and then with *Costa*, case 6/64 (where European community law is no longer imputed to international law). We must only give a good doctrinal seal to such novel and promising construction. It is a constitution!—the judges say. But what kind of constitution is it?—the scholars ask and try to find out.

2 Supranational Constitutionalism

There now are entire libraries filled to the brim with books and articles offering an answer to this question. Several strategies have been tried. There are attempts at equating a rule of law system or just an ordinary legal order with a constitution. A community of law such as the character given to the European community by its being monitored by an independent judiciary will in this way seen as based on a fundamental rule, the Treaties. These thus acquire the dignity of a higher norm, that is, a *constitution*. Constitution would here mean the highest applicable norm applied by the highest competent judge. The interpretative competence given to the European Court of Justice already in the Treaty of Rome, being doctrinally re-shaped in terms of a *Kompetenz-Kompetenz*, makes of this court sort of a constitutional judge, and modifies the Treaty in something functionally equivalent to a true constitution.[5]

There are, on the other hand, scholars treading an alternative and, perhaps, more promising path, that of constructing a "societal constitutionalism" out of extra-political relationships, from *lex mercatoria* to information or cognitive and functional networks. This new form of constitutionalism moves from the idea that is

[4]Weiler (2011), pp. 303–311.

[5]Grimm (2016), p. 9 ff., p. 121 ff.

possible to detach a constitution from the State, and that is possible at a supranational level because of an emerging global society made of autonomous subsystems.

Or pluralism is invoked to purify national constitutionalism and make it worth aspiring to the realm of supranationality. We can have a multi-level or "counter-punctual" order where the *Kompetenz-Kompetenz* is a matter of occasional, when not of occasionalist judicial decisions. There is no need to establish once for all where this preemptive authority will lay. The movement is everything, provided the end is already given (this being the "ever closer union"), and such movement is a pendular one, sometimes described and recommended as dialogue between courts.

There is moreover defended another view, that a constitution can be leveled up with *constitutionalism*, and this would be embedded in a doctrine of legal reasoning and more specifically by judicial case-law and its rationale. It would suffice to have general principles of the rule of law limiting political sovereignty (namely constitutionalism) applied by judicial agencies to produce an effective constitution or something functionally equivalent to it. Under conditions especially of supranationality or of globalization, separation of power would in the end be given through a special doctrine of jurisdiction. Institutional design and functioning are thus shaped through judicial decisions and the principles underlying them. These will therefore be eventually the core of any concept and practice of a constitution.

However, all these solutions to the constitutional *problématique* of European law suffer of a normative sting. To be plausible they must somehow disconnect constitution from democracy as political deliberation and decision, that is, from *citizenship*, as the meta-sovereignty of people expected to follow collective rules, and especially from *solidarity*, an inclusive mutual demand and offer of dignity, the "fraternité" that grants citizenship a redistributive role. Or else, those solutions need give a shortened and summary reconstruction of a democracy as the one, for example, that proposes to interpret judicial review in terms of "argumentative representation", where representation in interpreted as the merely ideal possibility that arguments used by judges are shared or supported by citizens. In any case, the context of all these views seems to be that of a policy that is given a constitution in a situation where one cannot explicitly refer to a collective actor that can be granted legitimacy and, at the same time, citizenship powers. Rules in all these reconstructions are mostly functionally, not deliberatively produced, and there is hardly a way to build a virtuous circle between the ruler and the ruled so that in principle the one could be re-placed by the other.

Modernity looks for the legitimacy of a novel political order mainly through a series of distinct strategies. A common one is a traditional liberal solution. Here you first have a to confront strong State with nearly absolute powers and competences. What you do in this case is challenging the sovereign State absolute claims by producing an alternative sphere of political action. In a sense, in such original liberal model, the State is the source of political legitimacy *a contrario*. You justify yourself as the producer of novel political order in so far as you fight against the State, and create a free zone limiting or downplaying its encompassing powers.

A second strategy has been invoking and mobilizing a social body that as such could be considered as the holder of true legitimacy. Such was the case of the French claim of a *Tiers État* as representing the entire nation. There is something that lies at the bottom of State, a community, a nation, that is more basic and original than the State, and this has a constituting force. There is constituent power that is the real source of the State, and we appeal to it. Here the constitution precedes the State; it is not just a reaction to it.

But what about the case, a historical contingency, where there is no consolidated and strong State to oppose, or in which we cannot rely on an integrated nation, on a "fraternité", a solidarity, to be mobilized to produce legitimacy? In both cases we do not have citizens, or political actors, but rather what we could define "economic subjects", individualist agents that do not share a common public space.

The phenomenology of the "economic subject" is somehow equivalent to that of a "naked man", devoid of a political community (either because such a community has yet to develop or because it has been wiped out by a historical catastrophe), of the man who only has egocentric, basic interests or "preferences" (because of this very nakedness) but no rights (because a political order or public discourse is absent). The *homo oeconomicus*' business is himself; all he wants is to be let alone and satisfy his own needs. "It's enough for a man to understand his own business, and not to interfere with other people's. Mine occupies me constantly"—Scrooge's words.[6] *Homines oeconomici*, who by definition do not act in concert, do not consider themselves as taking part in a common endeavor. They cannot be a real "power", since "power corresponds to the human ability not just to act but to act in concert".[7] Now, egocentric agents are reluctant to solidarity. Acting in concert implies helping each other, and somehow mutually compensating weaknesses and redistributing resources among participants. Individuals driven only by their own personal preferences seem therefore to be unable to operate as the bearers of a constitutional legitimacy, because they are not capable to create a "power", much less a "constituent power".

Now, this strong emergency of a radical individualistic anthropology is a situation which, I would say, we especially find as politically relevant in two historical contexts. The first is where we have a national community that cannot be trusted as a democratic subject, either because of its unsteady commitment to democracy, or because it has been impacted by some historical catastrophe (a lost war, for instance), or it is deeply socially divided or territorially split. The latter, paradigmatically, would be a context where several nations are called or expected to build a common body politic, but they cannot be given real citizenship powers, since they have not yet developed a common political sphere nor concrete, strong bonds of solidarity. This would be the second of the two historical contexts I am referring to. Now, the first case might be exemplified by West Germany after the Second World War; while we could find a case of the second in Western Europe in the late Forties and early Fifties of last century, where nation States had exited the war as deeply aggrieved and divided and the European Economic Community project was

[6]Dickens (1984), p. 51.

[7]Arendt (1970), p. 44.

thus intended to gather in a functional framework countries that only 10 years before had bitterly fought the one against the other.

We want and need a common political community, but we do not have a political collective base for it, we cannot refer to a legitimate and operative constituent power. What we dispose of are only single-minded and egocentrically oriented actors. What should we do then? Now, a possible strategy could be circumventing the legitimacy ground required. The idea would be that a political constitution might be found in initially igniting and ten building an "economic constitution", that is, a specific economic order, hoping this would then produce a more or less integrated political order. This strategy could be followed both at a national and at a supranational level. Around this solution converged different social forces, ideologies and doctrines. To this purpose in West Germany an intelligent scheme was offered by Ordo-liberalism. This successfully drafted a project for a politics without politics, a State without State, a Constitution without Constitution: self-made vertical statesmanship. This script was then rehearsed, when thinking about and shaping the institutional framework of a post-war European integration.

3 Constitution Without Constitution

Ordo-liberals are not enthusiasts about the merits of capitalism. Indeed, they have a more skeptical view about the virtues of the free market. Though they believe that a free market is a sort of Husserlian "essence", the basic norm of a functioning economic system, and that it offers the most reliable and normatively accomplished base for the setting of market prices, they do not believe in an invisible hand that, providentially, can steer market transactions to the best of their possible outcomes. The market should somehow be produced and then permanently monitored, "policed" by a public hand, and this public hand should be visible and operate through law. A market society here is envisaged as eminently a rule of law society, *Privatrechtsgesellschaft*,[8] or a *Rechtsgemeinschaft*. This however is only possible if backer buy a political "comprehensive decision", an *ordnungspolitische Gesamtentscheidung*, establishing a specific (economic) constitution, as it is claimed by Walter Eucken, the great founding father of Ordo-liberalism.[9]

For Ordo-liberals there cannot be a market in the real world without a strong normative regulation prohibiting the possible concentration of economic powers, backed by the rule of law. There is an "essence" of the market that is the business of law to enforce trough the legal process. The State's main role should be bringing about the framework within which the pure form laws of an undistorted market competition could be freely displayed. This is said by Franz Böhm, the legal mind of Ordo-liberalism, in his monograph *Wettbewerb und Monopolkampf*, published 1933.

[8]See Böhm (1966), pp. 75–151.

[9]Eucken (1990), p. 250.

According to him the State's main mission concerning market laws is: "Producing the political and legal conditions that are necessary for such laws to be displayed according to the desired purity and reliableness".[10]

Moreover, in the nature of market—it is argued—we find a core that is equivalent to democracy: consumers choose every day what they think can best satisfy their wishes and preferences; they select, or "elect", what is most suitable to them. Markets operate by a mechanism, the dynamic of demand and offer, that is a functionally equivalent to democratic political elections. People by buying express their preferences, choose, select and thus elect. "As matter of fact – says Franz Böhm –, market laws and social order connections have the character of a daily elective and voting procedure [In Wahrheit handelt es sich aber bei den Marktgesetzlichkeiten um soziale Ordnungzsammenhänge, die den Charakter von *täglichen Abstimmungs- und Wahlvorgängen* haben]".[11] The market is a "plébiscite de tous les jours". In this sense, it is therefore capable of producing legitimacy, since it is in itself a democratic procedure, "weil sie in sich selbst ein demokratischer Vorgang ist",[12] but if only it can be shaped according to its pure "essence". This, however, is the business of law.

You cannot have an economic sovereign or, better, a political sovereign governing economy by commanding: traditional liberalism and Ordo-liberalism agree on this point, a "curse", in Foucault's words, cast on the modern State. However, for the Ordo-liberal this claim reflects a "nature" of the economy we find in the world always put at risk, at peril. We therefore still need a political sovereign not just (this being the traditional liberal view) to protect or not to interfere in the *homo oeconomicus* default position. We need a political sovereign, this basically needed by the way to offer the much looked for political legitimacy, to transform the "essence" of market into a concrete process in the world. And it will be this transformation, and only this, that will ultimately confer fundamental political legitimacy, which will be thus measured by an output, not an input, by consequences, not by principles or an existential source. We will not have political legitimacy because of a privileged actor produces it, but more modestly because of a "nature" restored and gauged by its outputs.

The public hand should thus be all but invisible; the public authority's business is to give operative force to the "essence" of an undistorted, free, highly competitive economy. And such public hand should be strong enough; as Carl Schmitt said in a speech given before an audience of German industrialists in 1932, in order to have a "gesunde Wirtschaft" we need a "starker Staat"; a healthy economy needs a strong

[10]Böhm (2010), p. 16: "Die politischen und rechtlichen Voraussetzungen zu schaffen, die erforderlich sind, damit sich diese Gesetzlichkeiten in der gewollten Reinheit und Zuverlässigkeit abspielen können". The most important legal-theoretical contribution by Böhm possibly is a work, a quite long article, published 1934, where Ordo-liberalism however is made compatible with a strong authoritarian, dictatorial State: "Recht und Macht" (1934), pp. 115–193.

[11]See Böhm (1950), p. 50.

[12]See Böhm (1950), p. 51.

State.[13] At the beginning of the Thirties of last century Schmitt, together with people like Walter Eucken, criticized the interventionist "total economic State", because it is by necessity a weak State: "Der totale Wirtschaftsstaat würde ein schwacher Staat sein".[14] It will be so, because a social interventionist State would have to be feeding the pluralism of social interests that are active in society, and to be accountable and in debt to the social groups and the masses that mobilize those interests. This thesis is reloaded after the war in Eucken's most influential work, *Grundsätze der Wirtschaftspolitik*: "Everywhere we are confronted with State authority being undermined through particularist powers, which represent particularist interests. And a specific character of modern developments is just that this loss of authority is connected with a quick expansion of State intervention".[15] Pluralism predates the State, and by expanding its domain of competences makes its authority much weaker. The way out here should be the State putting the brakes to such predominance of particular groups and powers, to the regime of pluralism, to what was called in the Twenties and Thirties of last century the "revolt of the masses" (by the way Ortega's book *La rebelión de las masas, The revolt of the masses*, is published 1930, just 2 years before Schmitt's and Eucken's pronouncements).

However, a strong State as guarantor of a "healthy economy"—one could object—would play a too not different role State than that one conferred to State by a socialist planned and centralized economy. There should be a minute intervention in the operation of economic actors in order to check their inclination to reach monopolistic positions; a free competition to be realized will rely on a constant monitoring by public agencies. Ordo-liberals indeed acknowledged that by their scheme we shall need such a pervasive operation by public agencies, a State force ordering national economy, "staatliche ordnende Kraft der Volkswirtschaft" in Walter Eucken's words,[16] or later "Staat als ordnende Potenz".[17] Alexander Rüstow, another influential scholar of Ordo-liberalism, underlines the need for free markets to be monitored by special policing through a strong and independent State power, "marktpolizeiliche Überwachung durch eine starke und unhabhängige Staatsgewalt".[18] This strong ordering authority, such independent market policing agency had better not be a delegated power by the democratic law-giver, or a branch of the ordinary executive power bound by parliamentary deliberation and subject to the interest pluralism they inevitably will have to give voice.

[13]See Schmitt (1995 [1932]), pp. 71–91.

[14]Eucken (1932), p. 319.

[15]Eucken (1990) p. 329: "Überall handelt sich um die Unterhölung der Staatsautorität durch partikulare Gewalten, die partikulare Interessen vertreten. Und eine Eigenart der modernenen Entwicklung ist es eben, das mit diesem Autoritätsverlust eine rasche Expansion der Staatstätigkeit verbunden ist".

[16]Eucken (1932), p. 321.

[17]Eucken (1990), p. 330.

[18]Rüstow (2001), p. 102.

Such differently shaped public hand, these authorities, such agencies will have to be independent authoritative bodies, no longer under the direct scrutiny of parliaments and executives. They will function like a kind of judiciary, only bound to the rule of law. Parliamentary politics will not have a say about their operations. Franz Böhm is quite explicit about this: "Should an administrative function however in such a way anchored in a law procedure, it would then in second place made it possible for the task of fighting against monopolies and controlling them to be disconnected from the ordinary scope of government functions and thus granted to an independent State authority, which will not be accountable to parliament not even to government, while – in the way of a court – not being given any political discretionary power, but – as for its rulings – being subject to the law".[19] For the ordering function of economy can be effectively fulfilled, only if the public hand assuming that function can be working detached from the influence of the general electorate, when it, the State finds it possible to free itself from the influences of the masses, "wenn er [the State] die Kraft findet, sich dem Einfluss der Massen frei zu machen".[20]

Suppose now a context where we do not have citizens, nor can we hope to develop them soon; we only have "naked human beings", *homines oeconomici*, people whose main business are themselves, their basic needs, food, shelter, heating, a job. Suppose a society that has lost its national integrative force, or a group of political actors, like nations or States, that are mutually suspicious, and are not capable of producing a common space of solidarity. Under such conditions, we have, in short, something that seems like a Juan Fernandez Island,[21] an island where people are starving and do interrelate only through their acute need satisfaction, thus highly competing the one against the other for survival. "Hunger would drive them to work".[22] This is a market *in embryo*, or that we could consider to be such, and deal with it accordingly. But this wild competition needs to be civilized, egoistic subjects have to be reeducated into markets operators, entrepreneurs and consumers. Basic needs satisfaction, demand and offer, have to be filtered by market rules. Such reeducation and transformation from a wild fight for survival into a civilized operating market is the constitutional mission of a strong State.

Now, by making of naked subjects market actors, through the State intervention, we might hope to produce an original, though limited or weak base, foundation, for political legitimacy. We need to start from *homines oeconomici*. To do so we have

---

[19]See Böhm (1950), p. 54: "Wenn aber eine Verwaltungsaufgabe dergestalt an eine gesetzliche Marschroute gebunden wird, dann wird es zweitens möglich gemacht, die Aufgabe der Monopolbekämpfung und Monopolkontrolle aus dem übrigen Kreis der Regierungsaufgaben herauszulösen und sie einer selbstständigen Staatsbehörde zu übertragen, die nicht dem Parlament und auch nicht der Regierung verantwortlich ist, dafür aber – wie ein Gericht – keine politische Entscheidungsfreiheit besitzt, sondern hinsichtlich seiner Massnahmen dem Gesetz unterworfen ist".

[20]Eucken (1932), p. 318.

[21]Polanyi (2001), pp. 117–119.

[22]Polanyi (2001), pp. 119–120.

not to work out a democratic constitution, we can easily do without it, we can skip it; a basic law, a *Grundgesetz*, or even a Treaty perhaps, will suffice. They will be all the same. Since a constituent power or a "people" as a political actor here is not still possibly available or operative, or not yet to be much relied upon, we have to look for a different source of legitimacy. The master of the constitution, of the basic law, could not here be played by a fragmented and unpolitical people. As a consequence the guardianship of such basic law could not be given to a body representative of that fragmented and radically plural people, but it should be reserved to some kind of "independent agency", for instance a distant tribunal in a site where it could work undisturbed by ordinary politics and its passions, Karlsruhe, Luxemburg, a Constitutional Court, or else an Executive Commission, or an independent central bank, in Brussels or Frankfurt, as a regulatory agency.

The result will be a constitution without constitution, a politics without politics, possibly a State without State, and everything guided by the essence, Eucken would say the "free form", "reine Form",[23] now made process, of a free, of a highly competitive interaction of entrepreneurs and consumers, permanently moving around, with no public barriers, or tariffs, and collective borders, offering and asking for labour, goods, services, and capital. Since we do not wish, or are not capable, to have a collective political enterprise, we will rely on the production of a self-regulated and anti-collectivist, that is, competitive, interaction. This is—according to Alfred Müller-Armack, an Ordoliberal economist that leaded the German representation in the preparatory talks to the EEC Treaty in 1957—what happened to European nation States negotiating a European community: "One wanted to protect oneself against the economic policy of other States and resolved to strongly limit the political economy leeway internally".[24] We shall thus have *self-made statesmanship*, in the sense both of statesmen that give up state intervention, and of statesmen without political representation, or even without a State, that are nonetheless self-appointed as true guardians of the *régime* so established.

The basic law, or Treaty, will be progressively given the force of a constitution, not by politics, but with*out politics*, by granting to the imaginary original position of free market actors a special constitutional status. From the beginning, indeed already in its very foundation, the European community was conceived fundamentally as a zone of free market competition, or so it was thought of by a few of its most influential "founding fathers", as Müller-Armack in 1964 tells us: "The order of the common market is thus internally defined as a highly competitive market".[25] We shall thus see that a supranational antidiscrimination principle (article 7 of the Treaty of Rome), indeed an integrative civilizing idea, is translated in a bundle of individual

[23]Eucken (1990), pp. 21–22.

[24]Müller-Armack (1965), p. 405: "Man wollte sich gegen die Wirtschaftspolitik der übrigen Staaten sichern und kamm dazu, den wirtschaftspolitischen Spielraum nach inner streng zu begrenzen". See also Röpke (1958), p. 38.

[25]Müller-Armack (1965), p. 405: "Die Ordnung des Gemeinsames Marktes ist so als ein streng wettbewerblicher Markt im Innern definiert".

rights with direct effect by the European Court of Justice (*Van Gend en Loos*, Case 26/62), that these rights are made prevail over non-economic rights (*Costa*, Case 6/64, etc.), and that that same principle is converted and epitomized (notably by ECJ jurisprudence starting with *Cassis de Dijon*, Case 120/78, and then "constitutionalized" in the Single European Act) in an anti-regulative provision and as a matter of fact in the natural law of a "highly competitive social market economy" (Article 3, paragraph 3, of the Treaty on European Union). The European Commission could proudly claim, in a communication to Parliament, Council etc., on October 10th, 2010, that "the construction of one big market is at the heart of the European project envisaged by the founding fathers".

Indeed, this was already in the Sixties at the core of the European Commission's plans about what a European Community should mean and be, and it is explicitly anticipated for instance in the following words of Hans von der Groeben, a powerful German European Commissioner: "In the action programme of the EEC-Commission is clearly stated that a competition economy or a market economy is the appropriate instrument to reach the Treaty's end".[26] That is, it is competition and free market that are the most appropriate tools to produce European integration. However, this should not mean to get back to the *laissez faire* ideology and its comfortable lassitude ("Gemeint ist damit aber nicht ein Rückfall in die Bequemlichkeit des *laissez faire*"[27]). Public authorities cannot make it easy. A tight, studious public hand intervention will have to support the market and allow it to remain faithful, conforming, to its essential competitive nature: "Der Wettbewerb muss durch eine aktive wirtschaftspolitische Ordungspolitik ergänzt werden".[28]

The opening of markets is a fundamental tenet of the economic constitution. This is why it should be a public hand's task. It is too serious a thing—as it's pointed out by Walter Eucken—to be left to the private decision: "Openness of markets has an economic constitutional meaning [. . .] It's part of an ordinamental policy that should not be left to private actors".[29]

[26]von der Groeben (1967), p. 35: "Im Aktionsprogramm der EWG-Kommission ist klar zum Ausdruck gebracht worden, dass die Wettbewerbswirtschaft oder Marktwirtschaft das geignete Instrument zur Erreichung des Zieles des Vertrages [. . .] ist".

[27]von der Groeben (1967), p. 35.

[28]von der Groeben (1967), p. 35.

[29]See Eucken (1981), p. 148: "Die Öffnung der Märkte hat einen wirtschaftsverfassungsrechtlichen Sinn [. . .] Sie gehört zur Ordungspolitik, die Privaten nich überlassen werden darf".

4 Market as Social Contract

Let me resume the main point of this paper. There has been a recent revival of the notion of "political right" in the legal doctrine. My understanding of it is that by this expression one intends to refer to the political origins of a constitutional order or of a State. In the modernity this is conceived as the outcome of a political decision or, if you prefer, of political constructivism. Such decision, or construction, is then differently presented according to the different doctrines of political modernity. As a matter of fact, decision and construction may more often than not be considered and operationalized as opposed foundational strategies. This issue, however, is not of much relevance in my discussion here.

Decision, or construction, could be seen as just an act of existential decision both by a special individual or by a special collective body. Or they might be conceived as the integrative program of a plurality of subjects that interacting and deliberating both produce a constituent power and a constitution. In this second view producing and produced are coterminous. Or we could think of first a *pactum unionis* and then a *pactum subjectionis*. But a *pactum*, a contract, should there be. In all these views there is assumed a more or less full legitimacy of the subjects involved to act as producers of a polity. Even in the case of a brutal state of nature that should be overcome through a civil state given by an absolute sovereign, even in the case of the contract concluded by nasty and brutish competitors as shaped by Thomas Hobbes' imagination, these nasty individuals are not so corrupted or malicious that their product, their deliberation, should irremediably be defective and marked of vice and sin. The state of nature is a condition of war of all against anyone, where *homo homini lupus* is the rule, but such *lupi*, those human wolves, nonetheless are somehow still holders of a spark of morality. They are entitled holders of moral rights; their brutishness did not make them undeserving or losing those rights. They are still moral subjects. And they, being still a source of morality, are available for a residual political legitimacy: their mutual agreement might well produce a legitimate public power.

But what about when we cannot assume that the state of nature inhabitants have maintained some spark of moral values. What if they are marked by the most terrible crimes of humanity? Suppose they are even candidates to morality, or that they are not *pre-moral* agents, that have not yet made the transition to normativity from their original prudential and egocentrically utilitarian stance. They are rather *immoral*, or, if you like, *post-moral* agents, since, though they already lived and found themselves within a context ruled by normativity, they have given up moral rules, or better (or worse) they have seriously infringed them.

On the other hand, both Hobbes and Locke, and all the doctrines of a political right, assume as solved the question of the boundaries (or, if you like, of the self-definition) of the people that will enter into the contract and produce the political order. That is, they presuppose as given a certain common identity of the people that start entering in negotiations and then end in having an agreement about a common sovereign. But what if these boundaries are not given, what if they are blurred, what if the people concerned are a miscellaneous collection of individuals randomly gathering from different regions and traditions, and no self-definition can be assumed? No ground for solidarity, or "fraternité", is thus there disposable.

Now, in such extremely precarious conditions of morality and identity, no traditional doctrine of political right could work. There is no base for decision or construction. Political right philosophies are not prepared for such extreme case of pluralist and disordered collections of people. Such an extreme case you will find paradigmatically at least in two occasions. The first is the one where you believe the plurality of interest makes impossible the identity, that is the definition of those borders identifying a group of people as constituent, as imputable of a decision or of a construction or else of a tradition. This might be the case of radical social pluralism as feared by conservatives in the Weimar Republic, or of an international society, a group of countries of States, that are fed by opposed and irreconcilable interests and views, as it was, or seemed to be, Europe after the Second World War.

But then there is the second paradigmatic and much more dramatic case, that of a society of immoral individuals, of people that could not claim to be holders of moral rights, or else of individuals gathering without a common origin and tradition. They are incapable of self-definition because they have forfeited the right to it. Now, this second case could have been envisaged in the situation of Germany after the defeat of the second world war. After its *debellatio* Germany was now a country whose people had been deeply soiled by the most terrible tyranny. And the country had been divided, split in two, and had moreover become sort of melting pot with millions of refugees from the Eastern regions now annexed to Soviet Union and Poland. Such a society could hardly express a legitimate basis for a constituent power or for an empowered collective subject. Ordo-liberalism was then ready to offer an alternative constitutional strategy.

In 1938 several liberal thinkers, mainly economists, among whom we might remember Friedrich Hayek, Ludwig von Mises, Alexander Rüstow, Wilhelm Röpke, Robert Marjolin, gathered in Paris convened by Walter Lippmann. It was the now famous and much discussed *Colloque Walter Lippmann*, where, before an acute crisis of capitalist economies after 1929, distinct schools of liberal thought confronted their views and proposed new analyses and strategies. Most of the scholars there meeting agreed about the weakness of traditional *laissez faire* capitalism, and on the necessity of considering a renewed fresh start (a view later canonized by Walter Eucken himself[30]). They nearly all concurred that the State should be granted a special role in the defense of free economies. Lippmann thus stressed that "since the laws are the State's creation, upon the State fall the responsibility of determining the legal regime that serves as the framework for the free

[30]See Eucken (1990), for instance p. 373.

development of economic activity".[31] The State had an important role to play in the sound functioning of a free market economy.

The question however was immediately raised of which State it was here to be spoken about. A main objection was put forward by an Ordo-liberal, Alexander Rüstow: "But what State? Can the democratic State with its current structure actually assume – in an effective manner – such responsibility?".[32] It couldn't indeed, or so they believed, since a in a democratic State the public hand was considered a constant source of benefits which all groups and lobbies can appeal to without ever minding the cost of such lavish solidarity, but as a matter of act by claiming that others' purses will pay for one's own whims. "In this way – this is Röpke's analysis – we got a situation where, once needs and desires made a loud noise, these were addressed to the 'State', without ever generally thinking that in this way we were asking all other people, often in a not gentle manner, to provide us something".[33]

This is a view generally shared by Ordo-liberals: Democracy easily equates with "Gruppenanarchie",[34] and its consequential welfarism will be a danger for a healthy market economy only ruled by the free interplay of offer and demand. "Il y a la dissolution de l'État par les intérêts particuliers. C'est cette désintégration de l'État même par les partis, par les intérêts, qui retient notre attention"—as it is said by Röpke at the final session of the Paris *Colloque*.[35] This view, that a democratic State by necessity is, so to say, vampirized and brought to financial irresponsibility and exhaustion by the political pluralism nurtured by this State needing widespread popular support, had been suggestively echoed by Carl Schmitt with the formula of *Parteienbundesstaat,* "federal State of political parties", just a few months before the fatal January 1933.[36]

Under condition of radical social pluralism, a constitution cannot be the outcome for a democratic subject or entity. This is the basic tenet of Ordo-liberal constitutional doctrine. There is no such entity, there is no democratic subject available, either because of the extreme pluralism of society, or because of its illegitimacy, of its being still a gathering of devils, a rabble without a soul. These devils cannot be the source of a legitimate political order. From Behemoth's *Volksgenossen*, comrades, we shall never get Leviathan's citizenship.[37] Behemoth's rabble has to be first

[31]See Audier (2012), p. 72. This was a view articulated at length in Lippmann's book, *The Good Society* (Little, Brown and Co., Boston 1938), that served as a basis for discussion in the Paris Colloque.

[32]See Audier (2012), p. 77.

[33]Röpke (1949), p. 185: "So ist es dem Zustand gekommen, dass, wo nur immer Wünsche und Begehren laut wurden, der erste Gedanken dem 'Staat' gilt, ohne dass den meisten noch der Gedanke käme, dass wir damit die Gesamtheit der anderen – oft sogar in recht unmanierlichen Art – bitten, uns etwas zuzulegen".

[34]Eucken (1990), p. 328.

[35]Audier (2012), p. 458.

[36]See Schmitt (1932), pp. 55–70.

[37]Neumann (1944).

civilized, and thus given a surrogate of legitimacy, that they still do not get and do not know how and where to get. The way to do so, the only possible strategy, is to make of them rational subjects, and the only rationality here available is the one offered through an undistorted competitive market—a strategic rationality that has the advantage to be fed and moved only by the self-interest. Devils will not be asked to become angels, nor to approach the dignity of a Hobbesian wolf with its narrow but certain claims of morality, but only to claim their own self-interest. In the framework of market rules and supervised by a strong State those interests will be channeled into a natural law regime of undistorted competition that will render those self-interested actors self-conscious and disciplined market agents and virtuous consumers and entrepreneurs.

If it is dubious that a people of devils will be able to build a legitimate State, it is likely that devils will willingly enter into the market and will abide by its iron law, once such laws are wisely shaped and monitored by a public agency in charge of such evolutionary and pedagogic task. The constitution of the country, under such conditions, that is in a Behemoth predicament, will have to be an *economic*, not a political one. The political right, to be eventually recovered, should first be functionally reshaped as an economic function, that of consumer and entrepreneur, of offer and demand of goods, to sell and to buy, as a *prima facie* consumer and entrepreneur of oneself. This will be the historical mission of a political power whose legitimacy will only be drawn *a posteriori* from the successful implementation of a highly competitive free market dispensing satisfaction, and whose blueprint is given by the "essence" of free market economy. This novel strategy is explicitly presented in a speech given by Ludwig Erhard in Frankfurt on April 21st, 1948, and can be summarized in the following statement: "The State has a moral legitimacy to speak in the name of the people only there, where freedom and duty become binding law. In concrete terms this means that [...] performance competition should be given the chance of developing also in an automatic way".[38] This speech is intelligently put under narrow scrutiny by Foucault in his 1979 College de France lectures.[39] Foucault resumes Erhard's views in the following way: "The institution of economic freedom will necessarily, will possibly function in any case, somehow in the way of a syphon, of a primer for the building of a political sovereignty".[40] Here, programmatically, "economy is creating public law".[41] The economic constitution would thus be emancipated from the political one.

It is not, however, as it happened in the traditional liberal model, that we have a market, a free economy, and this is strong enough to build a legitimate political

[38]Erhard (1981a), p. 40.

[39]Foucault (2004), p. 82. Cf. also what Röpke wrote about the "German question" 1946, recommending *free trade* as a disciplining order "to compel Germans to bring into play exceptional resourcefulness, adaptability, and abstinence". Röpke (1946), p. 213.

[40]Foucault (2004), p. 84: "L'institution de la liberté économique va devoir, va pouvoir en tout cas fonctionner, en quelque sorte, comme un siphon, comme une amorce pour la formation d'une souveraineté politique".

[41]Foucault (2004), p. 86: "L'economie est créatrice du droit public".

power that is expected to guarantee the private rights already effectively practiced and mutually acknowledged by private economic subjects. In the Ordo-liberal scheme, echoed by Erhard's speech, there is yet no market to move from. Market is seen as a target and a possible achievement. Political power will be only legitimate, and there will be again a political sovereignty viable to be generally acknowledged as such, if it is able to produce a functioning market on the base of a free and competitive supply-demand mechanism. The State here is not a superstructure moved by the economic structure. It is the other way around; it is the State the structure, the ordering agency, that through rules of an idiosyncratic constitutionalism referring to free price formation, will give shape to the market and make of devils tamed economic actors. Liberalism is in this way founded through authority and it permanently refers to such authority. It is this, authority, that, through a specific normative architecture, an "ordo", a "fundamental law", and the corresponding policy, *Ordnungspolitik*, makes economic freedoms, and civilized intercourse between people, in the short run practicable.[42]

References

Arendt, H. (1951). *The burden of our time*. London: Secker & Warburg.

Arendt, H. (1970). *On violence*. Orlando, FL: Harcourt Books.

Audier, S. (2012). *Le colloque Lippmann*. Paris: Le bord de l'eau.

Böhm, F. (1934). Recht und Macht. *Die Tatwelt, 10*, 115–193.

Böhm, F. (1950). *Wirtschaftsordnung und Staatsverfassung*. Tübingen: Mohr.

Böhm, F. (1966). Privatrechtsgesellschaft und Marktswirtschaft. *Ordo—Jahrbuch für die Ordnung von Wirtschaft und Gesellschaft, 17*, 75–151.

Böhm, F. (2010). In E.-J. Mestmäcker (Ed.), *Wettbewerb und Monopolkampf. Eine Untersuchung zur Frage des wirtschaftlichen Kampfrechts und zur Frage der rechtlichen Struktur der geltenden Wirtschaftsordung* (2nd ed.). Baden-Baden: Nomos.

Dickens, C. (1984). A Christmas Carol. In M. Slater (Ed.), *The Christmas books* (1st ed.). Harmondsworth: Penguin.

Erhard, L. (1981a). Das Programm der Wirtschaftsreform. In *Grundtexte der sozialen Marktwirtschaft*, Zeugnisse aus 200 Jahren ordnungspolitischen Diskussion. Stuttgart: Fischer Verlag.

Erhard, L. (1981b). Die neuen Tatsachen (1948). In *Grundtexte der sozialen Marktwirtschaft*, Zeugnisse aus 200 Jahren ordnungspolitischen Diskussion. Stuttgart: Fischer Verlag.

Eucken, W. (1932). Staatliche Strukturwandlungen und die Krisis des Kapitalismus. *Weltwirtschaftliches Archiv, 36*, 297:323.

Eucken W (1981) Die Politik zur Herstellung der Wettbewerbsordung. In: Grundtexte der sozialen Marktwirtschaft, ed. by W. Stützel, Ch. Watrin, Hans Willgerodt, and Karl Hohmann. Gustav Fischer Verlag, Stuttgart

[42]See Erhard (1981b) where an appraisal is given of the recent German political and economic reform: "Es gab nur noch einen zusammengewürfelten, seelenlosen, verantwortungslosen Haufen von Lebensangst geplagter Individuen, wo, jeder, so gut er konnte, seine rein physische Existenz zu bewahren suchte. Diesen Zustand haben wir überwunden".

Eucken, W. (1990). In E.-J. Mestmäcker (Ed.), *Grundsätze der Wirtschaftspolitik* (6 revised ed.). Tübingen: Mohr.
Foucault, M. (2004). *Naissance de la biopolitique*. Paris: Gallimard.
Grimm, D. (2016). *Europa ja – aber welches? Zur Verfassung der europäischen Demokratie*. München: C.H. Beck.
Müller-Armack, A. (1965). Die Wirtschaftsordnung der Gemeinsamen Marktes. In E. Schneider (Ed.), *Weltwirtschaftliche Probleme der Gegenwart*. Berlin.
Neumann, F. L. (1944). *Behemoth: The structure and practice of national socialism, 1933–1944*. Oxford: Oxford University Press.
Polanyi, K. (2001). *The great transformation. The political and economic origins of our time*. Boston: Beacon Press.
Röpke, W. (1946). *The German question* (E. W. Dickes, Trans.). London: George Allen & Unwin.
Röpke, W. (1949). *Civitas humana – Grundfragen der Wirtschafts- und Gesellschaftsreform* (3rd ed.). Stuttgart: Bern.
Röpke, W. (1958). Gemeinsamer Markt und Freihandelzone 28 Thesen als Richtpunkte. *Ordo, 10*, 31–62.
Rüstow, A. (2001). *Die Religion der Marktwirtschaft*. Walter Eucken Archiv - Reihe Zweite Aufklärung, Münster
Schmitt, C. (1932). Konstruktive Verfassungsprobleme. now. In G. Maschke (Ed.), *Id: Staat, Großraum, Nomos—Arbeiten aus den Jahren 1916-1969*. Berlin: Duncker & Humblot.
Schmitt C (1995) Starker Staat, gesunde Wirtschaft (1932). In: Schmitt C, Staat, Großraum, Nomos—Arbeiten aus den Jahren 1916–1969, G. Maschke. Duncker & Humblot, Berlin.
von der Groeben, H. (1967). Die Europäische Wirtschaftsgemeinschaft und unsere Wirtschafts- und Gesellschaftsordnung. In *Europa—Plan und Wirklichkeit—Reden, Berichte, Aufsätze zur europäischen Politik*. Baden-Baden: Nomos.
Weiler, J. H. H. (2011). 60 years since the First European Community – reflections on political messianism. *European Journal of International Law, 22*, 303–311.

Massimo La Torre is Professor at the Department of Law of the Universitá di Catanzaro (Italy) and at the University of Tallinn (Estonia). Before that, he taught in Florence, Bologna, Murcia, and Hull. He had numerous visiting professional fellowships at European and American Universities, and he was fellow of the Alliance Française, the Consiglio Nazionale delle Richerche, the British Council and the Alexander von Humboldt Foundation. La Torre was honored with the Research Award of the Alexander von Humboldt Foundation. His publications include *Norme, Istituzioni, Valori* (Laterza, 2008), *La Lucha contra el Derecho Subjetivo* (Dykinson, 2008) and *Constitutionalism and Legal Reasoning* (Springer, 2007).

In Capital We Trust: The Eurozone: A Congeries of Material Norms Without a Constitution?

Agustín José Menéndez

Contents

Abstract This chapter reconstructs the content of the key norms and practices constituting and disciplining public power in the Eurozone. On the one hand, the fundamental substantive norms uphold the primacy of private property, entrepreneurial freedom and sound money. On the other hand, a series of procedural norms fragment, enervate and pulverise the power held by representative institutions and decision-making processes, and result in the selective empowerment of collectives of executives, central banks and key actors in the financial sector. The abstract and concrete weight assigned to economic freedoms, the multiplication of decision-making procedures alternative to representative decision-making, and the entrenchment of structural biases in favour of private property and entrepreneurial freedom

---

A. J. Menéndez (✉)
Universidad Autónoma de Madrid, Madrid, Spain
e-mail: agustin.menendez@uam.es

© Springer Nature Switzerland AG 2020

M. Nogueira de Brito, L. Pereira Coutinho (eds.), *The Political Dimension of Constitutional Law*, https://doi.org/10.1007/978-3-030-38459-3_9

have largely "taken the risk out of democracy" by fragmenting, enervating and pulverising public power.

> 'Whereas it is true that the emergence of modern democracy results from the development of capitalism, modern democracy is the antithesis of capitalism, and in no way its political expression'—(Basso 1958, p. 33, my translation).
>
> "It's true," Di Blasi said, "every society produces the particular kind of imposture that suits it best, so to speak. Our society is a fraud, a judicial, literary, human fraud – yes, I would say human too, for it is fraudulent in its very essence. So our society has produced, quite simply and naturally, a reverse fraud"—(Sciasia 1988, p. 592; English translation, Sciascia 2016, p. 109).

1 Introduction

This chapter reconstructs the content of the key norms and practices constituting and disciplining public power in the Eurozone. The object of the essay is thus the set of norms that contain the fundamental choices regarding the shape of the economic and political order of the Eurozone.

It is my claim the organisation of public power in Europe is characterised by the primacy assigned to private property, entrepreneurial freedom and sound money, and by the limitation, both substantive and procedural, of democratic decision-making which results in part in the fragmentation and pulverisation of public power and, as a result, in the empowerment of public but non-representative institutions and of private actors. As a result, it is possible to distinguish a *ceto dirigente*, but one whose discretion is itself programmed in a specific substantive form through the assignment of very high abstract and concrete weight to *some types* of private property, *some kinds* of entrepreneurial freedom, and *some variants* of "welfare-maximising" economic organisation.

The structure of the essays is as follows. In the first part, I consider the key substantive fundamental norms defining the European economic and political structure, namely sound money and economic freedoms. In the second part, I consider norm- and decision-making, both in terms of the general rule, and even more decisively, the exceptions to the principle of democratic and representative decision-making, through which public power is fragmented and pulverised. In addition, I show how the division of labour between decision-making processes and the division of competences between the Eurozone and the Member States combine to create a structural bias that reinforces the ascendancy of private property and entrepreneurial freedom, programming all power holders, including those exerting "exceptional" powers. The last part holds the conclusions.

One caveat is perhaps due. The object of this chapter could be said to be the study of the material constitution of the Eurozone. At least, it shares with the literature on the material constitution the willingness to transcend formal rules when analysing the actual content of law and the keen concern with power and the exertion of power. However, in the following I avoid as much as possible the words constitution or constitutional. In such a way, I hope to leave open the questions of what kind of polity the Eurozone is, and what kind of legal order European Union law is, questions to which I come back in the conclusions. Then I will plea for taking seriously the agenda of the material constitution, but dropping the confusing reference to "constitution" and favouring the more neutral "structural organisation of power".

2 Framing Democracy: Sound Money and Economic Freedoms

In this first section, I consider the fundamental principles characterising the European economic and political orders. Such principles are those defining the scope of what can be validly decided, or what is the same, the principles determining the possible contents of any new statute, policy, administrative decision or judicial ruling.

It is my claim that there are two sets of such principles, namely sound money and economic freedoms. In both cases, the principles have been inscribed in the European Union Treaties. In both cases, however, to make sense of the actual practices, we have to consider not only the formal legal norms, but also a set of social and economic practices (such as those defining money and monetary policy) and the implications of formal norms and social and economic practices in their wider social, economic, political and cultural context. Moreover, the institutions and processes through which these two yardsticks of validity came about first, and are enforced now are very different. While economic freedoms have been shaped and reshaped by the Commission and the European Court of Justice, which remain the fundamental actors empowering the holders of such rights, sound money evolved out of a very specific constellation in the seventies, and has been defined and is brought to bear in practice by an increasingly asymmetric European Council, by the European Central Bank and last, but not least, by (key actors in) financial markets.

2.1 Sound Money

The principle of "sound money" requires the guarantee of the stability of the currency, which should not get suddenly appreciated or depreciated in value, but rather maintain its purchasing power over time. To put it differently, it is paramount that the currency serves as a store of value, so that the worth of cumulated capital is not diminished, and so that the possibility of cumulating further capital is left unimpeded.[1]

[1]It is the latter that may render necessary strong and massive public intervention to guarantee and eventually restore the stability of the financial system; in operative terms, its liquidity).

This entails opting for one among different possible ways of constituting money, and of unfolding the constitutive effects of money (Desan 2014).

At first sight, the principle of sound money may be regarded as hopelessly outdated, belonging to a bygone era, that of commodity currencies, whose value was ultimately guaranteed by the intrinsic worth of the coins, or by the convertibility of banknotes or other forms of money into a precious commodity. The euro, like all contemporary currencies, is based on trust (a fiat currency) so "soundness" is said to be assured differently. In concrete, by a set of principles disciplining monetary and economic policy. Three of such principles are of outstanding importance: monetary stability as the paramount goal of monetary policy, monetary dominance and financial stability.

2.1.1 Monetary Stability as the Paramount Goal of Monetary Policy

Monetary stability has been established as the paramount goal of monetary policy. The principle emerged and became entrenched as a quasi-necessary consequence of the monetary arrangements predating EMU, in particular the European Monetary System (EMS). Formally speaking, the EMS "only" required Member States to keep the relative value of its currency vis-à-vis the rest of European currencies. However, to do so in a context marked by floating exchanges rates with parities ultimately fixed by offer and demand in financial markets, vast disparities in the relative power of the different states, and the lack of genuinely common European funds to manage exchanges, created the conditions under which most Member States were forced to mimic the monetary policy of the hegemonic monetary power, Germany, which happened to be the country with an independent central bank committed to monetary stability. The features of the EMS (including its easy reversibility) set limits to the unconditional character of monetary stability. Still, the principle came to permeate the design not only of monetary policy but also economic policy, and was ultimately codified in the Treaty of Maastricht.

Article 119.2 TEU now states that:

> Concurrently with the foregoing [the consistency and objectives of economic policy], and as provided in the Treaties and in accordance with the procedures set out therein, these activities shall include a single currency, the euro, and the definition and conduct of a single monetary policy and exchange-rate policy the primary objective of both of which shall be to maintain price stability and, without prejudice to this objective, to support the general economic policies in the Union, in accordance with the principle of an open market economy with free competition (my italics).

Among other things, this entails that the active use of monetary policy to achieve wider socio-economic goals, such as full employment, distributive or social justice, is to be subordinated to the previous achievement of monetary stability. In other words, other socio-economic goals can only be pursued once monetary stability is achieved, and without imperilling it.

The primacy of monetary stability has been further confirmed since the beginning of the financial, economic and fiscal crises, most importantly through the emergence of constitutional conventions that provide new (and as we will see alternative) guarantees of public debt being a "safe asset". Two developments are especially relevant:

- Firstly, default not only on internal but also on external debt has been ruled out. In particular, a constitutional convention has emerged according to which Eurozone states are now precluded from defaulting on their public debt. Doing so in a unilateral fashion is expected to result on the state being expelled from the Eurozone, most likely without any form of support or assistance from the remaining Member States of the Eurozone (something which is assumed would result in lasting economic damage, the perspective of which would deter any state from even contemplating "Euroexit"). The different stages in the Greek fiscal crisis, especially in the spring of 2015, constitute evidence in that regard.
- Secondly, constitutional practices or even explicit norms have been established ensuring the absolute priority of the repayment of principal and interest of public debt. In the case of Spain, the priority has been formally made part of the Constitution (article 135.3 of the Spanish Constitution). The subjection of the issue of Greek debt to English law, or the generalisation of collective action clauses in the issue of the debt of periphery states have further weakened the power of states to restructure debt unilaterally.

2.1.2 Monetary Dominance

Monetary dominance entails that the achievement of monetary stability is a precondition for the pursuit of goals other than monetary stability itself through not only monetary policy, but also through fiscal, social or tax policies. This entails that monetary stability is the ultimate principle to be pursued in the execution of all economic policies, the *stella polaris* of economic policy as a whole. Thus, one specific conception of the good monetary policy *comes to determine* the possible conceptions of fiscal policy, under the specific label of sound budgetary policies. Playing with words (but only a little) sound money dictates sound budgetary policies.

The expansion of sound money into sound budgetary policies was more than implicit in the asymmetrical structure of economic and monetary union.

To start with, the coherence of a single centralised monetary policy and a plurality of national fiscal policies was to be guaranteed by setting limits to fiscal, not to monetary policy, thus relegating the goals of fiscal policy to those of monetary policy. There and then emerged the most obvious component of the "sound budgetary" canon, the first two fiscal rules setting ceilings to the stocks of public debt (60% GDP) and to public deficits (3% GDP). At the same time, the fixation of the inflation target was left in the hands of the European Central Bank, or what is the same, there was no inflation rule (the 2% target was "self-imposed" by the ECB). A clear sign that discretion did not disappear, but was shifted in terms of policy domain and of the actor exerting it.

Crucially, EMU did away with the power of Member States to constitute their currencies. Not only the definition and execution of monetary policy was shifted to a federal and independent central bank, but states were prohibited from funding themselves through the central bank, imposing coerced loans on private financial institutions or, for that matter, receiving funds from other Member States. In such a way, states were forced into funding themselves either through taxes or through loans at rates decided exclusively by private actors in financial markets. In the momentous decisions taken in *Pringle* and *OMT*, the ECJ has come to characterise the elimination of the power that constituted the ultimate guarantee of the safety of public debt as an asset as key to ensure "sound budgetary policy".

> It is apparent from the preparatory work relating to the Treaty of Maastricht that the aim of Article 125 TFEU is to ensure that the Member States follow a sound budgetary policy (see Draft treaty amending the Treaty establishing the European Economic Community with a view to achieving economic and monetary union, *Bulletin of the European Communities*, Supplement 2/91, pp. 24 and 54). The prohibition laid down in Article 125 TFEU ensures that the Member States remain subject to the logic of the market when they enter into debt, since that ought to prompt them to maintain budgetary discipline. Compliance with such discipline contributes at Union level to the attainment of a higher objective, namely maintaining the financial stability of the monetary union (European Court of Justice 2012, par. 135).

In parallel, free movement of capital was extended to third countries, a move not only not required by the creation of an internal market, but potentially in conflict with it (and with a good many public policy objectives, not least fighting against tax fraud). The point was, quite explicitly, to enable capital markets (and de facto, key actors within capital markets) to further restrain the set of feasible budgetary policy alternatives (Article 73B TEC, as amended by Article G D 15 of the Treaty of Maastricht), in the hope that markets would favour "sound budgetary policies".

After the crises, the ascendancy of monetary stability over economic policy as a whole has been further reinforced, while new arrangements have emerged with a view to stabilise the resulting socio-economic order.

On the one hand, the so-called "new economic governance" has resulted in more fiscal rules (including the deficit reduction path rule, the debt reduction path rule, and the automatic expenditure cuts, genuine automatic stabilisers in reverse), further subordinating fiscal to monetary policy. By the same token, a set of "macroeconomic indicators" has been defined with a view to limit the discretion of Member States in the overall design of their social and economic policies. Furthermore, the "new economic governance" also extends to a new procedure for the monitoring of states' compliance with fiscal rules and macroeconomic indicators, backed up by sanctions that are now procedurally easier to apply (as they require being supported by a minority, not a majority of Member States, something to which I return in Section II) (see Menéndez 2014).

On the other hand, the room for discretionality and flexibility lost on the side of fiscal policy has been further transferred to monetary policy. A constitutional convention has emerged according to which the *remit* of monetary policy is to be as wide as necessary to achieve the *goals* of monetary policy, independently of the (narrow) legitimacy basis of the European Central Bank. At the very same time, the *goals* of monetary policy have been wildly expanded, as they include not only *ordinary* monetary policy, but also *extraordinary* monetary policy, the monetary policy needed to ensure that there would be a *future* monetary policy, or what is the same, the *extraordinary* monetary policy needed to keep the Eurozone whole, to avoid the collapse of the Eurozone (despite its incompleteness). This was endorsed by the ECJ in its OMT ruling. In the paradigmatic terms of the conclusions of the Advocate General in the case at hand:

> The ECB must accordingly be afforded a broad discretion for the purpose of *framing and implementing* the Union's monetary policy. The Courts, when reviewing the ECB's activity, must therefore avoid the risk of supplanting the Bank, by venturing into a highly technical terrain in which it is necessary to have an expertise and experience which, according to the Treaties, devolves solely upon the ECB. Therefore, the intensity of judicial review of the ECB's activity, its mandatory nature aside, must be characterised by a considerable degree of caution [my italics] European Court of Justice (2014a, par 111).

Among many other things, this implies that the ECB can decide on the scope of its monetary policy independently of whether or not this affects the conduct of national fiscal policies, while the reverse does not hold.

2.1.3 Financial Stability

Public institutions are expected to play a major role in preserving the stability of the financial system as a whole, something that may well require state intervention to underpin the value of financial assets when there is a serious risk (now labelled a "systemic risk") that the market will undermine itself and capital will, as a consequence, lose its value. While the role of the state as lender of last resort of financial institutions is far from being a new one, the breadth and scope of the responsibilities of states has expanded geometrically under EMU, despite the fact that public institutions were supposed to have their role limited to the guarantee of monetary, not financial stability. The spectacular failure of the assumption that financial markets tended to stabilise themselves led to a pragmatic return to state intervention from 2007. As a result:

- The ECB has become the lender of last resort of financial institutions, either stabilising the conditions under which financial markets operate (acting thus as a "market maker") or fully or partially substituting financial markets themselves. Since 2007, allocation of capital in the European Union has been constantly mediated by the ECB, through massive refinancing operations from which financial institutions have constantly profited. This entails that the principle of capital allocation through markets (ex Article 127 TFUE) is de facto suspended. (Tuori 2016).

- A convention has emerged that allocates responsibility for cross-border financial loans to state where the debtor is established or resides (*debtor state as guarantor of last resort*). This emerged with great force during the Greek and Irish fiscal crises.
- A convention has developed regarding the obligation of states to underpin systemic financial institutions, ruling out imposing losses on shareholders and creditors of such institutions. This was clearly the practice followed during the 2007–2008 financial crisis. The so-called "bail in" directive[2] is supposed to impose a rather different pattern of distribution of the costs resulting from the crisis of financial institutions, in particular ensuring that the losses are suffered by private shareholders. As a matter of fact, however, its actual effects are rather different. To avoid the "severe disruption of the functioning of financial markets", article 27.5 c) of Regulation 806/2014[3] codifies the different treatment to be granted to "systemic" banks. While the shareholders and creditors of ordinary bankers should be the first to suffer losses, the same is not the case when the bank is a systemic one. Then public money can be used to bail out the financial institution so as to avoid "contagion" to the financial system. The different way in which the crises of the small "banche popolari" on the one hand and the Monte dei Paschi di Siena on the other were handled is very telling in this respect.

2.2 *Economic Freedoms*

The validity of all norms approved, and decisions taken in Europe is to be determined by establishing that they do not undermine the fundamental economic freedoms and the principle of undistorted competition that, together, make the substantive core of the single market.

As is well known, a set of economic freedoms was enshrined in the founding Treaty of the European Economic Community. From their very codification, economic freedoms were deeply ambivalent. On the one hand, they could be constructed as the combination of a principle aimed at guiding legislative action and a formal subjective right, entitling physical and legal persons to non-discriminatory treatment. On the other hand, economic freedoms could be

[2]Directive 2014/59/EU of the European Parliament and of the Council of 15 May 2014 establishing a framework for the recovery and resolution of credit institutions and investment firms and amending Council Directive 82/891/EEC, and Directives 2001/24/EC, 2002/47/EC, 2004/25/EC, 2005/56/EC, 2007/36/EC, 2011/35/EU, 2012/30/EU and 2013/36/EU, and Regulations (EU) No 1093/2010 and (EU) No 648/2012, of the European Parliament and of the Council Text with EEA relevance, OJ L 173, 12.6.2014, pp. 190–348.

[3]Regulation (EU) No 806/2014 of the European Parliament and of the Council of 15 July 2014 establishing uniform rules and a uniform procedure for the resolution of credit institutions and certain investment firms in the framework of a Single Resolution Mechanism and a Single Resolution Fund and amending Regulation (EU) No 1093/2010, OJ L 225, 30.7.2014, pp. 1–90.

said to be full-blown subjective rights, operationalising a substantive conception of private property and entrepreneurial freedom, as was characteristically the case in the liberist tradition, which very much influenced nineteenth century apolitical constitutionalism.

In the sixties and seventies, the former interpretation prevailed. The realisation of an internal market was assumed to imply the creation of a *common* market, in which national economic borders were not dismantled but rendered porous, so as to facilitate cross-border economic activity.[4] This meant firstly and foremostly eliminating customs duties, quantitative restrictions and measures having an equivalent effect, so as to facilitate the growth of trade in goods, which would boost overall economic growth. All through, it was assumed that economic and political integration were to go hand in hand. This was directly reflected in the founding principles governing the institutional setup and decision-making processes of the Communities.[5] Under such arrangements, economic freedoms were socio-economic principles to be progressively fleshed out, and they were regarded as the operationalisation of the right not to be discriminated on the basis of nationality; they were thus formal, not substantive rights. Moreover, not all four economic freedoms were equal, given the different drafting and systematic position within the Treaties. The strongest by far, legally and politically, was the right to free movement of goods, reflecting the key political choices underpinning the emerging European political and economic orders, and in particular the mix of liberalisation of trade in goods and the sheltering of the power of states to implement autonomous socio-economic policy choices, which were regarded as requiring limiting the movement of capital. As a result, economic freedoms did not predetermine which policy choices Member States were to make, as long as the choices resulted in the same rights being acknowledged to nationals and to Community nationals.

In the mid to late seventies, however, the way in which the Commission and the Court of Justice conceptualised economic freedoms changed. A double transformation took place.

Firstly, the right to free movement of goods was no longer understood as a *formal right*, that is, as the operationalisation of the principle of non-discrimination on the basis of nationality, but as a self-standing, *substantive right.* Consequently, the right to freedom of movement would be breached not only by means of discriminatory

---

[4]Indeed, the norms, institutions and mechanisms through public authorities organised their economic activity (public enterprises) or regulated private economic activity were deeply inter-twinned with the norms, institutions and mechanisms through which national borders were made and maintained. This was why the point of European integration was not to get rid of borders per se, and certainly not in one stroke, but rather to reconfigure them.

[5]The key role of the Council of Ministers, the intergovernmental under currents in the composition and operation of the Commission, and in the composition of the European Court of Justice, reflected the extent to which the legitimacy of European integration had to be derived from the democratic legitimacy of national institutions, very critically, of executives supported and controlled by democratically elected parliaments. From this perspective, the Luxembourg compromise only reinforced a pattern that was part of constitutional and political design of the European communities.

treatment, by customs duties, quantitative restrictions and measures having an equivalent effect, but also by any national laws or decisions that placed obstacles to the exercise of the right, even if those obstacles were non-discriminatory (European Court of Justice 1979a). Secondly, and progressively, the other three economic freedoms, despite the differences in literal tenor and systematic position within the Treaties, came to be constructed in the semblance of the new understanding of free movement of goods (European Court of Justice 1991a, 1995a, b, c).

The drive towards monetary union amplified the transformation. As was already partially noted, free movement of capital, originally limited to free movement of payments of non-financial transactions, came to be not only a full-fledged economic freedom on the basis of Directive 88/361,[6] but one whose reach extended to third countries. Moreover, the abstract weight assigned to free movement of capital is such that free movement of capital prevails over the normative requirements enshrined in the Treaties themselves, and in particular, article 345 TFEU (European Court of Justice 2002a).

Finally, the abstract weight of economic freedoms may be further increased if the suggestion made by some Advocates General of the Court to make fundamental freedoms prevail over the singleness of the single market is accepted (European Court of Justice 2017: par. 228; but the Court did not follow the AG, see European Court of Justice 2018; which does not mean the issue is over; cf. European Court of Justice 2019a, b).

As a result, economic freedoms are now interpreted as subjective fundamental rights to:

- move capital, both within and outside the European Union, which entails the full freedom to decide whether to invest capital, and where to do so (and either into financial or non-financial activities);
- incorporate, or to establish the necessary elements to engage into economic activity anywhere within the European Union;
- provide and to receive services;
- import and export goods unimpeded, without suffering any sort of obstacle;
- movement of economically active persons (but not of non-economically active persons) (European Court of Justice 2014b, 2015).

2.3 Undistorted Competition

The principle of undistorted competition prescribes that the allocation of goods and services must take place through competitive markets, so that the welfare of the consumer is maximised. The principle was originally interpreted as constraining

[6]Council Directive 88/361/EEC of 24 June 1988 for the implementation of Article 67 of the Treaty, OJ L 178, 8.7.1988, pp. 5–18.

private activity that could undermine the effectiveness of economic freedoms, for example through the abuse of market power with a view to render difficult access to different national markets European Court of Justice (1979b, 1983, 1973, 1966, 1985). Since the eighties, it has also (and perhaps mainly) become a yardstick that determines the validity of public regulation of economic activity, and above all, the direct public engagement in the provision of goods and services (for example, through public ownership of corporations) (European Court of Justice 1991b, c, 2002b, 2013; Court of First Instance 2000). A parallel transformation has taken place in the substantive understanding of the principle. While the original target of the enforcement of competition law was economic power, now the emphasis lays with consumer welfare maximisation (Hovenkamp 2006).

The malleability of the principle of undistorted competition, as shaped in the image and semblance of consumer welfare, has been abundantly proven during the financial crisis. If barely some years before the crisis regional German banks were deprived of the state guarantee in the name of ensuring a levelled playing field to all financial institutions (European Commission 2002), competition rules were de facto suspended during the crises, resulting in massive injections of public capital through the acquisition of toxic assets, the provision of guarantees or direct public aid to scores of financial institutions (European Council 2009; for the detailed set of Commission decisions, see Menéndez 2012).

2.4 Implications

Economic freedoms have become very powerful battering rams in the hands of capital holders, service providers, traders and mobile economic actors, with which to attack all national norms setting obstacles to the exercise of their economic freedoms, independently of whether the point and purpose of such national norms is at all related to cross-border economic activity. In parallel, sound money has become a key principle which legitimises massive policy interventions by the European Central Bank, while serving as the yardstick by reference to which the European Commission and the Eurogroup monitor national fiscal, social and tax policies.

It is only when the effects of the two sets of principles are added up that one gets a full picture of the extent to which public power has been fragmented and enervated in Europe, while, at the same time, major new tasks (such as macroeconomic stability or the stability of the financial system) are now expected to be discharged by some specific power holders, some formally public (the European Court of Justice, the European Commission, the European Central Bank, different collegiate executive organs, such as the Euro Summit and the Eurogroup), some private (key actors in international financial markets). The outcome is not only contradictory, but revealing of the actual power structure in place. A question to which we turn in some more depth in the next section.

3 Calling the European Shots: Exceptions to Democratic Rule

The European Union identifies itself as a democratic polity, as do the Member States (Article 2 TEU) Formally speaking, the fundamental supranational decision-making processes are said to be so structured as to ensure democratic representation. In particular, the paradigmatically representative institution, the European Parliament, is not only said to have been a net gainer in successive Treaty amendments, but more decisively, to have become a full-blown co-legislator after the entry into force of the Treaty of Lisbon. To the point that some have reiterated their claims that the European Union would be a democratic polity in the making (Eriksen 2009).

The most obvious objections to such a conclusion are very well known. Indeed, many authors have enumerated the shortcomings of the European institutional structure and decision-making arrangements from a democratic perspective (Grimm 2017). The European Parliament has a limited control over the legislative agenda, lacking any power of legislative initiative. European political parties have only nominally come into existence. Furthermore, it remains the case that the European Parliament is not an equal co-legislator to the Council of Ministers on many decisive issues, including taxation or spending. Similarly, parliamentary control over foreign and security policy, defence policy or relevant elements of commercial policy is far and between. By the same token, powerful arguments have been made regarding the absence of vibrant supranational political discussion, something that is unlikely to happen until some basic democratic preconditions are met.

Further and deeper objections could however be made. In this section, I approach the issue from a different perspective, namely the one resulting from considering the different sets of decision-making processes that have come to affirm itself as alternative to those formally prescribed in the Treaties. Each of them throws some doubts on the strength of representative democracy at the European level. Altogether, they require reconsidering to what extent we can claim that supranational decision-making proceeds in compliance with the minimal requirements of representative democracy. At the same time, such exceptions confirm the *dramatis personae* of key actors and groups wielding fundamental power in Europe that emerged from the systematic analysis of the fundamental norms organising public power.

3.1 Euro-Legalism as an Alternative to Political Decision-Making

It is important to stress that the shift from the common market to the single market paradigm (as considered in Section I.2) has not only led to the characterisation of economic freedoms as operationalisations of private property and entrepreneurial freedom, but has also favoured a radical shift in terms of the institutional structures and procedures through which supranational decision-making proceeds.

The characterisation of economic freedoms as subjective rights opened up a new path of "Europeanisation" of national norms, which may be called, slightly taken an already coined term out of context, "Euro-legalism". Instead of politically mediated decisions agreed in the intergovernmental Council of Ministers, "integration" came to be also the result of legal or physical persons challenging national norms on the basis of economic freedoms, as interpreted by the Commission and the European Court of Justice.

As a result, the relationship in which the legal and political systems stand within the internal market has radically changed. Instead of complementing the rights of those engaging in cross-border economic and social interactions, economic freedoms have become battering rams fitted to attack national policy choices that set obstacles to the exercise of economic freedoms. Such dynamic radically altered the European power equation. Despite the fact that the single market is said to be brought about by the "mutual recognition" of national norms (European Commission 1979), it actually has resulted in the unleashing of a process of regulatory competition, which may serve as a functional substitute of politically mediated harmonising legislation. But with massively different socio-economic and political consequences. Instead of the proclaimed "mutual recognition" we are confronted with the "forced mutual concurrence" of all national normative solutions, with owners and managers of mobile capital having quite some power to decide which of the norms ultimately prevails and becomes the "common standard", or in other terms, which is the preferred collective solution. In particular, those economic actors routinely operating across borders (i.e., multinationals) have been not only repeated players before the European Court of Justice and national courts, but by now design their institutional and operational structures taking into account the possibilities opened by the internal market.

3.2 Trilogues[7]

The empowerment of the European Parliament as co-legislator has been the result of adding new steps to an already complex decision-making procedure. This would tend to not only increase the time needed to reach a decision, but also to reduce the extent to which combined indirect (Council) and direct legitimacy would lead to a convergence of views on the substantive content of legislation.

As a result, major functional pressures have resulted in a *de facto* streamlining of the decision-making procedure through the creation of mixed institutional structures (the so-called "trilogues") in which the main institutions with legislative responsibilities, the Council of Ministers, the Parliament and the Commission iron out their differences, and strive to reach an agreement.

This has rendered decision-making more effective, but at a severe legitimacy cost. The "trilogues" result in the formation of a group of parliamentarians that represent

[7]This section is much indebted to Stie (2012).

the Parliament as whole, or what is the same, in the doubling of the democratic legitimacy chain. Minority groups tend be under-represented in "trilogues", while some parliamentarians emerge as repeated players. A Parliament within the Parliament is thus not only created, but made to repeatedly interact with collegiate executive groups. That changes the very institutional identity of such representatives, very especially because the "trilogues" proceed at closed doors. At once and at the same time undermining the achievements of the increased transparency of the workings of Parliament and Council.

3.3 Epistocratic Decision-Making

A substantive set of the powers and competences that have been shifted from the Member States to the European Union have been assigned to institutions whose legitimacy basis is, by design, not democratic, but epistocratic, that is, grounded on the "expert knowledge" produced by office holders. In addition, we can observe the proliferation of instances in which such "epistocratic" institutions can constrain or set the parameters within which representative institutions intervene and take decisions.

The European Central Bank is the paradigmatic instance of such a supranational epistocratic institution. In the terms of the Maastricht ruling of the German Constitutional Court, the assignment of monetary power to an independent central bank constitutes a clear exception to the principle of the democratic foundation of all public power (German Constitutional Court 1994, especially par. 96). Such exception, the same Court has argued (and keeps on arguing) is at the end of the day based on the expert knowledge ensured by the selection procedures of central bankers (and the administrative personnel) and by the internal decision-making procedures followed within the bank. It is their expert knowledge, their *episteme*, that justifies excepting the democratic principle. While according to the just referred Maastricht ruling of the German Constitutional Court, this would call for a strict definition of the breadth and scope of the power of the ECB, as well as the setting of the objectives to be pursued by the institution, in practice we have observed rather the opposite transformation, as pointed in section I.1. Unsurprisingly, the ECB has seen the breadth and scope of its "old" competences expand, while new competences have been assigned to it, more specifically the macro and micro prudential supervision of financial institutions, something that entails a massive concentration of power.[8]

Equally important is the constitution of new independent authorities with an epistocratic legitimacy basis, which produce data and statistics that constrain the

[8]Whether this is the result of growing trust on the cumulated "technical" knowledge of the ECB, or rather signals mounting distrust in representative institutions or more simply, the lack of political agreement on how to organise the prudential supervision of Eurozone banks is rather immaterial.

range of policy options of the Member States. One of the measures that were said to be fundamental in avoiding a replay of the fiscal crises was the creation of independent fiscal authorities, that would not only reinforce the "credibility" of the key figures on which stability programmes and annual budgets are based, but also produce reports assessing the fiscal costs of alternative policy options. Not only such independent authorities have been established, but they have already constituted a European network of independent fiscal authorities. In addition, plans have been put forward to create independent "competitiveness" authorities, with a broader mandate, extending to the analysis of policy options to strengthen the "competitiveness" of the national economy (European Union 2016).

Last, but not least, the IMF has been acknowledged, both de jure and even more so de facto, key powers in the process of granting financial assistance to Eurozone states, and monitoring compliance with the economic programmes to which the said assistance is conditioned.

3.4 Minoritarian Decision-Making

The legitimacy of representative democracy is crucially tied to majority rule. It can be discussed, and *indeed* it has been discussed, *which* majority is required for collective action and decision-making. Different forms of qualified majority voting, or the combination of different procedures and institutional structures to verify the strength of the collective will are characteristic in democratic constitutions. While majority rule may be restricted institutionally or procedurally, all such limits and constrains are both exceptional and tend to be ultimately justified on the very basis of the *higher* democratic legitimacy of the grounds on which counter-majoritarian institutions or decision-making processes base their decisions (for a systematic review of the literature, see Troper 2003).

The original institutional structure and decision-making setup of the European Communities were geared towards the strongest possible forms of qualified majority: unanimity. Thus, the institution that was assigned most of the decision-making power, the Council of Ministers, had as its default decision-making rule unanimity voting.

Since the mid-seventies, the new interpretation of economic freedoms favoured the conditions under which a minority of states, of even a single state, could impose its regulatory preferences upon all remaining states. A clear illustration can be found in the impact that the decision taken by the United Kingdom to liberalise capital movements in 1979 had on other Member States. It would be disingenuous to deny that the effectiveness of capital controls had already eroded significantly by 1979. But the British decision clearly accelerated the process, and combined with the emerging interpretation of economic freedoms coming from the European Court of Justice which was already mentioned, dramatically narrowed the policy choices available to other Member States. Quite similarly, and as described in Section I, the conditions under which the EMS was agreed turned the Bundesbank into the hegemonic central bank within the Communities. The other EMS central banks were forced to follow suit after each and every decision taken by the Bundesbank. A further, and more recent example, can be found in the Irish decision, early in the financial crisis of 2008, to increase the public guarantee on public deposits.[9] Massive flows of capital towards Ireland ensued, something that created a major incentive for all Member States to follow Irish suit, well before a European common decision limited the scope for competition for deposits (Economist 2008).

By the same token, the crises have amplified the asymmetries of power, and as a result, have widened the set of issues regarding which we can de facto speak of minority or single rule. What some political scientists call the "new" intergovernmentalism is based not on the equality between Member States, but actually on the inequality among states. "Creditor" states (which happened to largely be the former strong currency states) have a disproportionate influence over the outcome of the decisions taken by the European Council, and perhaps even more so when we consider the formation of the European Council that only includes Eurozone states, the Euro Summit. These inequalities are in the process of being formalised, as reflected in the voting rules applicable to the granting of aid under the European Stability Mechanism (especially Article 4.4 of the ESM Treaty), and even more so, to decisions concerning the monitoring of the execution of national fiscal and macroeconomic policy, including the application of sanctions, as established in the amended Stability and Growth Pact, and as amplified by the Fiscal Compact (Article 7 of the Fiscal Compact). It is difficult to avoid the conclusions that such norms entail the formalization of minority rule.

3.5 Emergency Decision-Making

Last, but not least, there has been a marked increase in the number of instances in which decision-making proceeds in an emergency mode.

In particular, alleged extraordinary and urgent circumstances have been assumed to justify a departure from well-established decision-making procedures, as not doing so would entail lasting damage to vital public interests. The fiscal crisis and the refugee crisis provide quite a number of examples in this regard. This is especially problematic because, contrary to what is the case in national constitutional orders, and to a certain extent to what was the case in the early years of European integration (e.g. the old Article 108.3 TEEC),[10] there are few and far between specific provisions governing "emergency" decisions.

---

[9]The Irish Act is available at http://www.oireachtas.ie/viewdoc.asp?fn=/documents/bills28/acts/2008/a1808.pdf. See also Carswell (2010).

[10]Article 108.3 TEEC determined the procedure to follow in a balance of payments crisis. It foresaw either multilateral financial assistance, or lacking an agreement to provide it, opened the way to Member States imposing (temporary and proportionate) unilateral restrictions on trade.

As a result, the Union tends to follow a characteristic cycle of procrastination, ineffective action, and emergency decision-making, with the latter proceeding without the declaration of the emergency (there is not even an obvious procedure that could be followed in such cases).

In this context, a tendency to twist legal arguments so as to provide legal cover to what factually and normatively amounts to the undermining of the existing laws can be discerned. This pattern can be observed in the "bilateral but coordinated" financial "assistance" provided to Greece, the "unconventional" measures adopted by the European Central Bank during the financial and fiscal crises, hard to reconcile with the limited mandate of the European Central Bank, or with the management of the refugee crisis, especially with the second Decision concerning the reallocation of refugees, of September 2015.[11] The obvious danger is that undeclared emergencies result in the selective and arbitrary breach of legal norms and in the maximisation of pre-existing power imbalances (which are slowly being codified into specific emergency norms, as already pointed). Moreover, undeclared emergencies blur the understanding of the structural causes of the problems, and foster an addiction to emergencies. Indeed, the main driver of the resort to the emergency mode is the very fragmentation of public power *caused* by the present fundamental norms. As long as taking ordinary effective decisions is close to impossible, decision-making only takes place during emergencies, and decision-makers start to internalise a new identity as emergency decision-makers.

The existence of structural conditions that foster *emergencies* results in the empowerment of those institutions that are structurally capable of deciding swiftly *and* quickly, i.e., basically executives or executive-like institutions. The central role of the European Central Bank and the Euro Summit and the Eurogroup in the European crises becomes not only predictable, but also bound to reinforce itself as long as the proclivity to crisis remains untackled.

4 The Structural Bias in Supranational Decision-Making

In this section, I turn to a third plank of the organisation of power in the Eurozone, which I refer as the structural substantive bias in supranational decision-making, and which relates very closely the substantive, the institutional and the procedural components of the organisation of public power in the Eurozone.

The structural bias stems from the fact that the division of labour between supranational decision-making procedures renders highly probable that the substantive outcome of "representative" European Union decision-making processes is one that fosters private property and entrepreneurial freedom at the cost of other socio-economic values, including the collective rights, collective goods and subjective

[11]Council Decision (EU) 2015/1601 of 22 September 2015 establishing provisional measures in the area of international protection for the benefit of Italy and Greece, OJ L 248, of 24.09.2015, 80–94.

rights at the heart of the "social" dimension of the Democratic and Social Rechtsstaat. To put it differently, there is a structural substantive basis built into the very structure of EU decision-making. Such bias is *coherent* with the actual allocation of power emerging from Sections I and II, while serving to fully programme the use of power by non-representative institutions in the terms described in Section II.

The progressive empowerment of the European Parliament (reflected in the transformation of co-decision into the "ordinary" supranational law-making process) is frequently said to have alleviated the democratic deficit of the European Union. That seems to imply that the more powers that accrue to the European Parliament, the less undemocratic the European Union is bound to be.

The democratic rationale of co-decision is at first sight simple. By shifting decision from intergovernmental to supranational procedures, it is possible to move from indirect to direct forms of democratic legitimacy, or to put it perhaps more precisely, but a trifle more pedantically, from exogenous to endogenous democratic legitimacy.[12] What such line of reasoning neglects is the fundamental fact that not even after the Lisbon Treaty, co-decision is not the only, not even the dominant procedure of supranational decision-making. In the last two decades, what has got affirmed is not the primacy of co-decision, but rather a specific division of labour between co-decision and intergovernmental procedures of formation of the European collective will. In the latter, it remains the case that the supranational will is formed if, and only if, a unanimous agreement is reached within the Council of Ministers. Quite obviously, it is more difficult to achieve unanimous agreement in the Council of Ministers, than, as co-decision requires, a qualified majority in the Council and a simple majority in Parliament. Moreover, the sheer probabilities of unanimous agreement have declined given the expansion of the number of Member States, and the growing social and economic heterogeneity across states.

If the criterion determining which matters are subject to co-decision and which ones to unanimity was random, this division of labour might render randomly difficult the adoption of decisions. But the division is not random. Market-making norms, amplifying the breadth and scope of economic freedoms, are decided through co-decision; while market-correcting norms have to be adopted through unanimity.

Two major consequences follow. The first is the artificial splitting of issues. Questions that were regarded as so inextricably intertwined as to require simultaneous legislation have been turned into separate questions by the division of labour between supranational decision-making processes, likely to be settled in different pieces of legislation and in different points in time, because decisions are subject to different procedures. The following examples illustrates the point. For many years, it was assumed that the liberalisation of capital movements should come hand in hand with specific coordination measures among tax authorities to avoid that as a result

[12]The usual line of reasoning goes as follows. Once states can be outvoted because the will of the Council is formed through qualified majority voting (that is, since the Single European Act), there is a loss in indirect democratic legitimacy. See Weiler (1999, pp. 68–80 and 232).

the chances of avoiding taxes (especially on capital income) would be dramatically increased. Once, however, the Single European Act was enacted, and qualified majority voting in the Council (re)introduced, it became possible (and indeed probable) that there would be liberalisation of capital movements without companion measures to fight tax evasion.

The second is that the balance of the European legislative scales is tilted in favour of private property and entrepreneurial freedom. This is so because the division of labour between decision-making processes facilitates the adoption of measures reinforcing the understanding of economic freedoms propelling the case law of the Court of Justice (as we considered in the first section), while hampering legislation aiming at regulating economic activity at the supranational level.

5 Concluding Remarks

The reconstruction of the fundamental norms governing public power in the Eurozone reveals the extent to which a profound mutation of the goals and purposes of the Eurozone has taken place in the last four decades, at an accelerated speed in the last one.

The validity of all laws, regulations, policy choices, judicial rulings and administrative acts is determined by reference to the triad of principles of sound money, economic freedoms and undistorted competition. Private property and entrepreneurial freedom, which had played a paramount role in the constitutions of old, but which had been relegated to a secondary position in postwar Democratic and Social States, have regained their privileged legal position. At the same time, we observed that the formal primacy of representative democracy knows five fundamental exceptions, that altogether cast serious doubts on the legitimacy credentials of the Union. The substantive and procedural legitimacy of supranational decision-making is further open to be questioned given the structural substantive biases in built in the division of labour between different supranational decision-making procedures. The subjection of market-making decisions to co-decision under qualified majority voting, while market-correcting requires unanimous voting in the Council of Minister, fosters not only negative integration, but integration geared towards the further realisation of the right to private property and entrepreneurial freedom.

This state of affairs renders extremely complex the question that was left open through this essay, namely whether we should speak of the European Union law as a constitutional legal order. While the object of European law has become undoubtedly constitutional, given the massive expansion of its breadth and scope, the grammar of European law is only formally similar to that of national constitutional orders. It is not only problematic, but I would say extremely dangerous, to characterise European law as a constitutional, if only because the idiom of constitutionalism has served, ingeniously or disingenuously, to cloak in plain sight the profound substantive mutation of the Eurozone.

In such circumstances, it seems to me that one is forced to reach a contradictory conclusion regarding the pertinence of studying the "material constitution" of the Eurozone.

On the one hand, I hope this chapter proves the extent to which a purely formal analysis of the norms "in the books" (that is, in the Treaties) is clearly not enough. The approach followed by Lassalle (1931) and Mortati (1940), among others, is to be vindicated out of sheer necessity. To make sense of how power is organised in Europe, we have to reconstruct not only the actual norms, the socially enforced conventions and practices, but also to do that keeping at least one eye on the way in which power is actually wielded, perhaps not so much in the "stanze dei bottoni" as in quite a number of different sites. We need to reconnect the study of the agency and the fundamental content of fundamental norms, and to do so without the many blinders that the mythology (or perhaps one should say mythologies) of European law imposes upon us.

On the other hand, using the term "constitution", even if in purely descriptive terms, runs the risk of projecting into the object qualities that it does not have, connotations that it does not deserve. Above all, there is a serious risk of devaluing the currency of democratic constitutional law, of concluding that European law and national constitutional law are part of a continuum, an assumption that cannot but end up in conceptual and normative confusion (as indeed it has been the case and remains the case). In addition, the conception of the material constitution (not least Mortati's) remains problematic on account of its origins, or to be more precise, its role model. However, let me insist, the agenda of the material constitution constitutes a powerful reminder of the importance of agency even in processes which are deeply mediated by heavy structural forces, such as the transformation of European Union law in the last four decades. It should constitute, among other things, a powerful warning against naïve formalism, and an incentive to bring into the scope of our analysis the key institutions through which private power is exerted, not least, financial markets.

What is needed, thus, if I am allowed to simplify by reference to authors, is to take on board the critical agenda which the material constitution can potentially lead to, but to pursue it in the laïc fashion that Salvatore D'Albergo proposed in his last writings (perhaps most clearly in D'Albergo 1991).

References

Basso, L. (1958). *Il principe senza scettro*. Milano: Feltrinelli.

Carswell, S. (2010, September 25). The big gamble: The inside story of the bank guarantee. *Irish Times*. Available at http://www.irishtimes.com/newspaper/weekend/2010/0925/1224279646952_pf.html

Court of First Instance. (2000). Ruling in case T-296/97, *Alitalia*, ECLI:EU:T:2000:289.

D'Albergo, S. (1991). *Costituzione e organizzazione del potere nell'ordinamento italiano*. Torino: Giappichelli.

Desan, C. (2014). *Making money. Coin, currency and the coming of capitalism*. Oxford: Oxford University Press.
Economist, The. (2008, October 4). On life support. *The Economist*. Available at http://www.economist.com/node/12342156?story_id=12342156
Eriksen, E. O. (2009). *The unfinished democratization of the European Union*. Oxford: Oxford University Press.
European Commission. (1979). Communication from the *Commission* concerning the consequences of the judgment given by the Court of Justice on 20 February 1979 in Case 120/78 ("*Cassis de Dijon*"). OJ C 256 of 3.10.1980, pp. 2–3.
European Commission. (2002, February 28). Germany agrees on the implementation of the understanding with the Commission on State guarantees for Landesbanken and Savings Banks. Available at http://europa.eu/rapid/press-release_IP-02-343_en.htm?locale=en
European Council. (2009). Conclusions of the Presidency. *European Council*, 15 and 16 October 2008, par. 5. Available at http://www.consilium.europa.eu/uedocs/cms_data/docs/pressdata/en/ec/103441.pdf.
European Court of Justice. (1966). Ruling in joined cases 56 and 58/64, *Consten Grundig*, ECLI:EU:C:1966:41.
European Court of Justice. (1973). Ruling in case 6/72 Continental Can, ECLI:EU:C:1973:22.
European Court of Justice. (1979a). Ruling in case 120/78, *Cassis de Dijon*, ECLI:EU:C:1979:42.
European Court of Justice. (1979b). Ruling in case 85/76, *Hoffmann*, ECLI:EU:C:1979:36.
European Court of Justice. (1983). Ruling in case 322/81, *Michelin*, ECLI:EU:C:1983:313.
European Court of Justice. (1985). Ruling in joined cases 25 and 26/84, *Ford vs. Commission*, ECLI:EU:C:1985:340.
European Court of Justice. (1991a). Ruling in case C-76/90, *Säger*, ECLI:EU:C:1991:331.
European Court of Justice. (1991b). Ruling in case 18/88, *Régie des télégraphes et des téléphones*, ECLI:EU:C:1991:474.
European Court of Justice. (1991c). Ruling in case C-41/90, *Höfner*, ECLI:EU:C:1991:161.
European Court of Justice. (1995a). Ruling in case C-55/94 *Gebhard*, ECLI:EU:C:1995:411.
European Court of Justice. (1995b). Ruling in case C-415/93 *Bosman*, ECLI:EU:C:1995:463.
European Court of Justice. (1995c). Ruling in case C-163/94, *Sanz de Lera*, ECLI:EU:C:1995:451.
European Court of Justice. (2002a). Ruling in case C-367/98, *Golden Shares*, ECLI:EU:C:2002:326.
European Court of Justice. (2002b). Ruling in case C-218/00, *Inail*, ECLI:EU:C:2002:36.
European Court of Justice. (2012). Ruling in case C-370/12, *Pringle*, ECLI:EU:C:2012:756, par. 135.
European Court of Justice. (2013). Ruling in joined cases C-399 and 401/10, *Bouygues*, ECLI:EU:C:2013:175.
European Court of Justice. (2014a). Conclusions of AG Cruz in case Case 62/14 (OMT), ECLI:EU:C:2015:7.
European Court of Justice. (2014b). Ruling in case C-33/13, Elisabeta Dano and Florin Dano v Jobcenter Leipzig, ECLI:EU:C:2014:2358.
European Court of Justice. (2015). Ruling in case C-67/14, Jobcenter Berlin Neukölln v Nazifa Alimanovic and Others, ECLI:EU:C:2015:59.
European Court of Justice. (2017). Conclusionsof AG Wathelet in case C-284/16, *Achmea*, ECLI:EU:C:2017:699.
European Court of Justice. (2018). Ruling in case C-284/16, *Achmea*, ECLI:EU:C:2018:158.
European Court of Justice. (2019a). Conclusions of AG Bot in case Opinion 1/17, on CETA, ECLI:EU:C:2019:72.
European Court of Justice. (2019b). Opinion 1/17 on CETA, ECLI:EU:C:2019:341.
European Union. (2016). Five Presidents' Report. Available at https://ec.europa.eu/commission/sites/beta-political/files/5-presidents-report_en.pdf
German Constitutional Court. (1994). Ruling in Brunning. Available at http://www.proyectos.cchs.csic.es/euroconstitution/library/Brunner_Sentence.pdf

Grimm, D. (2017). *The constitution of European democracy*. Oxford: Oxford University Press.
Hovenkamp, H. (2006). *The antitrust enterprise: Principle and execution*. Cambridge: Harvard University Press.
Lassalle, F. (1931). *¿Qué es una Constitución?* Madrid: Cenit.
Menéndez, A. J. (2012). *De la Crisis Económica a la Crisis Constitucional*. León: Eolas.
Menéndez, A. J. (2014). A European Union in constitutional mutation? *European Law Journal, 20*, 127–141.
Mortati, C. (1940). *La Costituzione in Senso Materiale*. Milano: Giuffrè.
Sciascia, L. (1988). *Opere I*. Milano: Bompiani.
Sciascia, L. (2016). *Il Consiglio d'Egitto* (A. Foulke, Trans.). London: Apollo Classics.
Stie, A. E. (2012). *Democratic decision-making in the EU: Technocracy in disguise?* London: Routledge.
Troper, M. (2003). The logic of justification of judicial review. *I.CON, 1*, 99–121.
Tuori, K. (2016). Has Euro area monetary policy become redistribution by monetary means? 'Unconventional' monetary policy as a hidden transfer mechanism. *European Law Journal, 22*, 838–868.
Weiler, J. H. H. (1999). *The constitution of Europe*. Oxford: Oxford University Press.

Agustín José Menéndez is Lecturer of legal theory and political philosophy at the Universidad Autónoma de Madrid and visiting fellow, Arena, University of Oslo. Author of *Justifying Taxes*, *The Constitution's Gift* (with John Erik Fossum), *De la Crisis Económica a la Crisis Constitucional* and *Challenging European Citizenship* (with Espen D.H. Olsen).

The Different Faces of Politics: Economic Governance and European Democracy

Pedro Lomba

Contents

Abstract Against a depoliticized position that views the monetary union as the realm of epistocracy, strong economic and political bias and emergency decision-making, this contribution seeks to present the overall political and democratic challenges emerging from a more centralized, expert-based and politically sensitive European economic and monetary union. Courts are already responding to these challenges. Rather than interpreting democratic politics at the national and the European level as the two clashing forces preventing each other, the view is that both are part of a continuum of political ruling that requires political sensitivity, a sense of political purpose and overall transparency. For this also, economic governance cannot be seen only as the embodiment of strict rules and compliance procedures.

1 Introduction

The legal organization of the Eurozone and the European economic and monetary union has been recently subject to increasing constitutional attention.[1] Its complex normative structure, its combination of both hard and soft law mechanisms, its

[1]See Federico Fabbrini (2016).

P. Lomba (✉)
Lisbon's School of Law, Lisbon University, Lisbon, Portugal

© Springer Nature Switzerland AG 2020

M. Nogueira de Brito, L. Pereira Coutinho (eds.), *The Political Dimension of Constitutional Law*, https://doi.org/10.1007/978-3-030-38459-3_10

general policy orientation, its centralizing tendencies, are all issues that have been a matter of an intense and unfinished debate. In his chapter, Agustin Menendez provocatively challenges the current situation of European law by critically focusing on the agenda of the "material constitution" of the Eurozone. His claim is that both the European Union and European law are going through a turn "which results in part in the fragmentation and pulverisation of public power and, as a result, in the empowerment of public but non-representative institutions and of private actors". This legal instability is undermining democratic politics as a result of a larger group of substantive transformations that have been dramatically reinforced by the European response to the recent financial crisis.

The critique of European law goes down to the very foundations of the European economic project and to its subsequent legal developments: the role and significance of monetary policy and the litigation action from private corporations using the deregulatory potential of the European economic freedoms. The argument is that the four freedoms and the internal market were manipulated into sources of systematic economic deregulation as well as means for pre-determining certain commitments without meaningful participation from the democratic polities. But Menendez's core attack in his chapter aims at the "new European economic governance" that was designed since 2011 to respond to the financial crisis in Europe. He claims that "the ascendancy of monetary stability over economic policy as a whole has been further reinforced, while new arrangements have emerged with a view to stabilise the resulting socio-economic order". Menendez describes this new governance as composed by non-representative mechanisms that have reduced the scope for democratic decision-making at the national and supranational levels and thus significantly restricted the democratic aspirations of European economic law. These non-representative mechanisms include distinctive manifestations described as "epistocratic", "technocratic", "minoritarian" and "emergency decision-making": the "concentration of power" under the European Central Bank and the emergence of "independent fiscal authorities with an epistocratic legitimacy basis".

Integration through law was a famous intellectual project that sought to explain European integration through the unifying and integrative role of law. By stressing the place of law, the rule of law and legal institutions in the process of European integration, the project countervailed the opposite view that looked at the European accomplishments as a mere by-product of politics.[2] Integration through law was the antidote to a divisive and more precarious form of integration through force and politics.

Yet, the critical vision we are exposing represented in this case by Agustin Menendez is that European law has been captured by forms of rule that are depoliticized, technocratic and non-responsive to democratic norms. Menendez claims that these forms are under the pervasive effect of a substantive economic bias, market and property oriented. The law in Europe has thus been de-democratized and depoliticized. Rather than being a factor of integration,

[2]Loic Azoulai (2016), pp. 449–463.

European economic law has and will become a force of disintegration. It can be said, somehow in opposition to the title of this series of essays, that European law is not experiencing a return of politics but an *escape from politics*.

My aim in this brief comment is to discuss the fundamental assumption that the law sustaining the new European economic governance is the suppression of democratic politics. While the view that the new economic governance is weakening the national democratic mediation of European policies is easily acceptable, more care seems to be necessary in taking the narrative of describing the European economic and monetary union as a depoliticized project. European politics presents itself in many faces. Because the domains of politics and law always remain in constant tension,[3] legalization and depoliticization are usually not that successful when seen as strategies to overcome politics. There are political and democratic challenges emerging from a more centralized, expert-based and politically sensitive European economic and monetary union.

2 In Search of European Democratic Politics

The initial line of contestation adopted by this view disputes the very significance of democratic politics in the construction of the European Union and the internal market. Because of the processes of regulatory harmonization through which the European Union impacts on its citizens, and their activities, works or goods, it is said that the European Union has been marginalizing democratic politics.

It is not entirely clear what we should mean by democratic politics, because often this concept is characterized with referential expressions such as "democratic decision-making", "representative democracy", "political choice" or "alternative socio-economic policy choices". Ultimately, all these categories point to different practices of democratic politics. The practices of deliberation, representation, participation, accountability, public discussion or confrontation between alternative policy choices are all practical forms of developing the democratic ideal of self-government and self-rule in a particular polity. They also presuppose different accounts of what democratic politics should be. Every democracy can be normatively defined by emphasizing some practices more strongly than others[4]: democracies can be defined with deliberative, participatory, competition or discursive models. For example, does the failure of the European political democracy affect the quality of its representation or deliberation processes,[5] as it was proclaimed throughout decades of analysis of the democratic deficit in the European Union,[6] or does it primarily

[3]Robert Post (2010).

[4]See Robert Dahl (1998), p. 37, on the normative standards that a democracy must accomplish.

[5]As pointed out by Mattias Kumm (2010), p. 16: "there is no public representation of an alternative Europe that you could support".

[6]See Follesdal and Hix (2006), pp. 533–562.

concern with the freedom of national constituencies to generate alternative political and economic choices?

The European constraints on fiscal, budgetary, and economic policy have been substantially reinforced since 2010, with profound impacts to the fiscal sovereignty of the Member States. These constraints naturally "impact directly on national decisions concerning the budget, situated at the heart of the political constitution[7]". Agustin Menendez asserts that these impacts have brought a de-democratizing effect, which is hijacking not only the European decision-making through the power of technocratic expertise but also the national legitimation processes in which democracy is based on. This effect is being achieved through the imposition of "monetary dominance" deprived of democratic legitimacy that forecloses the national space for pursuing different economic policies, and notably policies that sustain meaningful social commitments. Menendez precisely writes in his chapter that "there is a structural substantive basis built into the very structure of EU decision-making that fosters private property and entrepreneurial freedom at the cost of other socio-economic values, including the collective rights, collective goods and subjective rights at the heart of the "social" dimension of the Democratic and Social Rechtsstaat".

If the failure of the European political democracy is primarily described as a diminishing freedom of national constituencies to generate and choose among alternative political choices under a normatively strengthened financial European framework, we are left with a disturbing paradox. First, it is well known how the European integration helped to promote democratic reforms in Portugal, Greece or Spain, to name three countries with strong isolationist pasts and where democracy took long time to gain roots. If European policies are now perceived by national electorates as a reason for internal contestation and disconnection, this can be easily converted into distrust of democracy itself. It is the national democratic processes that will be sanctioned for any shortcomings arising from European policies. There is now a trend in the academic literature focused on the deconsolidation effect of democracies resulting from anti-system politics and anti-establishment parties.[8]

The second concern is with the prospects of democratic legitimation of the Union itself. Democratic rule depends upon authorial choices made by a particular community. But European governance aspired to set out a different and complex form of political agency which could not simply be based on the authorship of collective decisions. The way to reconcile this historical contrast between democratic politics and post-national forms of governance was achieved by structuring a multi-structure chain of legitimation involving both European and national democratic processes. For this reason, national democratic requirements have been central to the European integration as they have ensured internal political legitimacy to the European actions.

[7]See Maduro et al. (2017).

[8]Foa and Mounk (2017).

Now, as also mentioned by Karlo Tuori, the Eurozone crisis has shown the extent to which "national democratic institutions are widely conceived as of mere executors of policies imposed from the outside[9]". We have seen this problem as generalized feature arising from the implementation of rescue packages and financial assistance programs. Citizens have been subject to the effects of these measures without a relevant sense of national intermediation. This poses a huge pressure for safeguarding an adequate level of democratic legitimation under a more complex and centralized European structure.

Courts are obviously aware of this need. As recognized by the German Constitutional Court in its rulings on the developments of the European financial framework, in which it is clearly pointed out that "the provisions of the European treaties do not conflict with the understanding of national budget autonomy as an essential competence, which cannot be relinquished, of the parliaments of the Member States which enjoy direct democratic legitimation, but *instead they presuppose it*[10]".

More recently, when asked to assess the constitutionality of the legislative framework regarding the European Banking Union the same German Constitutional Court has exposed its reservations to "the diminished level of democratic legitimation in the domain of banking supervision that results from the independence of the European Central Bank" as well as its broad monetary policy mandate.[11] However, the national Court added that this would still be "acceptable because it is compensated *by specific safeguards serving democratic accountability*". Such specific safeguards, accountability mechanisms and "reporting obligations of the European Central Bank vis-à-vis the European Union organs and the national parliaments" must be present in the implementation of the banking union.

Although the vision of democracy as accountability may be insufficient and too procedural for substantive democratic aspirations, the argument shows how much courts are concerned with maintaining the multilevel chain of legitimacy and with reinforcing the democratic safeguards of the new economic governance.

3 The Faces of European Politics

3.1 Politics and Expertise

It is thus possible to assert that even courts and particularly constitutional courts, although acting as bulwarks of legal expertise, were forced to assess the levels of democratic legitimation implied in the policies of the Union. The project of integration through law was never authorized to relinquish the necessary procedures of

[9]Tuori (2014), p. 17.

[10]See the Judgment of the Second Senate of 7 September 2011, 2 BvR 87/10, 2 BvR 1485/10, 2 BvR 1099/10 (our emphasis). See also Tuori (2014), p. 16.

[11]See Judgment of 30 July 2019, 2 BvR 1685/14, 2 BvR 2631/14.

internal legitimation coming from the Member-States. Legalization did not mean depoliticization.

For this reason, the reconstruction of European law as a structurally biased project is an attempt not only to protect democratic credentials in Europe, but also to rescue politics—and particularly social politics—from the increasing role of expert bodies acting in the non-political areas of financial and monetary policy. In here, the argument is that the main threat does not come from overzealous legal officials taking over the discretion of national legislators, but from opaque financial experts—the "epistocrats"—empowered to the position where they control and supervise the whole financial and monetary system. The consequences of this are that only certain policies—stabilizing, market-oriented—are allowed in the European Union, and only one institution, the European Central Bank, is permitted to define the terms of monetary policy binding the fiscal policies of the Member States.

As is well-known, monetary and currency policy in Europe were entrusted to an independent body of experts who should be immune to political control and influence. The inspiration came from the independent German Bundesbank which also reflected a cultural tradition with broad support, because of the past experiences of Germany with hyperinflation.[12] However, as demonstrated by the german constitutional scholar Bockenforde, "this kind of setup reflects a certain kind of monetary and currency policy which is itself a factor of the general politics of a community organized as a state[13]". This permeation of the legal setup explains why it has been so supported in Germany: the tradition reflects a collective commitment. Thus, went Bockenforde, "it is an audacious experiment to communitize monetary and currency policy as an isolated sphere, disconnected from other spheres of politics, as though it were possible to abstract them from the overall political realities like a technical–functional construct[14]".

The risks of creating a centralized monetary structure without the appropriate channels for political correction have been in our eyes with the various endemic crises in the Eurozone. But Bockenforde's insight can be remembered in this context when the monetary union, despite being borne in isolation from politics, was forced to intervene politically in order to protect the hidden collective commitments of the common currency. In that sense, and to put the question differently, the problem may be no longer whether epistemic independence is intrinsically the negation of democratic politics, but whether and how we should think about rational ways in which epistemic governance must be exercised to reinforce democratic politics and political commitments.

We have a strong example of this. In his famous speech at the Global Investment Conference in London in 2012, Mario Draghi precisely said that: "when people talk about the fragility of the euro and the increasing fragility of the euro, and perhaps the crisis of the euro, very often non-euro area member states or leaders, *underestimate*

[12]Widdig (2001).

[13]See Bockenforde (2017), pp. 355–356.

[14]*Ibidem*, p. 356.

the amount of political capital that is being invested in the euro" and that "within our mandate, the ECB is ready *to do whatever it takes to preserve the euro*.[15] While this can be perceived as the manifestation of an arrogant epistocrat declaring that he would act through all means to maintain a particular technical and economic construct, his reference to the *amount of political capital* invested in the adoption of the common currency is quite telling of the fundamental concern with issues of democratic trust and the need to protect the collective commitments behind the euro.[16] Draghi and the action pursued by the European Central Bank understood politically what the failure of the euro would mean as a permanent and irreversible damage to the European Union.[17]

3.2 Politics and Emergency

The way independent epistemic authorities may resort, in a quite similar position to courts,[18] to moments of statesmanship brings us to a last comment. The "addiction to emergency" that has emerged in the European Union as a consequence of the financial crisis may be described as antagonistic to politics, in the same way as we may think about authoritarian politics as opposed to democratic politics.

The larger question that deserves to be answered is: what should be the place of emergency in the maintenance of democratic politics? The regular politics of a democracy is composed of collective moments of discussion, deliberation and coordination. These are the most common instances of achieving collective action in a functioning democracy. But there are also moments when we may collectively recognize that coordination "*does not lead to a decision*", as said in the quotation of Jean Monnet, which means you still need a decision in face of a *real* problem.

Europe went through "different states of emergency" in dealing with the financial crisis. The different rescue packages and financial mechanisms—from the Greek loan facility in May 2010 to the launch of the European Stability Mechanism in 2012—have brought fundamental changes into the Eurozone, mainly with respect to the observation of the no-bailout provision and the underlying principle of exclusive Member State fiscal liability. However, instead of pure political *diktat*, emergencies may be also perceived as self-reflection and self-individualization of the kind of polity we purport to be. Democracy is not only about self-rule, but also about

---

[15]See the Verbatim of the remarks made by Mario Draghi, at the Global Investment Conference in London 26 July 2012, at https://www.ecb.europa.eu/press/key/date/2012/html/sp120726.en.html.

[16]See also Cafaro (2017), pp. 231–232.

[17]In a less quoted piece published in a German newspaper, Draghi (2012) also wrote: "The challenges of having a single monetary policy but loosely coordinated fiscal, economic and financial policies have been clearly revealed by the crisis. As Jean Monnet said, coordination "*is a method which promotes discussion, but it does not lead to a decision.*" And strong decisions have to be made to manage the world's second most important currency".

[18]See Siegel (2008), p. 959.

self-reflection and self-maturation. In this sense, emergency may instigate democratic reflection and maturation, and not democratic avoidance and circumvention.

Consider also the refugee crisis. It may be said that emergency decision-making ended a process first of procrastination, and then of improper action, because the Member-states were firstly exposed to the problem and manifestly impotent to respond. But whatever is our assessment of the causes behind the delayed response in Europe, it is unquestionable that the refugee crisis forced the Union to define itself in some way, to define its common commitments towards the world. Emergency foster political acts that are also productive in a way that may create a sense of solidarity and purpose.

3.3 Final Note

That is also why the risk of legalizing the economic and monetary governance in Europe does not come from absent politics and arbitrariness, but from a purely arrangement of rules and compliance mechanisms[19] deprived of good government purposes. The primary ambition of constitutional political economy was to create, design and justify the rules that would bring politics closer to the economy.[20] We should be concerned that this project may be on its way to become what the French theorist, Pierre Manent, has called "despotism of rules[21]", in the sense that political life, and human life, has been increasingly transformed into pure compliance with rules and regulations. Rules that amount to, and this is again Manent, "organised immobility". Providing citizens nothing but a prospect of rules and supervision, will be, after all, a very impoverishing form of what it means to live in a democratic community. Reacting against this phenomenon will require high doses of imagination and political sensitivity. We will have to be able to articulate and make transparent our political challenges.

References

Azoulai, L. (2016, April). "Integration through law" and us. *International Journal of Constitutional Law, 14*(2), 449–463.

Bockenforde, E. (2017). Which path Europe is taking (1997). In *Constitutional and political theory – selected writings*. Oxford University Press.

Buchanan, J. M. (2010). *The reason of rules*. Liberty Fund.

[19]For a discussion, see Maduro et al. (2017).

[20]See Buchanan (2010).

[21]Manent (2017), pp. 9–18: "we speak a lot today of the limited capacities of national governments, and of the loss of legitimacy to which that leads. But it will not take long to appreciate the ineffectiveness of the despotism of Rules".

Cafaro, S. (2017). How the ECB reinterpreted its mandate during the Euro-crisis (and why it was right in doing so). In L. Daniele, P. Simone, & R. Cisotta (Eds.), *Democracy in the EMU in the aftermath of the crisis*. Springer.

Dahl, R. (1998). *On democracy*. Yale University Press.

Draghi, M. (2012, August 29). The future of the Euro: Stability through change. *Die Zeit*. Available at https://www.ecb.europa.eu/press/key/date/2012/html/sp120829.en.html

Fabbrini, F. (2016). *Economic governance in Europe: Comparative paradoxes and constitutional challenges*. Oxford University Press.

Foa, R. S., & Mounk, Y. (2017, January). The signs of deconsolidation. *Journal of Democracy, 28*(1), 5–16.

Follesdal, A., & Hix, S. (2006). Why there is a democratic deficit in the EU: A response to Majone and Moravcsik. *Journal of Common Market Studies, 44*(3), 533–562.

Kumm, M. (2010). *Democratic challenges arising from the eurocrisis: What kind of a constitutional crisis is Europe in and what should be done about it?* Brussels: European Parliament, Directorate General for Internal Policies – Policy Department C: Citizens' Rights and Constitutional Affairs.

Maduro, M. P., Frada, A., & Pierdominici, L. (2017, May). Crisis between crises: Placing the Portuguese constitutional jurisprudence of crisis in context. *e-publica, 4*(1).

Manent, P. (2017, June). Populist demagogy and the fanaticism of the center. *American Affairs, 1*(2), 9–18.

Post, R. (2010). Theorizing disagreement: Reconceiving the relationship between law and politics. *California Law Review, 98*, 1319–1350.

Siegel, N. (2008). The virtue of judicial statesmanship. *Texas Law Review, 86*, 959–1032.

Tuori, K. (2014). The Eurozone crisis as a constitutional crisis. In M. Fichera, S. Hanninen, & K. Tuori (Eds.), *Polity and crisis reflections on the European Odyssey*. Ashgate.

Widdig, B. (2001). *Culture and inflation in Weimar Germany*, (Weimar and Now: German Cultural Criticism). University of California Press.

Pedro Lomba Assistant Professor at the University of Lisbon's School of Law. He is the author of *Teoria da Responsabilidade Política* (Coimbra, 2008).

The manufacturer's authorised representative in the EU is Springer Nature Customer Service Centre GmbH, Europaplatz 3, 69115 Heidelberg, Germany. If you have any concerns regarding our products, please contact ProductSafety@springernature.com

Printed and bound by CPI Group (UK) Ltd, Croydon, CR0 4YY
30/09/2026
02225644-0018